HISTORY'S GREATEST BATTLES

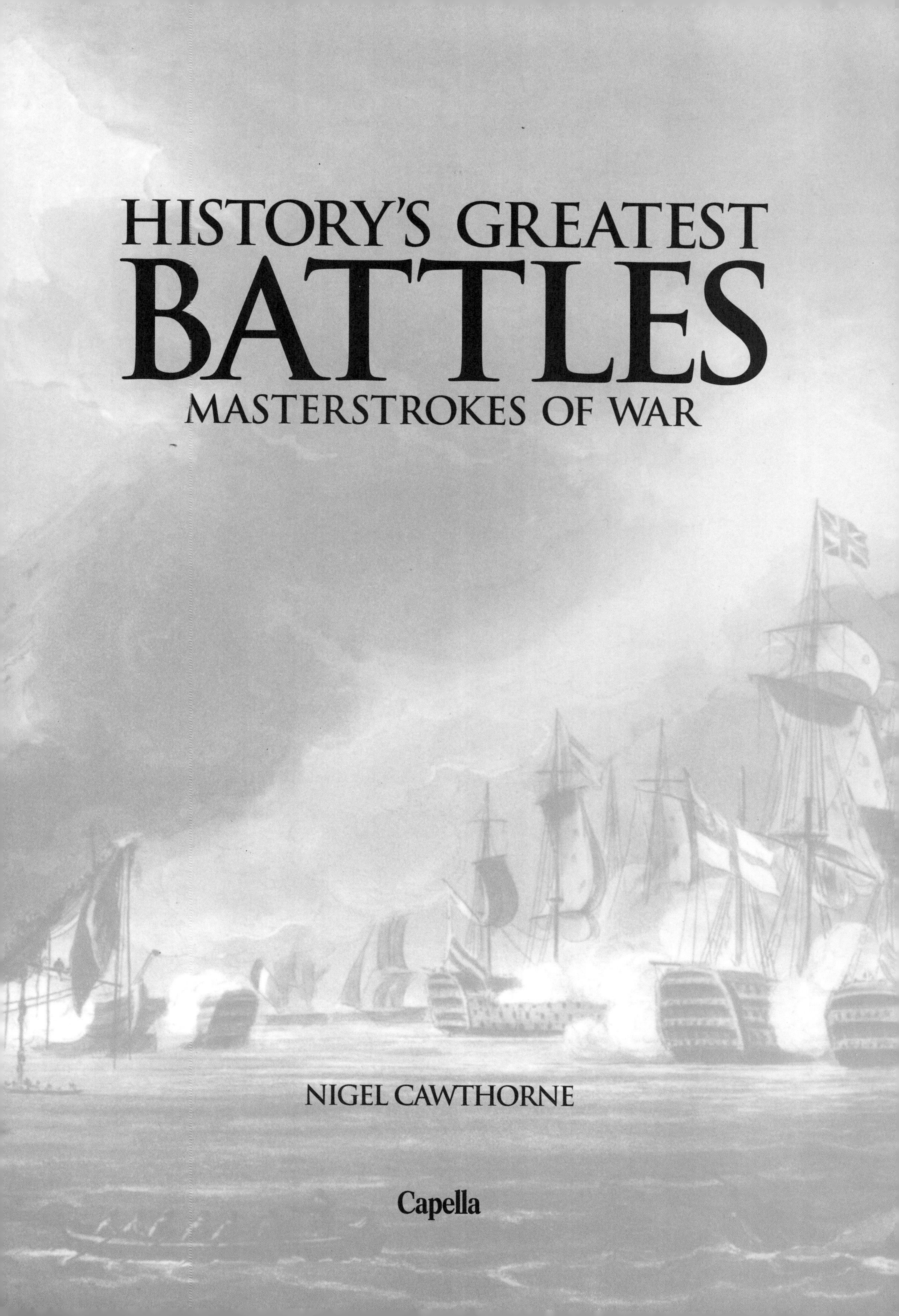

HISTORY'S GREATEST BATTLES

MASTERSTROKES OF WAR

NIGEL CAWTHORNE

Capella

Contents

This edition printed in 2007 by Arcturus Publishing Limited
26/27 Bickels Yard, 151–153 Bermondsey Street,
London SE1 3HA

ISBN 978-1-84193-865-3

Printed in China

Editor: Paul Whittle
Designer: Alex Ingr
Cover design: Peter Ridley and Beatriz Waller
Cartography: Rupert Matthews
www.rupertmatthews.com

Introduction

Great battles mark history's turning points. They occur at the times and places where cultures and ideologies clash. Marathon in 490 BC showed that the nascent Greek civilization could throw back the might of east. And at Granicus in 334 BC, the tide turned against the great eastern empire. We can, perhaps, see this as the beginning of a struggle between east and west continued throughout history, right up to the present day.

Cannae showed Rome that its military might was not unchallenged and led, ultimately, to the destruction of Carthage. At Alesia, Julius Caeser finally crushed Gaul, making Roman civilization the paramount force in western culture. The Roman defeat at the Teutoburger Wald halted the Empire's expansion to the north, while the crushing of resistance in Jerusalem in AD 70 reasserted Roman power in the east and remains the most significant event in the Jewish diaspora.

The Huns' advance was blunted at Châlons-sur-Marne, while the Muslim invasion of Europe was halted at Tours. However, the Muslim world itself achieved a lasting victory by taking Constantinople in 1453, a city founded as the capital of a Christian Empire.

Indeed, all the great battles in this book are pivotal in history. If any one of them had gone the other way, the world would have been a very different place. And none of them – with the exception, perhaps, of Iwo Jima and Berlin – was a foregone conclusion. Even Iwo Jima and Berlin mark significant points in larger conflicts whose results could easily, and catastrophically, have gone the other way. It is easy to forget how different a world we would be living in without the miracle of Dunkirk.

Some of the battles in this book were won by inspired leaders. Alexander the Great, Julius Caesar, Marlborough, Wolfe, Napoleon, Nelson, Washington, Grant and other victors are names that echo down the ages. In some battles, new technology influenced the outcome. Crécy and Agincourt were won by English longbowmen, ordinary folk who could, literally, put two fingers up at the French aristocracy, while at Yorktown ordinary American backwoodsmen, with a little help from the French, defeated the most powerful nation on earth.

But the true victors were always the ordinary soldiers who, through their courage, determination and sacrifice, changed the course of history. Lest we forget…

Marathon

The Greek Defeat of Persia

490 BC

At Marathon, a small force of Greeks threw back the massive Persian army in a battle that would alter the balance of power between east and west. It is commemorated today, nearly 2,500 years later, by a famous race.

THE GREEKS SETTLED on the Aegean coast of Asia in around 1000 BC. In the sixth century BC they were drawn into conflict with the Persians. Under Cyrus the Great (c.600–529 BC), the Persian Empire expanded westwards as far as the coast of Anatolia and by 550 BC it had swallowed up the small city-states of Ionian Greece.

In 546 BC Athens came under the control of the popularly-elected tyrant Hippias. Seeking to regain power, the Athenian aristocracy made an alliance with the Spartans, who then invaded Athens in 510 BC. Hippias was removed from power but he managed to flee to Persia, where he was granted sanctuary. Afterwards, the Athenians rose up and drove the Spartan garrison out.

Fearing a Spartan counterattack, the Athenians invited the new Persian king, Darius I, to form an alliance with them. As part of the subsequent negotiations, the Greeks were required to undergo

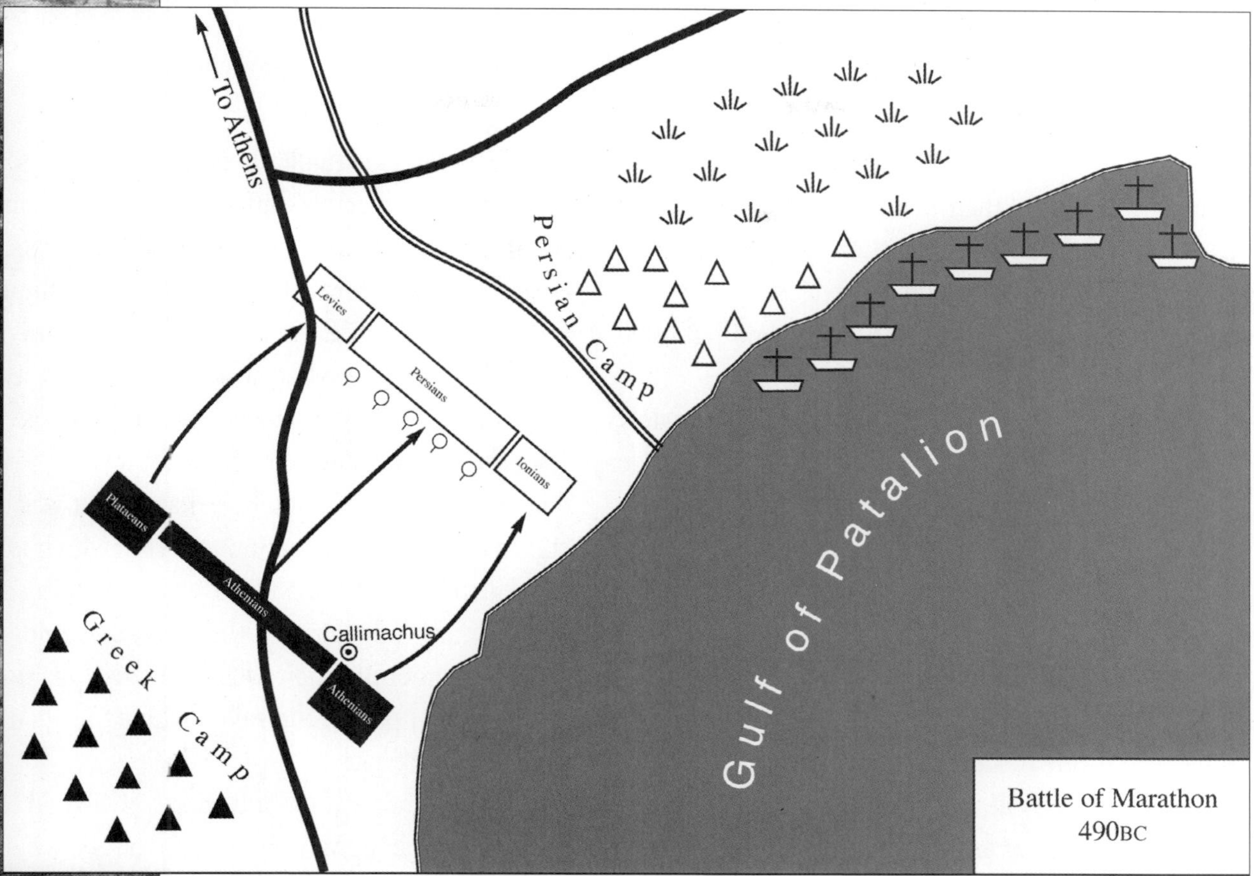

The Battle of Marathon proved that a small Greek force could overcome a huge Persian army using guile. It was a lesson that would stand the Greeks in good stead for another three hundred years.

what they considered to be an empty ritual – the handing over of water and earth. To the Persians, however, this ceremony meant that the Athenians were surrendering their territory to Darius.

Two years after making the alliance, the Athenians fought off a Spartan counterattack without Persian help. The regime in Athens changed once again and the new leaders considered the treaty with Persia to be null and void. At the time, the Persians were involved in campaigns in the Indus valley and Scythia, now part of the Ukraine, and so took little notice. The city-states of Ionian Greece seized the opportunity to rebel but although the Athenians went to their aid the revolt was quickly crushed.

The Persians now had a score to settle with Athens and in 492 BC they tried to invade Greece from the north, but their fleet was wrecked by a storm. They attacked again in the summer of 490 BC. This time 600 galleys worked their way through the Cycladic group of islands from the south. Their aim was to take over Athens and restore Hippias to power.

Athens was a walled city that stood a little way inland, which protected it from direct attack from the sea. On the advice of Hippias, the Persian commander Datis landed the invasion force in a bay near Marathon, some twenty-five miles to the north of Athens. Beyond the beach there was a broad plain, which was perfect terrain for the Persian cavalry.

The Athenians had a choice. They could either remain within their city walls and wait for the Persians to besiege them or they could emerge and face the foe. One of the Athenian generals, Miltiades, was from the Gallipoli Peninsula, which was then part of the Persian Empire. He had fought alongside the Persians in the Scythian campaign but had betrayed them, afterwards fleeing to Greece. Because Miltiades had a strong motivation to fight and knew the Persian way of war the Athenians made him commander-in-chief. He decided that it would be best to take the battle to the enemy and meet the Persians at their beachhead.

The Athenians raised an army of 10,000 men –

practically every able-bodied man in the city. The Spartans promised their help, but only after the end of the month: they had important religious festivals to attend to. Of Athens' fellow Greek city-states only tiny Plataea assisted the Athenians, sending 1,000 hoplites (heavily-armed infantrymen).

The Persians landed an army of approximately 25,000 men against this tiny force, including large contingents of archers and cavalry. The horsemen would sometimes carry bows but they were more usually equipped with armour, lances and javelins. This huge army drew up along the shoreline with the Persian fleet behind it.

When the Greeks arrived after their twenty-six-mile march down the path from Athens, they took up their positions at the inland end of the valley. It was narrower there and their flanks were protected by rocky hills on either side. Miltiades knew that the Persian tactics would be to use cavalry to attack the Greek phalanx on its flanks, thereby forcing the formation towards the centre where it could be overcome by heavy infantry. Accordingly, he instructed the Greeks to strengthen their flanks by cutting down trees and sharpening the branches, to create dangerous obstacles known as *abatis*.

There was a delay before the battle started. Ancient sources put the length of the hiatus at between three and eight days. Certainly it was not in Miltiades' interest to attack. With the road to Athens blocked by his men the city was safe and the longer he delayed the more chance there was of the Spartans arriving.

It is not known why the Persians hesitated. Perhaps they were considering re-embarking their troops and landing elsewhere. If so, it is unlikely that this strategy would have succeeded because transferring troops and horses from shore to ship and back again is time-consuming. Also, the Greeks had lookouts all down the coast and Miltiades and his army would have been waiting for the Persians wherever they landed.

The battle eventually began with volley after volley of Persian arrows, after which the Persian line began to advance with its cavalry on the flanks. The Greek historian Herodotus, who was born about six years after the battle, wrote that the Greeks then ran at the Persian line when it was still almost a mile away. This seems unlikely because Greek foot soldiers were heavily armed, so if they ran for any distance they would soon be exhausted. It was difficult to maintain a formation at a run, which is why Greek armies traditionally closed at a walking pace. Besides, any advance by the Greeks would have meant abandoning their well-protected position in the narrowest part of the valley, where they had prepared their defences.

As the Persian line advanced it would have become increasingly clear to Datis that he would be unable to use his cavalry. His infantry line began to fill the entire width of the plain as the valley narrowed, so there was no suitable terrain on either side for the horsemen to negotiate. By the time the two armies closed, the cavalry was forced to fall behind the infantry line and so could not be employed in its traditional role of attacking the enemy flanks.

Heavily outnumbered, Miltiades had to prevent his force from being encircled by deploying more troops on the flanks, thereby weakening the centre of his army. Also, he would have needed to move forward at some point, in order to give his heavy flanks enough room to pivot before falling upon the Persian centre. It was necessary for this move to be timed perfectly. If it were executed too early the flanks would be exposed to attack by the Persian cavalry; if it took place too late the Persian infantry would be able to cut the Greek army in two.

In the opinion of present-day military experts, the Greeks had arrived at the Persian line in good order and with plenty of energy left to fight and Miltiades had given the order to attack at the run when the Persians were about 200 yards away. The Persians began to push the Greeks back in the centre, where their forces were at their weakest. The centre, commanded by the veterans Artistides and Themistocles, fell back for a considerable distance but as it did so a funnel was created. While this was happening, the Persian infantry created an obstacle that protected the Greeks from the Persian cavalry.

Artistides and Themistocles then rallied their men and the Greeks launched a counterattack within the centre. At the same time, the flanks pivoted. The extended Persian centre then found itself under attack from three sides. The line broke and the Persians ran for the beach.

The fighting was far from over. Individual Persian units held their ground, rallied and even counterattacked. The monument to the Greek dead, the Soros, is around 1,000 yards from where the battle began. It is thought that this is where the Greek phalanx overwhelmed the last of the Persian resistance.

Traditionally, the Greeks did not pursue their enemies once they had driven them from the battlefield. In this case, however, they chased the Persians down to the shore and captured seven of their galleys, the Persians fighting a rearguard action to prevent the Greeks from setting fire to the other ships. One of the Greek commanders, Callimachus, was killed and another Greek had his arm chopped off while he was hanging on to a Persian ship as it pulled away.

Back on the battlefield, the extent of the Greek victory was dreadfully obvious. The Persians had suffered 6,400 casualties but the Greeks had only lost 192 men.

Even the Spartans were grudgingly impressed when they eventually turned up to view the battlefield. Miltiades was all too aware, however, that his decision to attack the Persians on the shoreline rather than let them besiege the city was controversial. There were even some Athenians who would have been happy to have seen the return of the tyrant Hippias.

As soon as possible, therefore, Miltiades ordered a messenger to run the twenty-six miles to Athens with news of his victory. This epic journey was the first marathon.

The Marathon defeat had only been a tactical setback for Datis, because he still had a massive force under his control. He sailed towards Athens, where he intended to make a second landing. While Aristides was left to guard the loot and the Persian prisoners of war – the Greeks traditionally treated their captives well – Miltiades led around 8,000 men on a forced march back to Athens.

When Datis sailed into the harbour at Athens, Miltiades and his army were lined up along the heights above it. The Persians could see that the military situation was impossible and so they sailed back to Anatolia. It is thought that Hippias died on the way. The Spartans arrived at Marathon a few days later, before the bodies had been buried, after a march of 150 miles in three days. All that remained for them to do was to offer their congratulations to the Athenians before marching away.

Marathon became a legendary victory and the Athenian treasury at Delphi was built out of its spoils. It is even said that the 192 figures on the Parthenon frieze – now part of the Elgin Marbles in the British Museum – represent the 192 Greek dead at Marathon.

The statue of Pheidippides, who ran the first marathon is placed next to the Marathon route, some 13 miles from Athens.

Granicus

Alexander Builds An Empire

334 BC

The Macedonian king Alexander the Great had already fought to take control of Greece. He then crossed into Asia and inflicted the first of a series of defeats on the Persian Empire at Granicus.

UNDETERRED BY THEIR DEFEAT at Marathon, the Persians returned in even greater numbers ten years later. They were led this time by Xerxes, who had succeeded his father Darius in 486 BC. The Greeks fell back to the narrow pass at Thermopylae, where the Spartan king Leonidas and 300 men faced a force of 200,000. They were eventually outflanked and slaughtered but this suicidal action delayed the Persians for three days, enough time for Athens to be evacuated. The Persians then took the city and pillaged it. However, the Athenian navy defeated the Persians at the battle of Salamis, which caused Xerxes to withdraw because he had no ships to bring supplies.

When Alexander the Great's father Philip II came to power in Macedonia in 359 BC, he sought to unite Greece and take the battle to the Persians. In 336 BC he sent an expeditionary force into Asia Minor under his general Parmenio, but he was assassinated before he could lead his main force into battle. After Alexander succeeded his father he stamped his own authority on Greece before crossing over into Asia Minor in 334 BC. Under his command were 35,000 men, including 5,000 cavalry. The bulk of the force were Macedonian veterans and the remainder of the troops were Greek, supplied under an alliance of the city-states called the League of Corinth.

Alexander's army was remarkable for its combination of arms. There were lightly-armed Cretan and Macedonian archers and Agrianian javelin men from Thrace. The well-disciplined and practically invincible 9,000-strong infantry phalanx carried shields and was armed with spears that were thirteen feet long. This main body of troops was supported by the 3,000 men of the royal bodyguard, known as the Hypaspistes, who fought on foot. Then there was the cavalry strike force.

While the Persians had a two-to-one cavalry advantage in Anatolia, Alexander's indomitable infantry phalanx outnumbered the Persian foot soldiers. After assessing the odds the Persians' general,

Alexander the Great was just twenty-one when he defeated the Persians on the river Granicus. It was the first of many victories that would leave him master of most of the known world by the time he died at the age of 32 in 323 BC.

Memnon of Rhodes, recommended adopting a scorched earth policy before withdrawing to the east. Memnon was a Greek mercenary, however, and the Persian satraps – provincial governors – did not trust him, nor did they want to see their provinces sacrificed. Accordingly the Persians dug in on the eastern bank of the river Granicus, now called the Kocabas, which flows into the Sea of Marmara, the ocean that separates Europe from Asia.

If Alexander moved to the south in order to liberate the Ionian towns of Ephesus and Miletus, the Persians could attack him from the rear. Alternatively, if he moved to the east against them they believed that their position was strong enough to withstand the attack of his larger army. The river was between sixty and ninety feet wide. It varied in depth and had a strong current and steep, irregular banks. This prevented an effective cavalry charge and ensured that an infantry assault would have experienced difficulty in holding its formation.

Alexander decided to move against the Persians directly. Before he joined them in battle, he visited Troy where, together with his friend and boyhood lover Hephaestion, he took part in funeral games for the Homeric heroes Achilles and Patroclus. Alexander claimed Achilles as an ancestor and Patroclus had been his friend. Accompanied by Hephaestion he made sacrifices to Athena, poured a libation in honour of the heroes and laid wreaths. At the tomb of Achilles, the two anointed themselves

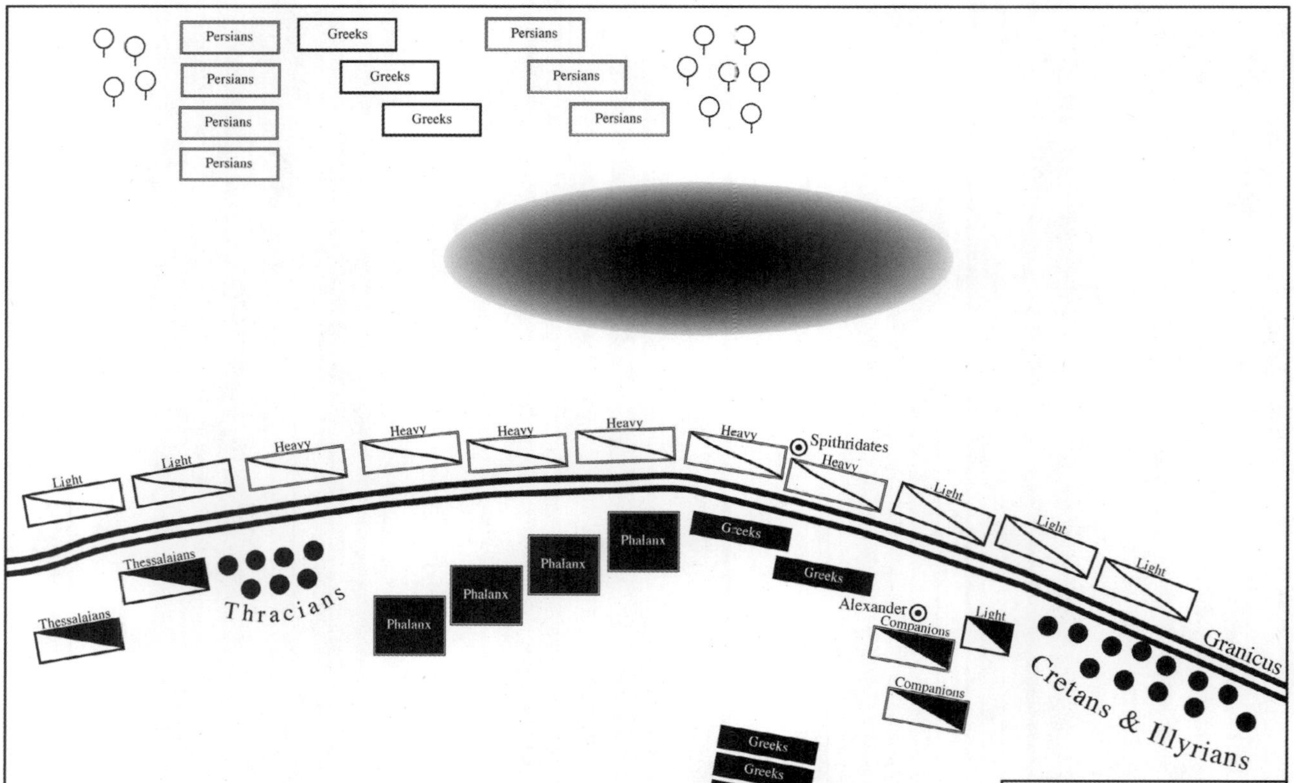

Battle of the Granicus
334BC

with oil and raced naked around the vault, in the traditional fashion. Alexander then recounted how lucky Achilles was to have had such a faithful friend in Patroclus while he was alive and no less a poet than Homer to immortalize him after his death. He was asked whether he wanted to see the lyre of Paris, whose seduction of Helen of Sparta, began the Trojan Wars. Alexander refused, saying that Paris had used it to accompany 'adulterous ditties such as captivate and bewitch the hearts of women'. He wanted instead to see the lyre that Achilles had used to 'sing the glorious deeds of brave heroes'. Alexander also took a sacred shield from the Trojan temple of Athena, which later saved his life in India.

Then Alexander selected 18,000 of his finest troops – 13,000 infantry and 5,000 cavalry – before marching to the River Granicus. He reached the river within three days, where he discovered that the Persians had already taken up strong defensive positions on the far bank; they occupied a front of some 7,500 feet or just over 1.4 miles. Strangely, the Persians put their cavalry in the front line along the riverbank, where there was little possibility of making a charge, with their infantry further back on high ground. It is thought that this was no tactical blunder, but rather an attempt to lure Alexander into ordering a cavalry charge across the river. The Persians knew that he would head such a charge and if they could cut him down in the first wave the battle – and the war – would be won.

They were very nearly right. Alexander wanted to begin by making a direct attack. As he marched towards the river he placed his infantry in the centre, with columns of cavalry on either flank, while the baggage train moved to the rear. He then advanced in a semi-deployed formation, behind a heavy screen of light cavalry and infantry, right up to the bank of the river.

But Parmenio and his other generals were fearful of the situation and raised religious objections. It was May – the Macedonian month of Daesius – when military campaigning was traditionally forbidden because men were needed to get the harvest in. So Alexander made a quick adjustment to the calendar and declared that it was not May at all, but a second Artemisius or April. Sources disagree about what happened next. The historian Diodorus of Sicily, who lived in the first century BC, wrote that Alexander's second-in-command Parmenio managed to persuade him to delay his attack until the following morning. There was good reason to do so. The Persians always began their day with dawn sacrifices. This would give the Macedonians the opportunity to surprise the Persians by moving downstream during the night before crossing over to the other bank in the morning.

On the other hand, the Greek writer Plutarch wrote, in the first century AD, that Alexander attacked straight away, saying that he would 'disgrace the Hellespont if he feared the Granicus'. Together with thirteen troops of horse, he is said to have braved a hail of javelins before scrambling up the muddy bank on the other side of the river. This more gung-ho account is echoed by other historians. However, it is based on the writings of Alexander's court historian, who had reason to be hostile to Parmenio, so Diodorus's more cautious account is probably closer to the truth.

Whether they attacked immediately or waited until the morning, the situation changed completely once Alexander's men were across the river. The two armies now faced each other on a flat plain, which was perfect terrain for Alexander's well-drilled army. The Persians were aware that their infantry did not stand a chance against the Macedonian phalanx, so they launched a cavalry charge, hoping to outflank the Macedonians on the left and then attack their rear. However, Parmenio thwarted the charge, while Alexander's archers and light infantry were sent against Memnon's Greek mercenaries on the right. This stretched the Persian line, a typical tactic of Alexander's.

Alexander then led his elite Companion cavalry in a decisive charge against the weakened centre. There was a furious battle and Alexander was in the thick of it. Easily identified by his splendid armour and the large white plumes on his helmet, Alexander was attacked by two Persian commanders, Rhosaces and his brother Spithridates. Alexander's lance broke on Rhosaces's body armour, but he had the presence of mind to jab the Persian in the face with the broken shaft. Meanwhile, Spithridates hit Alexander on the head with a battle-axe, chopping off one of his plumes and slicing through the helmet to the scalp. Spithridates was about to deliver the fatal blow when Alexander's comrade-in-arms, Cleitus, ran him through with a spear while Alexander finished off Rhosaces with a sword.

With the death of Spithridates and Rhosaces the Persian line broke and the Macedonian phalanx poured through. The Persian infantry took flight but the Macedonians did not bother to pursue them. Instead they turned on the Greek mercenaries, slaughtering between 3,000 and 4,000 where they stood. Another 2,000 troops surrendered and were sent back to Greece to be sold into slavery. Memnon miraculously escaped although he died soon after, seemingly of natural causes. Alexander later took Memnon's widow as his mistress.

A Greek historian of the second century AD, asserts the battle was over so swiftly that the only losses suffered by the Macedonians were eighty-five cavalry and thirty infantry. No doubt the number of wounded was considerably higher. Persia lost a total of 4,000 troops, including around 1,000 cavalry.

Alexander moved quickly to liberate the Ionian Greek cities, installing his own satraps and garrisoning them with Greek soldiers. He had no personal use for the Greeks, preferring to use his Macedonians for fighting.

After the Macedonian victory at the River Granicus, written sources claim that Parmenio was able to take Dascylium, the capital of Hellespontine Phrygia, without a fight. However, there is considerable archaeological evidence to suggest that the city put up a struggle. Alexander then received the surrender of Sardis, the capital of the wealthy satrapy of Lydia, which allowed him to pay his troops. He afterwards marched on Miletus, the largest Greek city on the eastern shore of the Aegean sea, which had an excellent harbour.

Alexander seized other coastal cities, thereby cutting off supplies to the Persian navy. Then he visited Gordium in Phrygia, where the fabled Gordian knot was kept. It had been tied around a pole by the Phrygian king Midas in the eighth century BC. According to legend it could only be undone by the future conqueror of Asia. Always fond of oracles and divine portents, Alexander tried his hand at untying it. When he failed, so the story goes, he drew his sword and sliced the knot into two parts, providing posterity with a potent metaphor. In another version of the story he pulled the pole out of the knot, thereby revealing its ends.

With Memnon dead, Alexander went on to face the Persian emperor at the Battle of Issus on the banks of the Pinarus river (either the present-day Payaz or the Deli river). The Persians were defeated again, although Darius escaped. Alexander then turned south and marched through Syria and Phoenicia – now Lebanon – depriving the Persians of their bases. After taking Egypt, Alexander returned to Mesopotamia where he faced Darius for one last time at the Battle of Gaugamela. Again the Persians lost and Darius, once the most powerful ruler in the world, was killed by his own men as they retreated from the battle. All Asia was now at Alexander's feet. He was just twenty-five.

Later, in a drunken brawl, Alexander killed Cleitus, the man who had saved his life in the Battle of Granicus.

Cannae

A Bloody Nose For Rome

216 BC

The Romans considered themselves unrivalled militarily. Then suddenly a young Carthaginian general named Hannibal from North Africa invaded Italy and threatened Rome itself. At Cannae he slaughtered two armies and taught the Romans a valuable lesson in tactics.

THE BATTLE OF CANNAE, which took place on 2 August, 216 BC, is still part of the teaching in military academies, because it represents the classic 'double-envelopment' manoeuvre in which an inferior force is able to defeat a superior one on open ground.

In the second and third centuries BC, Rome and the North African city of Carthage, near modern Tunis, were rivals for the control of the western Mediterranean. A dispute over Sicily and Corsica led to the First Punic War, which lasted from 264 BC to 241 BC. It was called 'Punic' after the language that the Carthaginians had inherited from their forebears, who came from Phoenicia (now Lebanon). In 221 BC, the sixteen-year-old Hannibal took command of the Carthaginian forces on the Iberian Peninsula. He then went on a two-year rampage, taking over the rest of Spain in breach of all the agreements between Rome and Carthage. In 218 BC, the Romans declared war – the Second Punic War – and demanded that Hannibal be handed over. But

Hannibal brought elephants over the Alps. Unfortunately, few of them survived the journey. They certainly frightened the Roman legionnaires, but it was Hannibal's superior command of tactics that won the day.

Hannibal went on the offensive. He left his brother in command of the armies in Spain and North Africa and headed off across the Pyrenees with 40,000 men and some forty elephants. By the time he had crossed the Alps and descended into the Po Valley he was left with 20,000 infantry, 6,000 cavalry and only a few of his elephants. This much-reduced force was inadequate for the task of suppressing Rome. However, Hannibal's superior cavalry got the better of the Roman forces at the Ticino River, costing the Romans 2,000 men.

At Trebia, Hannibal killed another 30,000 Romans and their allies and at Lake Trasimere he destroyed another 15,000 and also took the life of an important Roman commander. A column of Roman reinforcements was also ambushed, accounting for another 4,000 deaths. Hannibal had cost the Romans some 50,000 troops in just two years. His army was now poised to mount an attack on the city of Rome itself.

But Hannibal did not attack because Rome still had considerable military resources. If he tried to besiege Rome, he would give the Romans time to recover. Instead, he kept on the move in the hope that some of Rome's Italian allies might come over to the Carthaginian side if he continued his series of victories in the field.

In shock from the losses it had sustained, the Senate suspended the republican form of government and put the fate of the city into the hands of a single dictator, Quintus Fabius. With its army and naval power, Rome was bound to win out in the end,

Fabius realized, as long as the allies stayed loyal.

The senate authorized the raising of eight new legions. Another eight were supplied by the allies, giving Fabius command of the biggest army Rome had ever put into the field. Fabius went out to find Hannibal once the defences of Rome had been strengthened, but he refused to engage him. Instead, he just maintained contact, always keeeping to the high ground. By this stage Hannibal was encumbered with prisoners, and a great deal of booty, so he could not outrun Fabius. Also, while the Romans had secure supply lines, Hannibal's army survived by foraging, so Fabius harassed Hannibal's foragers.

Unable to draw Fabius into battle, Hannibal adopted the tactic of taking over the towns that belonged to Rome's allies in Italy. He then killed all the Roman men of military age. The Romans' women and children would be carried off, but the local Italians would be left alone. Hannibal hoped that this would encourage them to defect. However, with a huge Roman army following up behind, few were tempted to go over to the Carthaginian side: they knew what retaliation Fabius would wreak.

Although Fabius's strategy was successful, he was mocked with the epithet *Cunctator* ('the Delayer'). Rome wanted action. A Roman dictator was elected to office for just one year and at the end of that time Fabius was removed. Command of the army was given to Lucius Aemilius Paullus and Caius Terentius Varro, who aimed to give Rome the quick victories to which she was accustomed.

On 2 August 216 BC, the Romans met Hannibal at Cannae – now Monte di Canne – in southern Italy. At around sunrise, the Romans formed up so that their right faced the Aufidus River, across from Hannibal's camp. They had 80,000 infantry and 6,000 cavalry. Of the cavalry, 2,000 horsemen under the command of Paullus were on the right, while the elite force of 4,000 horsemen – patricians, knights and their sons –were on the left, under Varro. The Roman infantry legions were drawn up into a narrow formation in the centre under the command of a proconsul called Servilius. The Roman plan was to concentrate the strength of the legions into a narrow front, inflict a hammer blow on the enemy's centre and then break clean through their lines.

Hannibal was heavily outnumbered with just 35,000 heavy infantry, a few thousand light infantry and a number of slingers. Added to that, his men were largely mercenaries who were paid to fight. However, with 11,000 horse he enjoyed superior cavalry numbers. Like the Romans, he put his cavalry on the wings, with 7,000 heavy Spanish and Celtic horsemen on the left under the trusted Hasdrubal and 4,000 Numidian light cavalry on the right under Maharbal (the best cavalry general on the field by a large margin). Hannibal put his weakest troops, light infantry from Gaul and Spain, in the centre; these were flanked by his African heavy infantry. They would be commanded by Hannibal himself and his younger brother Mago.

Despite the reverses the Romans had suffered at the hands of Hannibal, morale was high. The Romans always depended on the strength of their legions to give them victory and they could see that Hannibal's forces were outnumbered by two to one.

When Varro's purple cloak was hung out as a signal for battle, said the Greek historian Plutarch:

> *...this boldness of the consul and the size of his army – double theirs – must have startled the Carthaginians. But Hannibal commanded them to their arms, and with a small train rode out to take a full prospect of the enemy as they were now forming in their ranks, from a rising ground not far distant. One of his followers, called Gisgo, a Carthaginian of equal rank with himself, told him that the numbers of the enemy were astonishing; to which Hannibal replied with a serious countenance: 'There is one thing, Gisgo, yet more astonishing, which you take no notice of.' And when Gisgo inquired what, he answered*

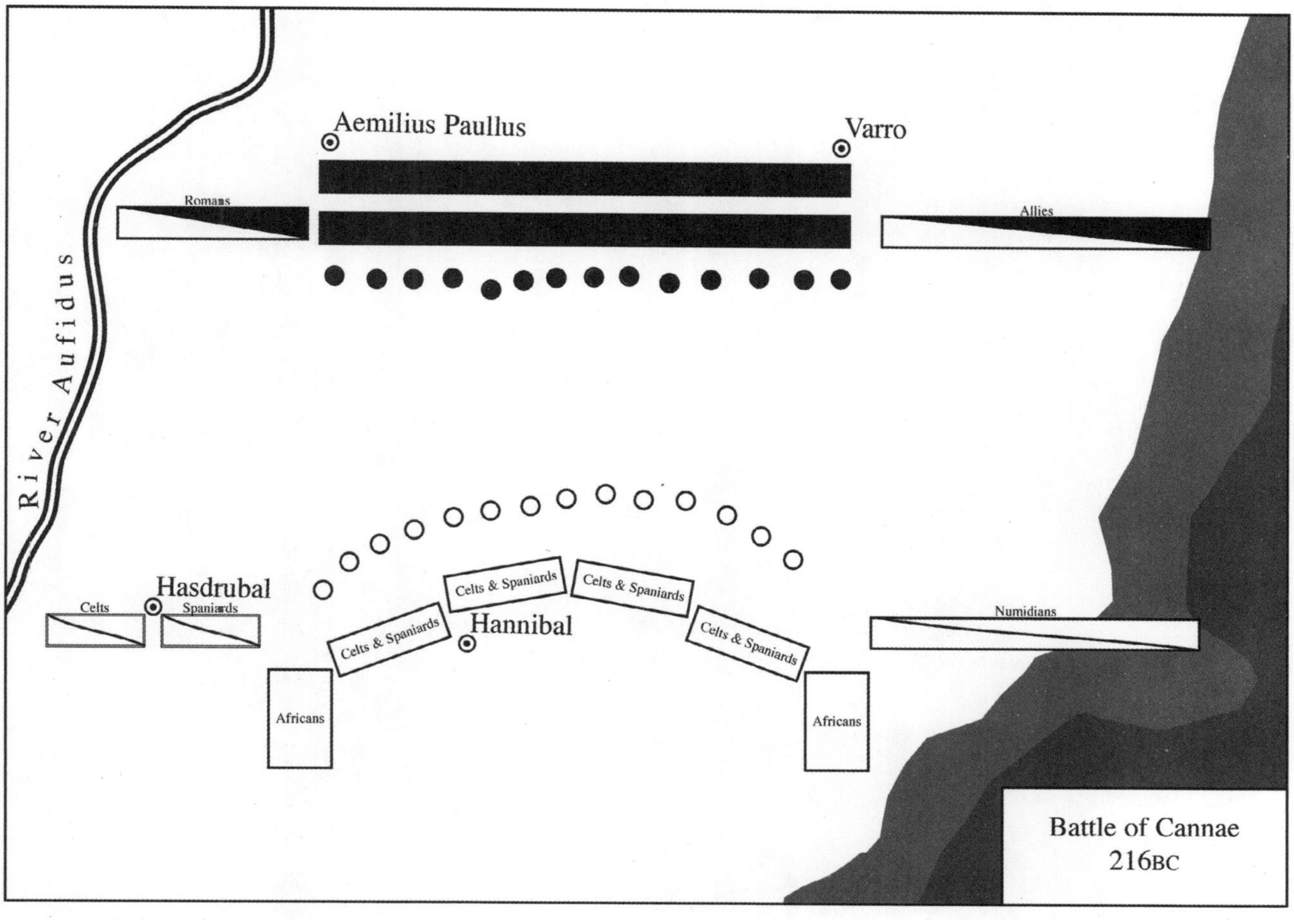

Battle of Cannae 216BC

that 'in all those great numbers before us, there is not one man called Gisgo'. This unexpected jest of their general made all the company laugh, and they told it to those whom they met, which caused a general laughter amongst them all.

Hannibal had some tricks up his sleeve, though. He pushed the weaker Gauls and Spaniards out immediately before the battle, while the stronger Africans were held back, thereby forming the infantry line into an arc. According to the Roman historian Livy, about 500 Numidians pretended to desert just before the battle started. They threw their shields and javelins to the ground and were conducted from the battlefield. However, they had swords under their robes and these weapons were suddenly pulled out during the battle. They struck at the Roman rear, 'causing terrible destruction, and even more panic and disorder'.

The battle began when skirmishers on each side hurled their javelins. Then, on the Carthaginian side, Balearic slingers rained stones and lead shot down upon the Romans. One of those projectiles seems to have hit Paullus on the head, wounding him. Then, with a mighty roar of opposing battle cries, the two armies moved towards one another.

The Spanish and Celtic horsemen on Hannibal's left quickly overcame the Roman cavalry, who were first trapped by the river and then slaughtered. Paullus was killed at that stage: Hannibal later honoured him by having his body buried with ceremonial rituals.

The Numidian cavalry held their own to the right. In the centre, Hannibal's light infantry, who were taking the full force of the Roman assault, began to give way. The Romans assumed that this was because of their superior strength, but Hannibal had ordered his men to retreat slowly, as if they were

The carnage at Cannae was appalling. The Romans were encircled completely by Hannibal's Carthaginians. Unable to retreat or manoeuvre, they were hacked down by the thousand.

being pushed back. The Roman formations, pushing up a slight incline, became compressed but the African units on either side stood firm and as the Carthaginian centre gave way, the Romans found themselves lured into Hannibal's trap.

Having destroyed the cavalry units on the right of the Roman line, Hasdrubal rode round to the back of the Roman infantry and attacked the Roman cavalry on the left wing from the rear. Besieged both at the front and the rear, the cavalry took flight.

Hasdrubal chased them from the battlefield so that they could play no further part in the action. Among the fleeing cavalrymen was Varro, so the Roman army was now effectively leaderless.

By this time the Roman infantry was so compressed that it cculd no longer manoeuvre. All it could do was continue forward, cutting its way through the Spanish and Celtic ranks – which only succeeded in drawing it deeper into the trap. Then, at the critical moment, the African phalanx that had been holding the ends of the Carthaginian line turned inwards to attack the Roman flanks. Returning from the chase the heavy cavalry under Hasdrubal ran into the back of the Roman formation. The Romans were now completely encircled. They could not manoeuvre to their flanks or to the rear. Only those on the outside of the formation could fight. In a matter of hours, 50,000 Romans had been slaughtered and another 5,000 had been taken prisoner. Those who escaped were hamstrung and later dispatched. Around 17,000 Romans had managed to break out and these troops raced back to their fortified camp. However, another 2,000 were killed there and the remaining 15,000 were taken prisoner.

Hannibal had lost 6,000 men, 4,000 of whom were the Gallic infantrymen who had held the centre of the line. Another 1500 Spanish and African infantrymen had died, along with 500 horsemen. Some 70,000 men lay dead in an area that was around the size of Hyde Park in London or Central Park in New York. The Roman historian Livy described the scene:

> *The morning after, as soon as it was light, they* [the Carthaginians] *pressed forward to collect their spoils and view the carnage, which was dreadful, even to enemies. There lay thousands upon thousands of Romans, foot and horse indiscriminately mingled, as chance had brought them together in the battle or rout. Here and there amid the slain, gory figures whose wounds began to throb with the chill of dawn got up, only to be cut down by their enemies. Some were discovered laying there alive with thighs and tendons slashed, baring their necks and bidding their conquerors to drain them of their last blood. Others were found with their heads buried in holes in the ground. They had apparently dug these pits themselves, and had tried to suffocate themselves by putting earth over their faces. But what drew the attention of all was a Numidian who was dragged out alive from under a dead Roman lying across. His nose and ears were lacerated as the Roman, no longer able to hold a weapon in his hand, had expired in a frenzy of rage tearing at his attacker with his teeth.*

The gold rings of the Roman knights were collected and later poured onto the floor of the senate in Carthage. Hannibal allowed to return home all the non-Roman prisoners, his hope being that this would encourage Rome's allies to rebel.

Hannibal had inflicted on Rome the largest defeat in its history. His generals now wanted to march on Rome itself, which was now defenceless but he refused. Maharbal is said to have complained: 'Hannibal, you understand how to win a battle; but you do not understand how to use your victory.'

The Romans had been defeated at Cannae because they had relied solely on the superiority of their legionaries, while Hannibal had employed complex manoeuvres that they could not counter. Until Cannae, Roman tactics had been non-existent. Now they had learned their lesson.

Cannae had made Hannibal master of the Italian peninsula, but the Romans had reverted to the successful tactics of Fabius. Although the victory had brought with it some defections among the Italian states, Hannibal was in no position to defend them. Starved of men and materiel by the Roman navy that dominated the Mediterranean, Hannibal's forces grew weaker. In 204 BC, the Roman general Scipio – later Scipio Africanus – attacked Carthage and Hannibal was forced to return to North Africa in order to defend his homeland. In 202 BC Scipio outmanoeuvred Hannibal at the Battle of Zama, after which Hannibal went into hiding. When he was eventually cornered in the Bithynian village of Libyssa in northern Anatolia in 183 BC he poisoned himself rather than be taken.

The dictator Quintus Fabius Maximus Cunctator was also the inspiration for the Fabian Society in England, which planned to introduce Socialism to the nation by similar gradualist tactics.

Alesia

Caesar Defeats the Gauls

52 BC

After ten years, Julius Caesar finally managed trap the Gallic leader Vercingetorix in a hill fort and surrounded him. He then fought off a second Gallic army that had come to break the siege.

IN THE WINTER OF 53–52 BC the Carnutes rebelled in Gaul, a region that had recently been annexed by Julius Caesar and his legions. The Carnutes were a Celtic tribe who gave their name to Chartres, which had been their Druidic headquarters. In their *oppidum* (fortified town) of Cenabum (now Orléans) they rose up and massacred all the Roman citizen traders, together with Caesar's supply officer. To the Senone people in the northeast this was a signal to form guerrilla forces and begin disrupting the Roman army's food supply.

Elsewhere other Gallic forces moved against the Roman legions in their winter quarters. At the time, Caesar was performing his magisterial duties in Cisalpine Gaul (now northern Italy). However, in

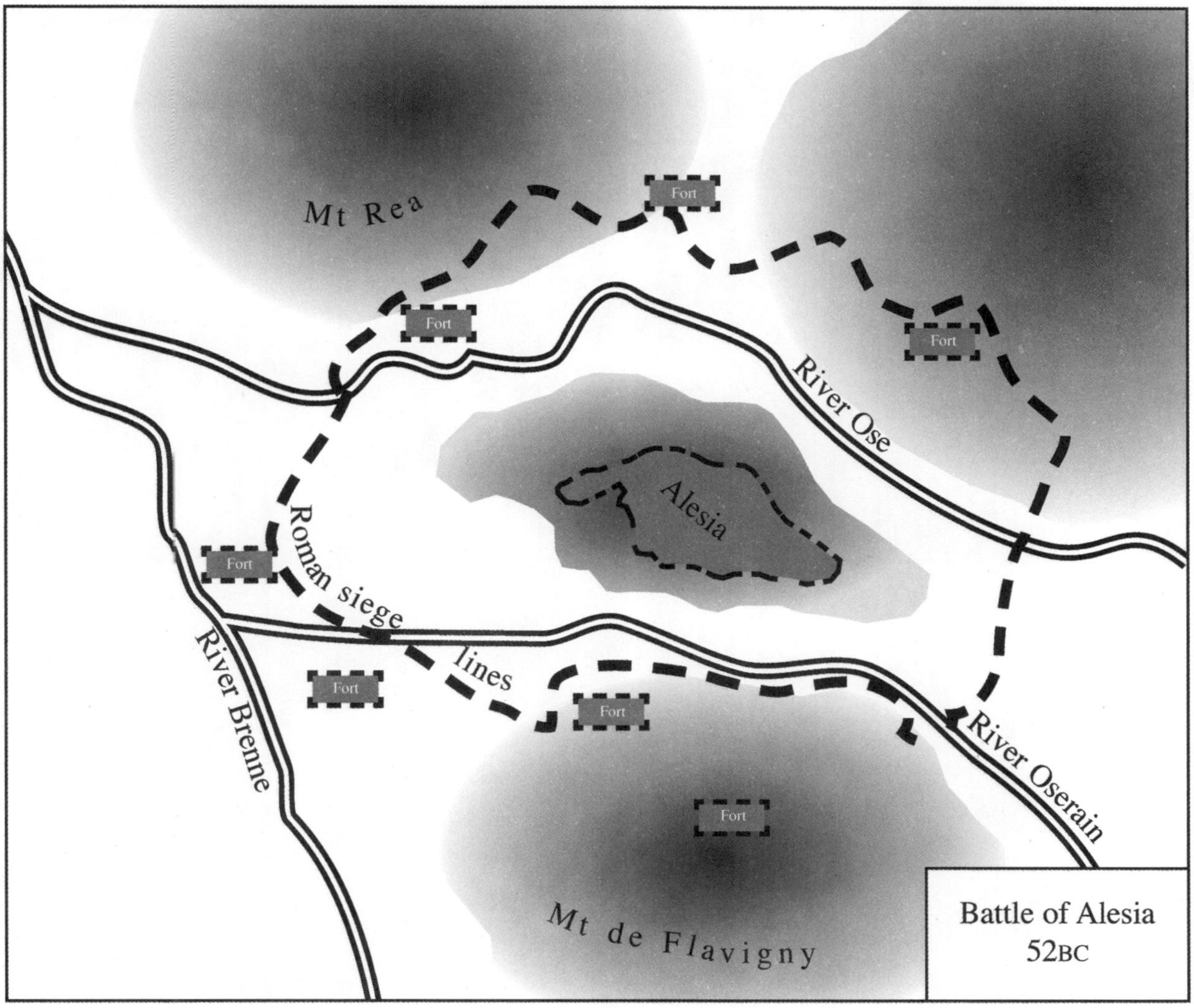

Battle of Alesia
52BC

Until Alesia, the Gauls had thought that they were safe inside their hill forts. Julius Caesar crushed Gallic resistance at Alesia by a massive display of military engineering.

late February he hurried across the Alps, defying heavy snows in the Cevennes mountains, to arrive unexpectedly at Agedincum (now Sens in Burgundy) where he mustered his legions. Titus Labienus was sent with four legions to suppress the Senones and the Parisii to the north, while Caesar himself led six legions towards Gergovia, the hilltop stronghold of the Arverni near what is now Clermont-Ferrand.

The Arverni's leader, Vercingetorix, was not just a formidable fighter. He was also a skilled politician and had secured the support of the Aedui tribe, Caesar's former allies, who had served for years as auxiliaries and were highly valued by Caesar as

cavalry. While Caesar was besieging Gergovia, the Aedui rebelled and massacred some of the Roman troops and all of the Roman citizens in Cabillonum, now Chalon-sur-Saône, to his rear. With his siege of Gergovia now placed in peril, Caesar attempted to take the hill fort by storm but was repulsed, at the cost of heavy losses. Vercingetorix had brought about Caesar's first outright defeat in Gaul, forcing him to withdraw.

Tribal leaders who had been loyal to Caesar switched their allegiance to Vercingetorix, who was elected commander-in-chief: some sources say he was named King of Gaul. It is thought that as many as forty-five tribes joined in the struggle against Rome. They set fire to the army depot at Noviodunum (now Nevers) and massacred the Roman merchants there.

The situation Caesar now found himself in was critical. His tribal allies had deserted him. The Arverni, elated by their victory at Gergovia, were at his rear; the Bituriges, from modern Bordeaux, were on his left flank; and the Aedui barred his front. According to the military theoretician J. F. C. Fuller, one of the pioneers of modern tank warfare: 'One thing alone saved him – his own invincibility.'

With his supply lines under attack Caesar fell back towards the Loire, where he was reunited with the legions of Labienus. He also replenished his cavalry with German auxiliaries. The Aedui, particularly, viewed their replacements with horror, considering them to be brutal barbarians. Vercingetorix was now in command of superior numbers, but Caesar managed to hold him off with his German horsemen.

That summer, Vercingetorix found it difficult to maintain his leadership without a clear victory. The tribes under his control were accustomed to warring with each other for territory and plunder; they found co-operation difficult at the best of times. However, Vercingetorix managed to persuade the tribal leaders to destroy their grain stores so that the Romans would be deprived of food during their campaign. The Bituriges burnt more than twenty of their own towns in one day but begged that Avaricum (now Bourges) be spared. It was, as Caesar said, 'the fairest city in the whole of Gaul' and they thought it could easily be defended. Caesar took it by storm within a month.

Vercingetorix was now on the defensive and he withdrew his huge army to the hillfort of Alesia, the capital of the Mandubrii. This *oppidum* was on the summit of Mont Auxois, just above the present-day village of Alise-Sainte-Reine, some thirty miles northwest of Dijon.

Caesar immediately grasped the changed situation, so he isolated Vercingetorix from his allies by surrounding Alesia. The key to Caesar's strategy was his army's engineering ability. The entire plateau of Alesia was quickly encircled by a series of walls, ten miles long in total. His men dug a ditch that was eighteen feet wide, at the side of which was a trench filled with water. 'Mantraps' were dug. A mantrap was a carefully concealed hole in the ground, several feet deep, with a sharpened spike in its centre. Anyone falling into the hole could well be impaled. Then a second wall, nine feet high and capped with breastworks, was built far behind the first line of defence. There were square towers at regular intervals where the awesome siege equipment of the Romans was mounted. This was all designed to keep Vercingetorix and his army trapped inside.

But Caesar also expected other Gauls to rally to the cause of Vercingetorix. So he began constructing an entire second line of fortifications which was parallel to the first and faced outwards. These defences were between thirteen and fifteen miles long. Caesar's army was now safe between the two rings of fortifications and the Gauls could scarcely believe their eyes when they saw the scale of this feat of military engineering.

Vercingetorix sent out cavalry detachments to harry the building work and the foraging parties while the construction was underway. As the siege tightened, there were cavalry battles in the three-miles-wide corridor between the outer wall of the hill-fort and the inner wall of Caesar's circumvallation. On the night before the Roman fortifications completely encircled Alesia, Vercingetorix sent out all his cavalry. Their mission was to return to their own tribes and conscript all the men of military age. The lives of 80,000 men inside the fort were in their hands. The horsemen escaped through the last gap in the Roman lines and galloped off to raise reinforcements.

After calculating that there was barely enough corn to hold out for a month, Vercingetorix introduced strict rationing. As stocks ran low all the townspeople who could not bear arms were marched from the hill fortress and into no-man's-land. The women and children and the aged cried out pitifully as they begged the Romans to take them as slaves, but that would have given the Romans the problem of feeding them. Caesar posted guards to ensure that his troops would refuse the women and children admission and they were left to starve between the lines.

Meanwhile, the other tribal chieftains arrived with what Caesar said was a quarter of a million men. Modern scholars believe that the warriors amounted to somewhere between 80,000 and 100,000. A great cheer went up inside Alesia at the sight of them. Vercingetorix and his men thought they had been saved.

As these fresh troops encamped on a hill that was a mile outside the Roman outer wall, Caesar and his lieutenants, including Gaius Trebonius and Mark Antony, braced themselves for a battle on two fronts.

The fighting began with a cavalry battle on the first day, which ended with a Roman victory thanks to the daring of the German horsemen. After a day's rest the Roman fortifications were simultaneously attacked from the inside and the outside, but they held firm.

According to Julius Caesar's *Commentary on the Gallic Wars*:

> *As long as the Gauls were at a distance from the entrenchments, the rain of javelins which they discharged gained them some advantage. But when they came nearer they suddenly found themselves pierced by the goads or tumbled into the pits and impaled themselves, while others*

were killed by heavy siege spears discharged from the rampart and towers. Their losses were everywhere heavy and when dawn came they had failed to penetrate the defences at any point...

The besieged lost much time in bringing out the implements that Vercingetorix had prepared for the sortie and in filling up the first stretches of trench, and before they reached the main fortifications heard of the retreat of the relief force, so they returned into the town without effecting anything.

At around midday on the fourth day the Gauls attacked again from both sides. After a terrible battle, the Romans won a great victory. As Caesar charged the relief force from the front the German cavalry hit them in the rear and they were scattered. Completely routed, they were pursued from the field by the German auxiliaries.

On the following day, with no hope of relief, Vercingetorix surrendered. He gathered the tribal leaders and told them that he had not made war for personal reasons but for the freedom of Gaul. Now they must decide whether to kill him in order to appease the Romans or hand him over alive. A deputation was sent to Caesar, who ordered the defeated Gauls to lay down their arms and bring their tribal chiefs to him. Then he sat on the fortification in front of his camp and waited.

Vercingetorix's surrender to Caesar is recorded by Plutarch:

Vercingetorix, after putting on his most beautiful armour and decorating his horse, rode out through the gates. Caesar was sitting down and Vercingetorix, after riding round him in a circle, leaped down from his horse, stripped off his armour, and sat at Caesar's feet silent and motionless, until he was taken away under arrest to be kept in custody for the triumph.

J.F.C. Fuller wrote:

Thus this remarkable siege was brought to an end by the simultaneous defeat of two armies by a single army, no greater than the one and incomparably smaller than the other. An army which not only was the besieger but itself was besieged, and which had to hold twenty-five miles of entrenchments in order, at one and the same time, to achieve its aim and secure itself against defeat. In spite of the paucity and frequent vagueness of details provided by Caesar, and the consequent difficulty in reconstructing some of the incidents, the siege of Alesia remains one of the most extraordinary operations recorded in military history.

Some 20,000 Aedui and Arverni were separated from the prisoners and returned to their tribes in an attempt to regain their loyalty. The Arverni also had to hand over some hostages in order to ensure their future good behaviour. The other survivors were divided among Caesar's soldiers and sold as slaves.

In Rome the Senate honoured Caesar with a twenty-day thanksgiving. Vercingetorix was taken to Rome in chains where he remained as an honoured prisoner for the next six years while Caesar fought Pompey in the Civil War. Once Caesar was in sole control of the Roman world, he had Vercingetorix exhibited in his Gallic triumph in 52 BC. Then, according to custom, the Gaul was strangled in the depths of the Mamartine Prison in Rome.

The defeat of Vercingetorix at Alesia essentially ended any hope of an independent Gaul. Caesar had two more years of mopping up before he had completed the pacification of the province and the Romanization of Gaul remains one of his most enduring achievements.

The ruins of the Alesia fortifications were rediscovered some nineteen centuries later. Mindful of the contribution of German cavalry to the defeat of

Vercingetorix, Emperor Napoleon III of France arranged for a massive statue of the Gallic leader to be erected on the site. Vercingetorix had come to symbolize the courage of France in fighting her enemies. Soon after that, Napoleon III fell from power having also been defeated by the Germans, this time at the Battle of Sedan in 1870.

Teutoburger Wald

Seizing The Roman Eagles

AD 9

Long after the expansion of the Roman Empire had been halted in the forests of Germany, Rome's first emperor, Caesar Augustus, would wander about his palace at night crying: 'Quincitilius Varus, give me back my legions.'

IN 12 BC THE ROMAN EMPEROR Caesar Augustus ordered his legions across the Rhine, from Roman-occupied Gaul and Germany as far as the Elbe. The area was pacified by his son-in-law, the future Emperor Tiberius, until he was recalled to Rome in 7 BC. Tiberius was replaced by Publius Quinctilius Varus, the former governor of Syria, a place known for its sexual and financial corruption. It seems that he brought profligate Syrian ways with him. Ancient sources accuse him of sexual misconduct with the sons and daughters of German nobles and profiting personally from the harsh taxes he imposed. He succeeded in alienating the German leaders who had sworn fealty to Rome.

One such was a young German called Arminius, who became chief of the Cherusci tribe. He joined the auxiliary forces of Rome with his brother Flavus, earning Roman citizenship and gaining equestrian rank. In the years immediately prior to the uprising he had served under Tiberius in Pannonia, the Roman province immediately to the southeast.

Back in Germany, Varus thought Arminius was a loyal ally and he entertained him as a guest at the Roman camp at Minden on the River Visurgis (now the Weser). But Arminius had a problem. He had fallen in love with Thusnelda, the daughter of his uncle Segestes, one of Varus's advisers. When Segestes opposed the match, Arminius and Thusnelda eloped. Segestes then accused Arminius of abducting his daughter. In the normal course of events this sort of charge would be heard by Varus, the Roman legate. The last thing that Arminius wanted, however, was the fate of his marriage being decided by a foreigner.

Given the general level of discontent in the country, there was a simple way for Arminius to solve the problem. Varus was preparing to move from his summer camp on the Weser to his winter quarters in the west – the Romans did not feel secure enough in Germany to overwinter too far from the Rhine. The move did not just entail the movement of troops but it also involved the displacement of thousands of wives, children, slaves and camp followers, along with their possessions.

News came that there had been a tribal rebellion along the route. This information probably came from Arminius himself, who offered to escort Varus with his Cheruscian auxiliaries. Although Segestes warned Varus that Arminius was plotting against him, Varus, with typical over-confidence, dismissed this as part of the family feud.

Varus had three legions under his command, some 18,000 men, plus three units of cavalry, another 900. However, some of them were away on other duties and it is estimated that he set off from Minden with between 12,000 and 18,000 men. With them were six cohorts of allied infantry, 3,500 to 4,000 men, and three squadrons of auxiliary cavalry, another 600, under Arminius's command. There were another 8,000 to 10,000 non-combatants. With supply wagons and baggage carts, the column stretched for nine miles.

They headed first for the Roman garrison at Aliso, near present-day Paderborn. The Romans had not built any paved roads in Germany, but the column followed a well-worn track that ran through a swampy region. On the second day, they moved into a heavily-wooded area. Seasonal rain had turned much of the area into a quagmire and movement was confined to a few dry tracks. Occasionally, trees had to be cut to build causeways so the engineers led the column. In these conditions, Varus did not order the army to draw up into a proper field march formation with fighting men at the front, even when Arminius suddenly disappeared from the column.

A storm broke, turning the track into mud. Falling trees added to the confusion. Suddenly Arminius attacked the Roman rear guard. All along the column, Germans began throwing spears from the safety of the trees. Varus called for his light cavalry – German auxiliaries – and found that they had deserted to a man.

The Germans had gone by the time the Romans had organized themselves into a fighting formation. The engineers quickly began to construct a field camp on a piece of dry, flat ground and Varus ordered the burning of all superfluous baggage. On the following morning the column formed up to march the twenty miles to Aliso, with the civilians and the supplies in the middle. Varus hoped to engage Arminius in a pitched battle by moving out into open ground, but the Germans hung back: they

The Romans were proud of their military prowess. Their defeat in the Teutoburger Forest was a great humiliation.

preferred small, harassing actions. The heavy Roman cavalry could keep larger formations from attacking the column, but without light cavalry there was no defence against small-scale ambushes and spears thrown from the undergrowth.

Towards the end of the day, the column reached a point where the trail entered another wooded area in the Teutoburger Forest, near present-day Bielefeld in Westphalia. The German attack intensified from the cover of the trees, so the Roman column stopped for the night in a new fortified camp.

The Romans found they had to move on or die at dawn on the next day. More German tribes were joining Arminius's army and together they threatened to overwhelm the Roman positions. The only possible salvation lay with the garrison at Aliso. What Varus did not know was that it, too, was under attack.

The column had to pass through the Dören Ravine in order to reach Aliso. There was a thickly-wooded slope on one side of the approach and a swamp on the other. It was the perfect place for an ambush. As the trail entered the ravine, it was crossed by swiftly-running streams. Not only was it muddy but Arminius had also spent the night felling trees to block the pathway.

As the column approached the ravine they were met by Germans who had fought in Pannonia and were, therefore, familiar with Roman close-order fighting. Other Germans hurled spears from the wooded hillside. Even so, the Romans made progress in the hope that they would find some shelter inside the ravine itself. Unfortunately, it began to rain again as soon as they reached their goal, turning the path into a sea of mud and inhibiting any further progress. In some places they could not even stand up, nor could they defend themselves. Their hide shields were soaked, making them too heavy to hold.

Unable to go forward, the Romans tried to return to the safety of their camp. At this point Arminius attacked. The targets of the first assault were the Romans' horses. Wounded animals panicked, bucking and falling and creating havoc amongst the infantry around them. The retreat, which had begun in good order, turned into a rout.

Varus was wounded so he committed suicide rather than fall into the hands of the Germans, who were known to torture victims and use them for human sacrifice. His servants buried him. Some Roman commanders followed Varus's example, while others fought on only to be slaughtered where they stood. All the non-combatants were also butchered.

Of the three Eagle standards of Varus's legions – the XVII, XVIII, and XIX – two were captured. The standard-bearer of the third legion plunged into a swamp with his standard to prevent the Germans from taking it. Those who were captured or who surrendered were crucified, buried alive or sacrificed to German gods in sacred groves; the heads of dead Romans were put on spears around the Germans' camp. Arminius ordered the body of Varus to be dug up and decapitated and the head was sent to Maroboduus of the Marcomanni as an inducement to join the revolt. Maroboduus remained neutral and sent the head to Augustus for burial. Thereafter, the story goes, the ageing Augustus would on occasion wander the halls of his palace at night, crying out: 'Quinctili Vare, legiones redde!' ('Quinctilius Varus, give me back my legions!').

Tiberius returned to Germany in the following year but Arminius would not engage in battle with him. Augustus died in AD 14, and was succeeded as Emperor by Tiberius. In the following year Tiberius's nephew Germanicus Caesar was sent to avenge Varus. The first-century Roman historian Tacitus describes what he found:

On the open ground were whitening bones, scattered where men had fled, heaped up where

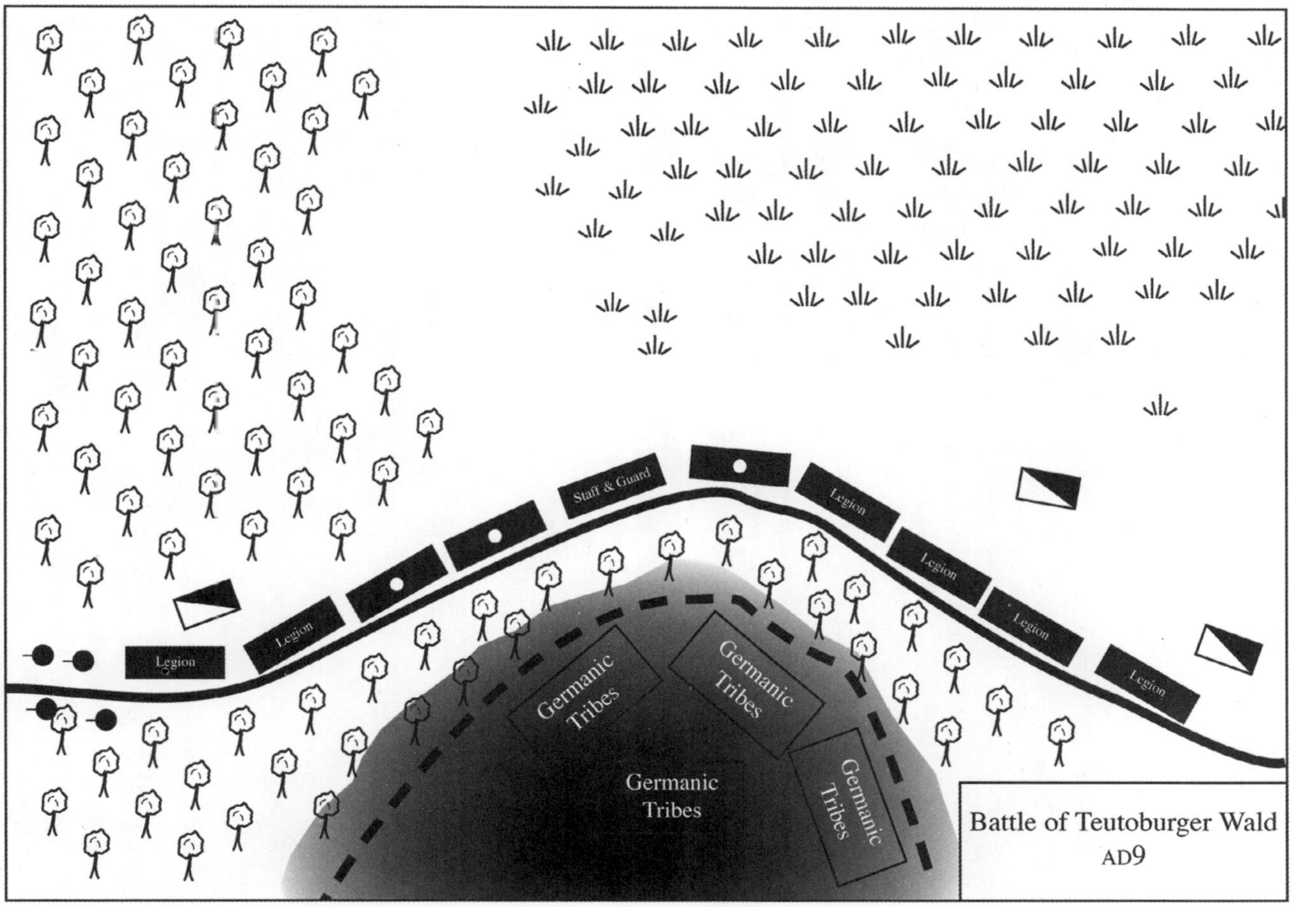

Battle of Teutoburger Wald AD9

they had stood and fought back. Fragments of spears and of horses' limbs lay there – also human heads, fastened to tree trunks. In groves nearby were the outlandish altars where the Germans had massacred the Roman colonels and senior company commanders.

Germanicus arranged for the bones to be buried with appropriate military honours, and the Eagle of the lost XIX Legion was recovered. He roamed across Germany for three years, killing men, women, children and the elderly but he did not catch up with Arminius. He was sometimes lured into the forests and swamps, however, where Arminius mauled him but never inflicted another decisive defeat. Germanicus managed to capture Arminius's wife Thusnelda, who was pregnant. She refused to betray her husband and was taken to Ravenna where she brought up their son, never seeing her husband again.

As the war continued, Arminius told his men: 'My fighting has been open, not treacherous and it has been against armed men and not pregnant women. The groves of Germany still display the Roman Eagles and standards which I hung there in honour of the gods of our fathers.' And he gave his followers a stark choice: 'Follow Segestes into shameful slavery or follow Arminius to glory and freedom.'

Germanicus was recalled by Tiberius in AD 17, leaving the Germans to fight a civil war, and Arminius was murdered by one of his allies in AD 19. He had not united the German people; he had, however, succeeded in keeping Germany out of the Roman Empire and so, as Tacitus called him, he was '*liberator haud dubie Germanie*' – 'unquestionably the liberator of Germany'.

Jerusalem

Defending The Temple

AD 70

By crushing Jewish resistance in Jerusalem, the Romans consolidated their eastern empire, driving Jews out of their homeland in a diaspora that has religious and political consequences to this day.

PALESTINE HAD LONG BEEN a client state of the Roman Empire but after the death of Herod the Great in AD 6, followed by the banishment of his son, it became the province of Judea and came under direct rule from Rome. There were sporadic riots against Roman rule in Jerusalem, but there was a period of relative calm under Caligula's protégé Herod Agrippa, grandson of Herod the Great. Rioting broke out again after Herod Agrippa's death in AD 44.

Things deteriorated under Gessius Florus, who was procurator from AD 64 to AD 66. His anti-Jewish stance encouraged the large Greek population of Caesarea Maritima (now Horbat Qesari, south of Haifa) to massacre the Jews there. Greeks in other towns within Palestine followed suit. The Jews responded by killing Gentiles in Galilee, Samaria and elsewhere and a full-scale revolt broke out.

Cestius Gallus, the Roman governor of Syria, advanced through Palestine and tried to besiege Jerusalem, but he was soundly defeated and was forced to withdraw. Utterly routed, Cestius aban-

The Jews put up a fanatical resistance, but they could not long defy the power of the mighty Roman Empire.

doned his baggage train and his siege engines. The city was free for three years and silver shekels minted during that period bear the legend 'Jerusalem the Holy'. A revolutionary government was set up which took control of the whole country.

Plainly the Romans could not let this situation continue. In AD 67 Nero dispatched the future emperor Vespasian with a force of 60,000 men, in an attempt to put down the revolt. He broke the resistance in the north and then besieged Jotapata, the strongest city in Galilee. The Jews repeatedly attacked the Romans' siege engines and earthworks, setting fire to them. They broke up a Roman testudo – the army's protective tortoise-shaped formation, made from overlapping shields – by pouring boiling oil over it; they also tripped up attackers by pouring boiled fenugreek over the planks they had laid across the rubble, making them slippery. The city held out for forty-seven days and fell only because it had been betrayed. A deserter told Vespasian that the defenders were exhausted and that the guard slept towards dawn. One foggy night Vespasian's son Titus (who also became emperor) led a party to scale the walls and take the city. According to the Jewish historian Joseph ben Matthias, who had survived the siege (his Romanized name was Flavius Josephus), only six Jews had died during the fighting although 300 were wounded. The Roman casualties, he said, were 'heavy'. Even Vespasian was wounded in the foot by an arrow.

The Romans then marched on Jerusalem, which had much stronger fortifications. Huge towers strengthened the walls and deep ravines made most of the fortifications unassailable. Even if an attack breached the outer walls there would be new lines of defence to be encountered within the inner divisions.

However, the inhabitants had a problem because they were divided against themselves in the new atmosphere of freedom. The rivalry between the different factions was so bitter that most of the city's vast food stores had been destroyed before the Romans arrived. There were fruit trees and small gardens within the city, but food needed to be smuggled in from the outside. This would present a pressing problem because the population was swollen by refugees.

On the other hand, the besiegers found themselves short of water. The limited supplies could not satisfy the demands of 60,000 soldiers and their numerous camp followers. That logistical problem would endure throughout the five months of the siege.

There was no shortage of water inside the city, however. Cisterns held millions of gallons and an extensive network of tunnels brought water in from underground springs outside the city.

Vespasian departed when the Romans reached Jerusalem in the early spring of AD 70, leaving the four legions in the hands of Titus. Just thirty years old, Titus had little military experience and he had no wish to besiege a city as strong as Jerusalem. So he sent an envoy, accompanied by Josephus, to negotiate a surrender. The Jews' answer was to shoot an arrow that wounded the messenger.

Titus then set out to reconnoitre the city in preparation for the siege. However, he was almost captured when a Jewish war party dashed out at his party. The Jews then launched a full-scale attack on the legion that was encamped on the Mount of Olives to the east and had almost routed it before Titus arrived with reinforcements.

The walls of Jerusalem were only vulnerable to siege engines at the northwest corner of the outer wall. The wall was not very strong at that point because it had been hastily completed when the war with the Romans broke out. Accordingly, Titus moved his main force there and set to work.

Archers and spearmen guarded the soldiers while they were building the siege works. The Romans also deployed arrow-firing and stone-hurling catapults along the wall. The largest of these could hurl a stone weighing 1,100 pounds over a distance of 500 yards. The defenders listened for the whizzing noise of the stones and also had spotters looking out for them. However, the Romans blackened the stones, making them more difficult to spot. The Jews also had catapults, which they had captured from Cestius, but they were not practised in their use and their firing of them was ineffective.

The Romans had completed their siege works in five days and they were close enough for their battering rams to reach the wall. The distance was measured using a lead weight attached to a line. The Jews made repeated attacks on the rams and Titus had to bring up reinforcements in order to prevent them from putting the rams out of action.

Titus's men also built great towers that were seventy-five feet high, which made them tall enough for the top to be out of range of any missiles that might be hurled by the Jews. The towers were covered by metal plates to protect them from fire and their great weight prevented them from being capsized. However, one of them collapsed under its own weight on one particular night, to the consternation of the Romans.

The wall was breached after ten days of battering. The defenders withdrew inside the second wall, abandoning the suburbs in between, and the Romans quickly cleared the houses there and moved up to just outside bow-range of the second wall. They began battering it in the centre, out of range of the Jewish artillery in the Antonia Fortress. The second wall took five days to breach after which

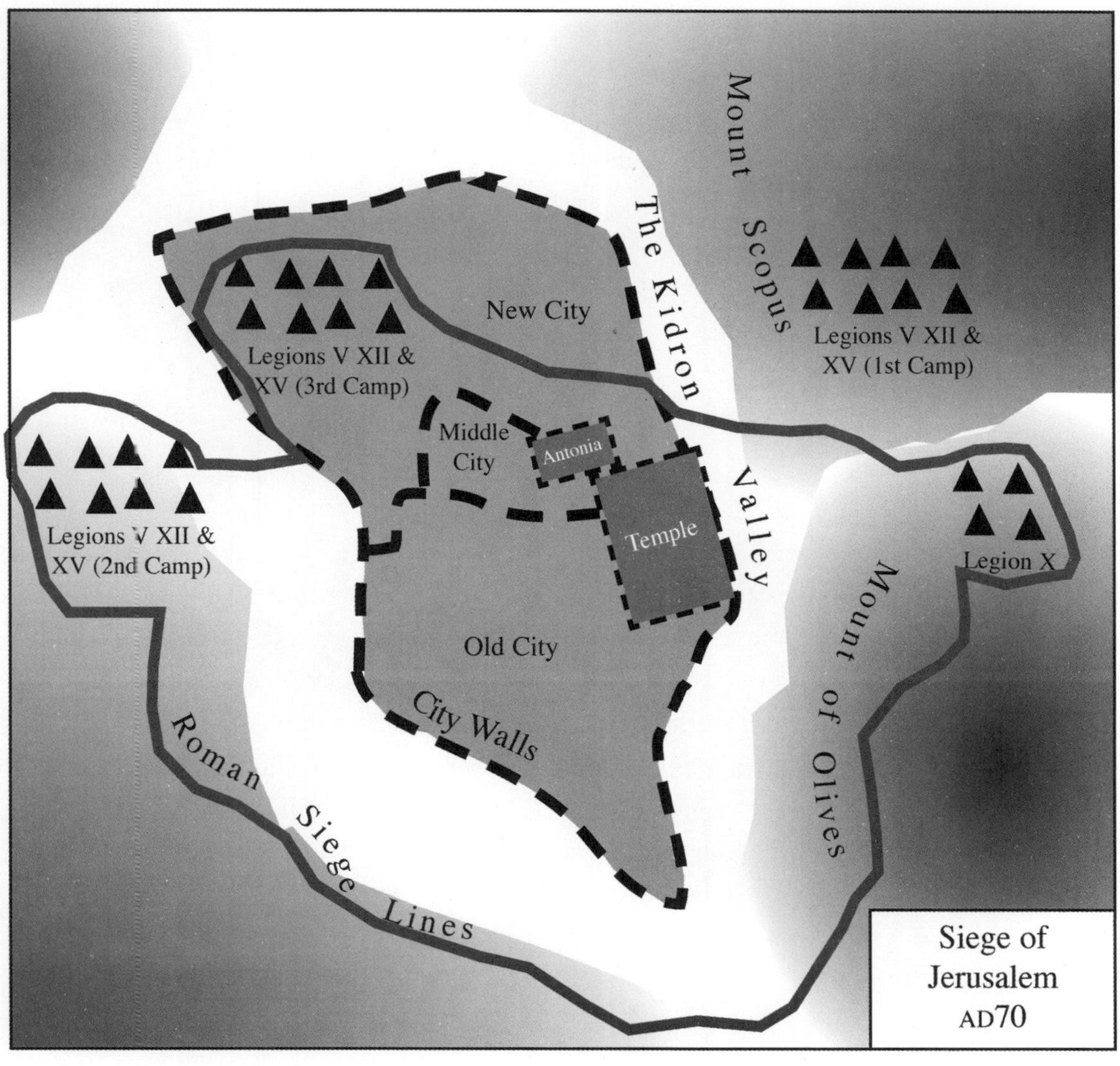

The Romans were equipped with huge siege engines, which Jewish raiding parties managed to sabotage several times. But eventually the Roman machines destroyed the city's defences.

the Jews retreated behind the first wall that protected the Upper City and the Temple Mount. These were the most strongly fortified areas of the city.

Titus prevented his soldiers from sacking the areas they had just taken in the hope that this would encourage the defenders to surrender. Instead the Jews launched a counterattack. The Romans were trapped in a maze of narrow streets because Titus had only left one narrow breach in the wall. It was only when he brought up archers to cover their retreat that they managed to escape. The Jews had succeeded in pushing the Romans back beyond the second wall.

It took three more days of hard fighting before the wall could be breached again. This time Titus made sure that it was razed before paying his men and waiting for four days. The breaching of the two outer walls had produced numerous desertions – although those that left might just have been non-combatants fleeing the cramped conditions of the area that was still in Jewish hands. In any case, the remaining defenders would need all the food they could get and some of the 'deserters' seem to have managed to sabotage the Roman water supplies. At this point the defenders in the Upper City and on Temple Mount refused to surrender.

Titus ordered more siege works after four days. Each of the four legions constructed its own ramps, two against the Upper City and two against the Antonia Fortress on the Temple Mount. The Jewish catapults became more effective now that the Romans were closer and the Jews rained arrows and stones down on the Romans. Titus still hoped for a surrender because, according to Josephus, he did not want the siege to end with the destruction of the temple. Josephus himself was sent as an envoy, but he had to stay out of bow-range when he shouted his pleas because the Jews considered him to be a Roman stooge.

The Jews deserted the city as the rations dwindled. At first the Roman soldiers tried to stop them in order to make the famine more intense for the defenders, but Titus ordered them to let the fleeing Jews through. Josephus wrote that the rich among them had swallowed gold coins which they used for the purchase of food outside the city once the cash had passed through their bowels. Poorer people found they were no better off outside the city. The Roman cavalry rode down anyone caught foraging and had them crucified.

It took a week for the new earthworks to be completed. The battering rams were then brought up but the Jews managed to undermine one of the ramps leading up to the Temple Mount, causing it to collapse. Three Jewish soldiers made a daring attack on the other three earthworks, setting fire to the battering rams. When the Romans tried to put the fires out, the Jews came pouring out of the city and drove them back. They then destroyed the ramps and attacked the Romans. They were held off by the camp guards, who faced the death penalty if they deserted their posts, allowing Titus to make a flanking attack with his crack troops. The troops managed to drive the Jews back into the city but seven days work had been lost.

The Romans were now at a loss as to what to do. Some wanted to make an all-out assault on the city, but Titus dismissed that as too costly. Others wanted to rebuild the ramps and try again. However, there was now a shortage of building materials in the area. Still others favoured a blockade, but the terrain around Jerusalem made it possible to smuggle food into the city and Titus feared that prolonged inactivity would sap the morale of his men.

Titus's answer was circumvallation. He would build another wall around the wall around Jerusalem, sealing the defenders inside the city. It would be five miles long, with thirteen towers on the outside that would effectively add another one and a quarter miles to its length. Titus set his legions to compete with each other in the race to build the different sections of the wall. Josephus writes that the wall was completed in three days. At that rate each legion would have built half a mile of wall a day.

Conditions were awful inside the city. A measure of grain cost 500kg of silver and people were reduced to eating offal and cow dung. Children were bloated with starvation and no-one had the strength to bury the dead. Titus was appalled by the sight of bodies that were thrown into the ravines with 'thick matter oozing from under the clammy carcasses'.

Now that the defenders were visibly weakened, Titus ordered huge new earthworks to be erected against the Antonia Fortress. The suburbs were stripped of building materials in the process. All the trees in the area had been felled and timber was brought from as far as nine miles away. Jerusalem, which once stood in fertile countryside, was now a fortress in a desert. So scarce was the material that the earthworks took twenty-one days to complete.

The Jews tried to attack it but they were now too weak to fight and they were pushed back by the Romans and their artillery. Eventually, the battering began but the Jewish defenders dropped boulders onto the rams. The Jews had also undermined one of the ramps and the weight of the stones caused it to collapse. However, this also weakened the wall. The Romans formed a testudo, made their way up to the wall and tried levering out stones with a crowbar. That night, the wall collapsed.

The Jews then hurriedly built another wall behind it. Although it was weak, the Romans were not keen to attack it and a speech by Titus failed to inspire his men. According to Josephus, one man volunteered to attack single-handedly. Only eleven others followed and they were easily beaten back. The Romans took the wall by stealth two days later. A small party scaled it at night, killed the guards and sounded trumpets as a signal for the rest of the army to follow.

The Jews fell back on the heavily-fortified Temple. Heavy fighting broke out, but the Romans could not break through. Instead they began dismantling the Antonia Fortress for the building material that would be needed when they besieged the Temple. Josephus said that Titus was reluctant to fight over the Temple itself and had tried to persuade the Jews to surrender. However, even though they had no more sheep to sacrifice, a ritual that had been maintained throughout the siege, the Jews' morale was not dented.

Titus then tried a night attack with a force made up from the thirty best troops from each century. It is said that he wanted to lead the assault himself, but was persuaded to watch from the Antonia Fortress. As it was, the Jewish guards were alerted. Fierce fighting went on for eight hours but still the Romans could not break through. Only several hours after dawn did Titus eventually call the attack off.

The Romans then set about clearing the area around the Temple. It took seven days to level the Antonia alone, then embankments were built along the west and north sides of the Temple. These efforts were hampered when the Romans were attacked by the Jews. By this time, the wood that was needed had to come from twelve miles away. Meanwhile the Romans pounded the western wall of the Temple with their catapults but little damage had been done after six days.

The Jews tried to protect themselves from the encroachment of the embankments by setting fire to the porticoes that faced the Antonia. When the Romans tried to chase them out of the western portico, the legionaries got trapped there and were burned to death.

With the embankments completed, the Romans deployed their battering rams. At the same time, some of the soldiers succeeded in prying stones from the foundation of the north gate, but the remaining stones continued to support it. By now the Jews had no more food and they were reduced to eating grass and leather. Josephus said that one women even killed her own baby and ate it. But still they held off the attackers.

The Romans set fire to the remaining gates and porticoes and fires blazed for a day and a night. The Romans then put them out. Moving into the inner court, they met stiff resistance and one of the Romans threw a burning stick into the Temple itself. Josephus wrote that Titus did not want the Temple burnt down – instead, it is thought, he wanted to turn it into a Roman Pantheon. But he was no longer in control of his men, who wanted vengeance. However, other authorities maintain that Titus ordered the burning of the temple and that he violated the sanctity of its innermost sanctum before the flames engulfed the building. His men then sacked and burned the city and the slaughter was terrible.

Some Jews escaped through underground tunnels and others made a last stand in the Upper City. It took a further eighteen days to build the earthworks from which to assail them there. When the battering rams completed their job in early September the Jews in the Upper City were too weak to put up any further resistance. They were sought out and massacred over the next few days and by 7 September the whole of the city was in Roman hands.

The Romans left three towers of the Temple standing as a monument to their conquest and for use by the victorious legions. Of the Jewish population, 110,000 were killed and 97,000 were taken prisoner. Thousands more were taken to Rome as slaves.

The destruction of the Temple is commemorated by the Jewish holiday of Tisha be-Av and the Arch of Titus, which still stands in Rome.

The fall of Jerusalem did not end Jewish resistance in Palestine. The Zealots, a passionately anti-Roman Jewish sect, held out in the mountain Fortress of Masada to the southeast, which they had seized in AD 66. Numbering just 1,000, including women and children, they held off a Roman army of 15,000 for two years. Again the Romans broke the siege by building huge ramps and battering the walls down but the Zealots preferred suicide to defeat. Only two women and five children survived after hiding in a water pipe. Masada fell on 7 April AD 73, but the destruction of Jerusalem that had taken place three years earlier had already marked the end of the last Jewish state in Palestine for almost 2,000 years.

Châlons-sur-Marne

The Defeat Of Attila the Hun

AD 451

Attila the Hun suffered the one defeat of his military career at Châlons-sur-Marne and believed he would die there. He was spared by the politically astute Roman general Flavius Aetius, but the Huns were soon a spent force.

BETWEEN 434 AND 449, Attila the Hun had led a series of successful onslaughts on the Eastern Empire, besieging Constantinople and forcing the Emperor Theodosius II to pay tribute and cede territory. Attila then turned his attention to the Western Empire, which was weaker. His excuse was that Honoria, the sister of the Emperor Valentinian, had sent him a ring. She had been having an affair with her steward, who had been executed. Now pregnant, she had sent the ring to the King of the

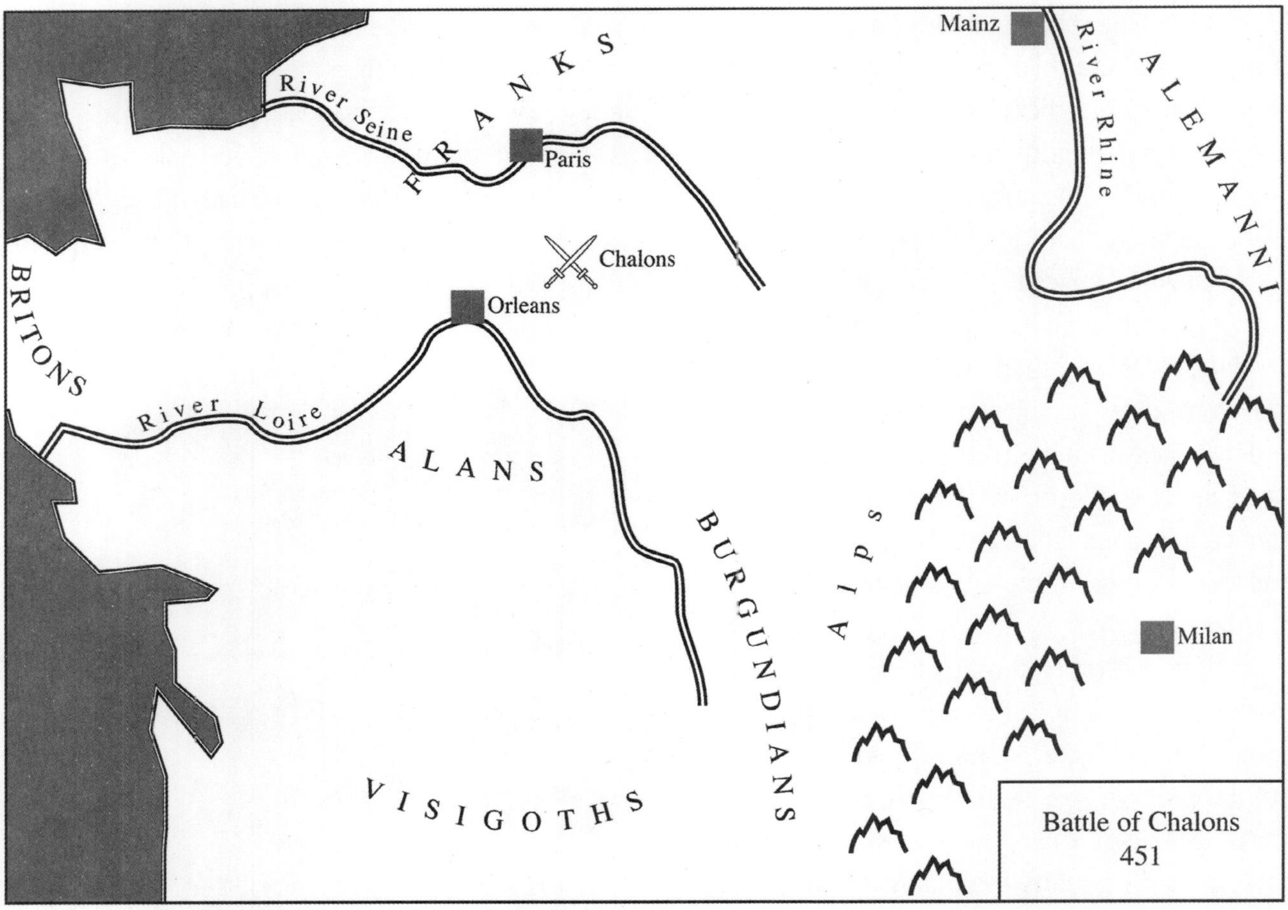

Huns and had begged him to rescue her. He had taken the ring as a marriage proposal and had asked for half of the Western Empire as her dowry.

In the spring of 451, Attila forged an alliance with the Franks and the Vandals and unleashed an attack on the heart of western Europe. He took Metz in April, with an army of between 300,000 and 700,000, and Reims, Mainz, Strasbourg, Cologne, Worms and Trier were destroyed. It was said that Paris was saved because St. Genevieve was in the city. Consequently, she became its patron saint.

However, Attila was stopped at Orléans. He was besieging the city when a Roman army under Flavius Aetius arrived, supported by the Visigothic King Theodoric I. For once, Attila abandoned his hit-and-run tactics and joined pitched battle on the plain of Châlons-sur-Marne. This vast area of flat ground was perfect for a cavalry battle, to the advantage of Attila's horsemen.

During the retreat from Orléans it is said that a Christian hermit approached Attila and told him: 'You are the Scourge of God for the chastisement of Christians.' Attila promptly assumed this as a title and was known from then on as '*Flagellum Dei*' ('Scourge of God').

The Christian forces drew themselves up with the Romans under Aetius; the Visigoths assembled under Theodoric on the left; and the Alani, whose loyalty was suspect, joined Sangipan in the centre. Attila himself commanded the middle part of the Hunnish forces with the Ostrogoths and other allies on the flanks. While Attila had the advantage in horse, Aetius was more adept at set-piece battles and fighting on foot. Before the armies engaged, a little skilled manoeuvring enabled him to occupy a sloping hill that overlooked the left flank of the Huns.

Attila quickly spotted the importance of the high ground and the battle began with a furious assault

The Huns were unrivalled horsemen, while the Romans were footsoldiers. Under the inspired generalship of Flavius Aetius, however, the superior tactics of the Romans routed Attila.

on the Roman positions there. However, even though he detached some of his best troops from the centre, Attila could not oust the Romans from their commanding position.

The right-hand side of Attila's army was then attacked by Visigoths, with Theodoric leading the charge. Theodoric was then struck down by a javelin and killed by his own cavalry who charged over him in the confusion. Despite the loss of their king, the Visigoths were not dispirited. Determined to avenge him they wheeled around on the centre, where the Alani were fighting a bloody, but indecisive battle with Attila's main force.

Fearing that they were about to be encircled, Attila's men pulled back to their camp and, from the safety of entrenchments and wagons, the Hun archers repulsed the Visigoth horsemen. But Aetius failed to press home his advantage on the right and when night fell the day had ended in a stalemate.

After a night of heavy drinking Attila was found dead of a nosebleed, drowned in his own blood

On the following morning, Attila put his best archers outside the fortifications and made every preparation for desperate resistance. Even so, he expected to lose so he resolved that no man would have the honour of either killing the 'Scourge of God' or taking him alive. Accordingly, he built a huge bonfire of Hunnish woollen saddles, on which he placed all the booty he had looted and the wives that he had brought along on the campaign, leaving a place on top for himself. There he would be burnt alive if the enemy succeeded in overwhelming his defences.

When dawn broke the plains were seen to be scattered with corpses, evidence of the level of resistance that had been mounted by the Huns. It soon seemed clear that Aetius's forces were not about to storm Attila's camp, nor did they make any attempt to blockade it. Attila was allowed to withdraw with the remnants of his army.

Although Aetius had apparently lost his nerve, some think that he was employing clever tactics. Perhaps he did not want the Visigoths to win too great a victory under their new king, Theodoric's son Thorismund. After all, the Visigoths themselves had sacked Rome under Alaric just forty-one years before in 410. Aetius managed to persuade Thorismund to return to his capital in Aquitaine, thereby ridding himself of a formidable foe and a dangerous friend.

Attila might have suffered his one and only defeat in battle, but he was far from finished. He regrouped his forces and invaded Italy the following year. It is said that Attila turned back before the gates of Rome because he was impressed by the holiness of Pope Leo I, who came out of the city to parlay. However, he may have retreated because the countryside was racked with disease and famine at the time and his troops, who lived by foraging, could barely support themselves. It is also possible he feared the return of the Roman legions fighting abroad.

The Huns collected their booty and turned back towards the north. The forty-seven-year-old Attila died on the way. He had taken a new wife named Ildico and, after a day of heavy drinking, he had withdrawn with his young bride on his wedding night. The next morning, he was found dead after a nosebleed, drowned in his own blood.

After Attila's death the Germanic tribes revolted and his sons fell out amongst themselves. Within twenty years, the Huns ceased to be a military power. Without the wide Asiatic plains to graze their horses, they were forced to fight on foot, like other European armies and they lost their edge. Plainly the Battle of Châlons-sur-Marne had dented the myth of the Huns' invincibility and, for the time being, the glory that was Rome was preserved.

Tours

The Advance of Islam Halted

732

If the Frankish general Charles Martel had failed to stop the Islamic army of Abd-ar-Rahman between Tours and Poitiers, Europe would now be Muslim and be speaking Arabic. This was not a crusade, but an invasion.

Charles Martel was already an accomplished general who had re-united the entire Frankish realm. His byname 'Martel' means 'the hammer'.

After the foundation of Islam by Muhammad in the seventh century AD, the faith quickly spread throughout Arabia, Syria and Persia and across Egypt, Cyrenaica, Tripolitania and the rest of the Maghrib in North Africa. In 711, an army of 10,000 Muslim warriors crossed the Strait of Gibraltar and crushed the Visigoths who had settled in Spain in 415.

Muslim forces then began raiding over the Pyrenees and, in 725, they reached Burgundy and sacked the town of Autun. Then, in 732, one hundred years after the death of the Prophet, a large army under the command of Abd-ar-Rahman, the governor of Córoba, marched into Bordeaux, defeated Eudes, the king of Aquitaine, and burnt down all the churches.

At that time the Franks were a divided people, but they quickly united behind one man: Charles Martel. A Frankish general, Martel was not his given name, rather it was a *nom-de-guerre* roughly translating as 'the hammer'. He already had a considerable reputation after fighting campaigns in Germany and France.

Abd-ar-Rahman now considered himself to be governor of southern France. His next objective was Poiters. From there he intended to capture Tours, which was celebrated throughout Christendom for the basilica of St Martin, where numerous priceless treasures were held. The Muslim army seemed unstoppable. They numbered between 60,000 and 400,000 and were mainly horsemen. Europe had

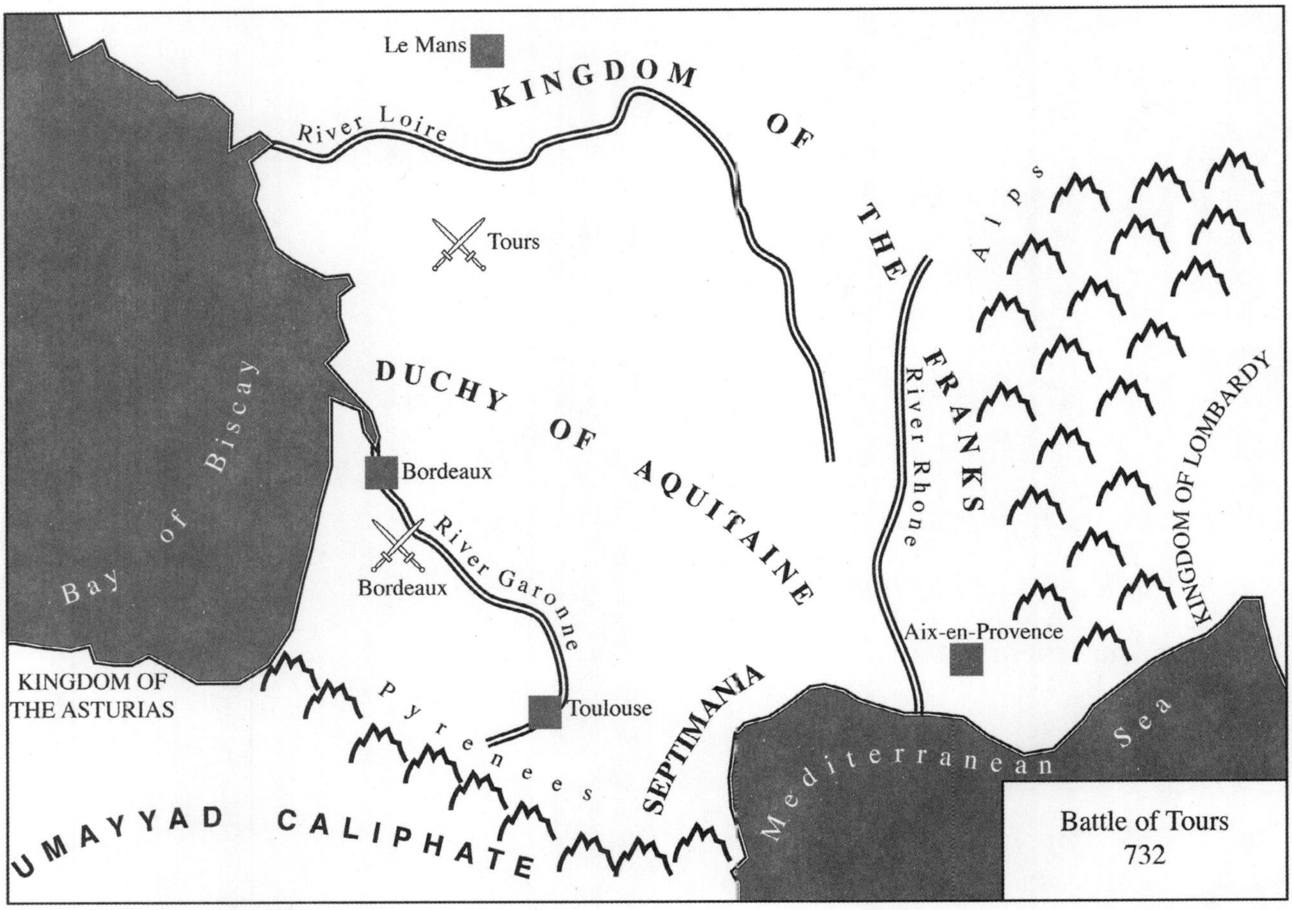

seen nothing like this since Attila the Hun had arrived with his mounted soldiers nearly 200 years earlier. In those days, only superb horsemen such as the Huns could ride into battle so European battles were traditionally fought on foot. However, recent improvements in saddles and harnesses had made cavalry engagements possible and Charles Martel's army also boasted cavalry alongside the infantry.

In October 732 the Franks and the Moors met on the road from Poitiers to Tours. Abd-ar-Rahman halted his army because he wanted to discover the strength of the enemy and he hoped they would attack. On unfamiliar territory, he did not want to chase after the enemy and risk losing his army among the forests and the streams.

Martel's forces also stopped and made camp at the edge of the forest because Martel knew that he could withdraw into it if he were attacked. Martel also had a reason for delaying any engagement. The weather was bitterly cold and the Moors were dressed in light clothing from their summer campaigns, while the Franks were warm in their wolf pelts. For seven days the two armies watched each other from a distance.

On the morning of the eighth day Abd-ar-Rahman could wait no longer and decided to attack. Martel formed his army into a hollow square which stood firm against the Moors' charge. Meanwhile, he sent riders through the forest to attack Abd-ar-Rahman's army from the rear.

The Franks enjoyed numerous advantages in the ensuing battle. The Arabs had been looting as they came through France and had a large amount of treasure to protect with them , while the Franks had no baggage train to hamper them. Also, the Arab horsemen were basically guerrilla warriors and were not accustomed to the type of pitched battle they had embarked on. On the other hand, the Franks were disciplined and trained in classical warfare and they had the Loire at their backs, so they could not retreat even if they wanted to.

However the Arabs also had an advantage: that of armour. They wore pointed helmets and chain mail that also covered their horses, making them practically invincible. As the battle progressed, the Franks began to weaken.

But Martel's men still knew how to divert the Moors. When the battle was almost lost, a column of Franks fought its way through to the Moors' treasure wagons. Seizing them, they began to drive them away. This caused the Moors to panic and they ran from the battlefield to recapture them. Abd-ar-Rahman ordered his men back into the fray, but he was struck down by a lance. The battle then resolved itself into a series of disparate cavalry engagements.

The Arab steeds were fiery but the Franks' mounts were bigger and Martel's men were bigger and heavier too. The Muslim horsemen were armed with scimitars but they were no match for the lances of the Frankish cavalry. Also, the Frankish infantry used heavy clubs and cudgels at close quarters. Wave upon wave of Moorish cavalry charges was cut down and the fighting continued in a confused fashion until night fell.

The two sides then withdrew to their camps. Throughout the night the Franks heard the clash of arms as Abd-ar-Rahman's lieutenants fought over the leadership, while others fought a small-scale civil war over the treasure carts. By dawn the sounds of fighting had ended. When the sun came up, Martel saw that his enemies had disappeared. They had taken their treasure and hurried off south.

The battle at Tours was a historic turning point. Through his victory over ar-Rahman, Martel had stopped the spread of Islam into Western Europe. As it was, however, Spain would remain in Muslim hands for another five centuries.

Hastings

The End of Anglo-Saxon England

1066

The Battle of Hastings was a crucial event in history for the English. It was the last time that the nation was overrun by hostile foreign forces. The English never suffered such an invasion again.

Edward the Confessor was the last king of the old English royal line. When he died childless in January 1066, there was a problem with the succession. Edward had almost certainly named William, Duke of Normandy, as his heir. However, Harold Godwineson, Earl of Wessex and Kent, and one of Edward's favourites, was crowned king of England instead.

In August 1066, William, a seasoned campaigner, assembled a force of 4,000 knights and 7,000 foot-soldiers at the mouth of the Dives river on the coast of Normandy. They were unable to embark, however, because the wind remained unfavourable. Harold feared an invasion all that summer, particularly in the Hastings-Pevensey area but by 8 September it was thought that the beginning of the autumn gales would rule out any seaborne attack. Accordingly, the English fleet was dispersed and the army disbanded.

That same day another claimant to the English throne, the Norwegian King Harald Hardraade, arrived in the Tyne estuary. Joining forces with Harold's embittered brother Tostig, the former Earl of Northumbria, Hardraade seized York on 20

The Battle of Hasting was of such significance for England that it is still re-enacted on the battlefield over nine hundred years later. The Norman Conquest also had the effect of drawing England into the mainstream of European history.

September. Harold hurriedly assembled an army of no more than 2,000 men and set off northwards, leaving the south of England totally undefended.

The English met the Norwegian forces at Stamford Bridge on 25 September and slaughtered them. Both Hardraade and Tostig were killed and of the 300 Viking ships that had arrived in the Tyne only twenty-four were needed to take the survivors home. William breathed a sigh of relief when he heard the news. He considered Hardraade to be a far more formidable foe than Harold.

Two days later, the wind in the Channel turned to the south. It seems that William planned to sail due north from Normandy and land on the Isle of Wight, giving him an offshore base for attacks on the mainland. However, a westerly squall blew him up the Channel to Pevensey, where he landed on 28 September. There on the beach he built a makeshift fort on the ruins of a Roman stronghold. Two days later, he moved his entire army ten miles to the east to the small fishing port of Hastings, which provided a much better base for an invasion. There, above the town, he built two wooden forts with palisaded ditches.

On 2 October, Harold heard that William had landed and he began his march south. In London he hastily assembled a force of some 7,000 men, who were poorly armed and mostly untrained. Although William was no real threat to London and the seat of power, his men were plundering Kent – Harold's own earldom – so Harold had little option but to march south and confront him.

Harold arrived outside Hastings on 13 October where he camped for the night. When William rode out of his Hastings stronghold at six a.m. on the following morning, half an hour before sunrise, he

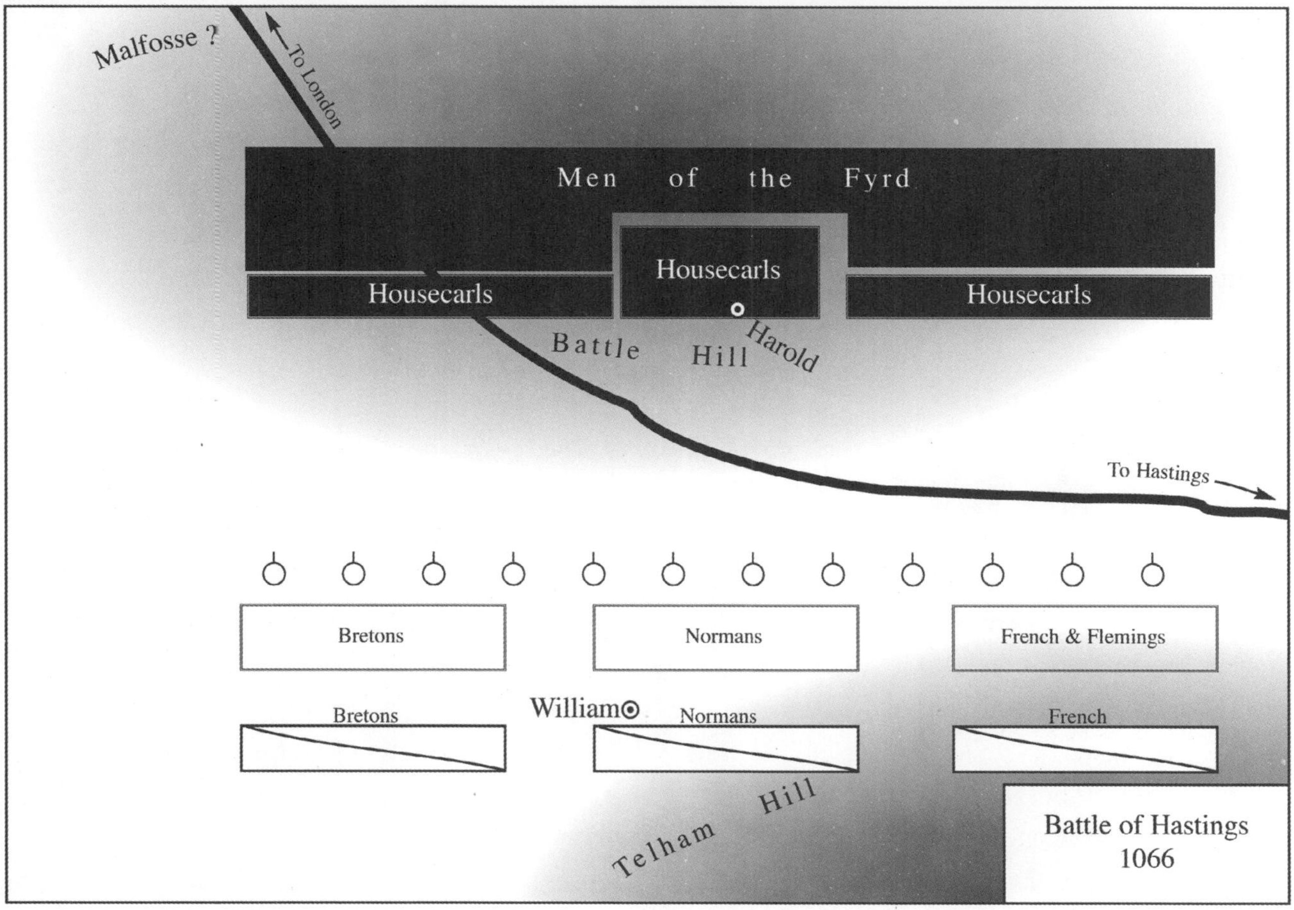

Malfosse ?
To London
Men of the Fyrd
Housecarls
Housecarls
Housecarls
Harold
Battle Hill
To Hastings
Bretons
Normans
French & Flemings
William
Bretons
Normans
French
Telham Hill
Battle of Hastings
1066

The Bayeux tapestry celebrates the Norman victory over the English at the Battle of Hastings. It is 231 feet long and 19.5 inches wide, with more than seventy scenes telling the story of the battle. Here, the English king Harold is killed by an arrow in the eye.

found Harold's army already formed up. They were ten or twelve ranks deep and spaced along a high ridge, blocking his path. The English flanks were protected by streams and hollows and their rear was shielded by a steep slope.

The ground was marshy at the bottom of the ridge. Only a narrow strip in the centre was firm enough for William's army to negotiate as they marched into battle. William sent his troops through this narrow gap and formed them up at the foot of the ridge – the French to the right, the Bretons to the left and his own Normans in the centre. This was a risky move, especially for those moving to the left because they presented their unshielded side to the enemy. The English could have swarmed down the slope and attacked at any time but Harold showed an unusual caution by maintaining his position on the high ground.

The Norman archers moved forward and fired at around 9.30 a.m. but the arrows were stopped by a wall of English shields and the archers, in their exposed position, suffered huge losses. The Norman infantry went in next. They were cut down by English two-handed battle-axes. Observing their plight, William sent in the cavalry, but its effectiveness was blunted by attacking uphill.

When the cavalry pulled back, however, the undisciplined English chased after them, crashing into the Norman infantry. The Norman line began to give and a rumour that William was dead began to circulate, causing some Normans to take flight. Sensing that this might turn into a rout, William lifted his helmet so that his men could see that he was alive. This put heart back into his troops. They attacked and fell back in turn, keeping relentless pressure on the English line while giving themselves periods of rest.

Occasional feints lured more Englishmen down the hill to their deaths but this tactic also cost a number of Norman lives. By evening, William knew that he had to win that day or surrender for Harold would have reinforcements by the next day, whereas he would have none. He ordered an all-out assault and this time the archers fired high into the sky and the falling arrows thinned the English ranks. The English were forced to shorten their line in order to maintain their shield wall, which left room for the Normans to mount the ridge on the flanks. At that stage, the Norman army turned into a killing machine but it took a further two hours for them to scythe their way through to where Harold had fallen, possibly killed by an arrow in the eye, although equally possibly, not. His brothers Gyrth and Leofwine died with him.

The retreating English staged a stout rearguard action at the edge of the forest of Andredsweald that covered much of Kent, but they were cut down to a man. The road to London was now open to William. Instead of making straight for the capital he encircled it, thereby isolating the city. The remaining English leaders surrendered to him at Berkhamstead, and William was crowned king in Westminster Abbey on Christmas Day 1066. Resistance to William continued until 1071, however, and a series of castles had to be built across the country to keep the people in subjugation.

William dispossessed the old Saxon lords and parcelled out their lands to his knights. Although he kept much of the old Saxon system of administration and law, it was overlaid with the feudal system that was practised on the Continent and a body of new Continental 'forest law' was introduced.

The conquest also broke England's traditional ties with Scandinavia and brought the country into western Europe politically. Vernacular English was replaced by Latin and Norman–French in official documents and other records and written English did not reappear until the thirteenth century.

Crécy

England Dominates Europe

1346

The victory of the English longbowmen over mounted French knights at Crécy made England the dominant power in Western Europe for the next one hundred years. It also united France into a single nation.

WHEN THE FRENCH KING Charles IV died in 1328, the French throne was claimed by Edward III of England on the grounds that Isabella, his mother, was Charles IV's sister. Edward was also Count of Ponthieu on the French coast and Duke of Guyenne, which was part of Aquitaine in southwest France.

However, according to the Salic Law of the Franks an inheritance could not pass down the female line. At that point, Philip de Valois, son of another branch of the family, also claimed the throne. An assembly of France was called to settle the question. They chose de Valois as Philip VI and Edward appeared to accept the decision. When Philip tried to confiscate Guyenne in 1337, however, Edward renewed his

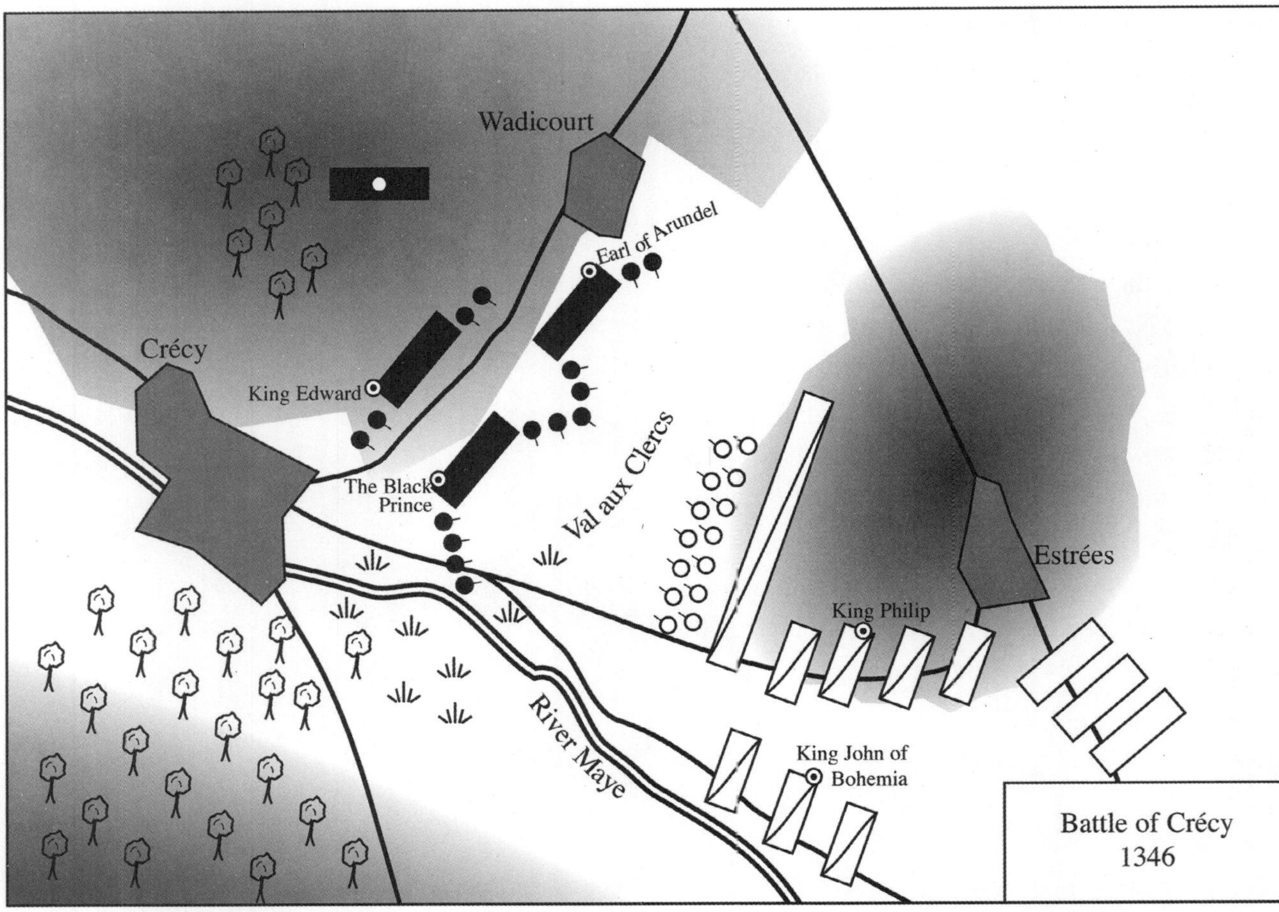

claim to the throne and went to war. The English seized the island of Cadzand, off the coast of Flanders, on 11 November and soon after made an alliance with the Flemish. This provided Edward with a bridgehead for a full-scale invasion. The prize was immense because France was the largest and richest country in Europe at the time, with a population of 20,000,000.

England's population was just 4,000,000, but it made a formidable foe. More united than France, its officers were loyal to the central state. They were experienced from fighting the Scots and their men were battle-hardened and disciplined. What is more, the English had longbows, which meant that a peasant archer could bring down the finest knight in France at long range.

The effectiveness of the English longbow had already been demonstrated against the Scots, first at the Battle of Dupplin Moor in 1332 and then at Halidon Hill in 1333. The Flemish crossbows were also no match for the English longbow at the Battle of Cadzand in 1337 and the French discovered its effectiveness in a naval battle at Sluys in 1340.

However, Edward's attempts to invade France proved unsuccessful in 1339 and 1340. He tried again in the July of 1346, landing near Cherbourg with his eldest son, Prince Edward the Black Prince. They advanced rapidly through Normandy, taking Caen after a brief siege. The English then headed for Rouen where they heard that Philip VI was massing an army near Paris. The war flag of France, the Oriflamme, had been taken from its place in the abbey of Saint-Denis. With the bridges across the Seine cut, Edward moved his army to the north to give him a clear line of retreat into Flanders. But his way was blocked by the River Somme which was in flood. Now a massive French army was on his tail. Eventually he made a crossing near Blanchetaque

At Crécy, the French horsemen rode down the Italian crossbowmen who joined them as mercenaries. However, they were not ready to meet the English longbow which rained down lethal clouds of arrows.

and then he turned to face the French outside the village of Crécy, in his own fiefdom of Ponthieu.

Vastly outnumbered, Edward deployed his army for a defensive battle in harrow formation, ready to receive the French charge. Near the village of Wadicourt on the left were 3,000 archers, 1,000 dismounted knights and some Welsh footsoldiers, under the Earls of Arundel and Northampton and the Bishop of Durham. On the right, near Crécy itself, there were another 3,000 archers, 1,000 men-at-arms and 1,000 Welsh infantry. They were under the command of sixteen-year-old Edward, Prince of Wales, who later found fame in his own right as the Black Prince. His commanders were Count Godfrey of Harcourt and the Earls of Oxford and Warwick, along with four knights of the garter – Lord Stafford, Lord Burghersh, Sir John Chandos and Sir Thomas Holland. Behind them, on a ridge, the King kept a reserve of 2,000 archers and 700 dismounted knights.

This modest force of just 10,000 faced an army of 60,000 Frenchmen, including 12,000 mounted men-at-arms. However, the French force was ill-disciplined and disorganized. As well as the troops that had been brought by the French nobility, there were foreign contingents under King Jaime II of Majorca, the Duke of Lorraine and Charles, King of the Romans, along with hundreds of German and

Bohemian knights under the blind King John of Bohemia. Even though it was already clear that the English longbow was superior to the Continental crossbows, the French knights were to be led into battle by 6,000 crossbowmen from Genoa, under the commanders Carlo Grimaldi and Odone Doria. It had been raining, however, and the strings of their crossbows were wet.

The footsoldiers had been marching for eighteen hours when the French spotted the English at around six o'clock in the evening. Philip wanted to make camp in order to allow the rest of the army to catch up, but the knights were eager to join battle. They cried out 'Kill!', giving the impression that battle had already begun. Unable to control his men, Philip decided to attack.

The Genoan crossbowmen started forward, followed by a line of knights under the command of the Count of Flanders and Count Charles II of Alençon, who was the King's brother. As they approached the English, the Genoans loosed their first volley of arrows, which fell short. When they began to reload, they were hit by a storm of English arrows. Some 60,000 rained down in the next sixty seconds. At the same time the Genoans were pounded by rocks and boulders that were being flung from English catapults.

The Genoans turned tail and ran, but they found their way blocked by a line of knights. The fleeing crossbowmen had also blocked the knights' advance and the piqued Philip ordered his knights to kill them. The English were then treated to the sight of the French slaughtering their own mercenaries while they were being pummelled by English arrows. When the French knights finally turned their wrath on the enemy, there were few left and they made little impact on the English lines.

The battlefield was strewn with the dead and the dying but no attempt was made to clear it. Disparate bands of knights charged straight at the English lines and were cut down; effectively leaderless, they did not manoeuvre or attempt any flanking movement. Even the blind King of Bohemia met his death by joining the charge with a knight chained on either side of himself.

Some of Alençon's men-at-arms broke into the left wing in an attempt to avoid the English arrows. Prince Edward was knocked to the ground, but was rescued by Richard Fitzsimmons, his standard bearer. Harcourt went to the King to ask for reinforcements, but Edward famously said: 'Let the boy win his spurs.' However, he quietly sent twenty knights to the prince's flank and Alençon's men were overpowered.

The King himself was knocked to the ground twice while he was engaged in single combat with the French knight Sir Eustace de Ribeaument, who was eventually taken prisoner. That night Sir Eustace dined with Edward, who gave him back his liberty and rewarded him for his bravery with a string of pearls.

By nightfall, the French had made fifteen charges, to no avail. Over 1,500 French men-at-arms lay dead, along with countless footsoldiers. The counts of Alençon and Flanders and Louis II of Nevers were among the dead. Philip himself was knocked off his horse twice during the fighting and eventually escaped wounded, but the English maintained their discipline and did not pursue him.

The English victory at Crécy put an end to the medieval order of battle that had been fought between mounted knights. After the battle, Edward went on to take Calais after a siege lasting for almost a year. The longbow made England the dominant power in Western Europe over the next hundred years, adding huge tracts of France to her possessions. However, the battle also had the effect of giving France a sense of nationhood. The supremacy of the English longbow lasted until the Battle of Formigy in 1453, when the English faced overwhelming French handguns and cannons. Calais would remain in English hands until 1558.

Agincourt
Victory of the English Longbow
1415

The English victory at Agincourt made Henry V a national hero. He won the hand of daughter of the French king and, had he lived long enough, the right to sit on the throne of France as well as England.

AT CRÉCY, the English longbowmen demonstrated their ability to overcome mounted knights. At Agincourt, they inflicted an even more telling defeat on the French dismounted knights. The English longbow again showed its worth, but English footsoldiers also demonstrated the havoc that could be wrought with swords and axes wielded by lightly armoured men.

When Henry V became king of England on 21 March 1413, he faced a full-scale uprising and a plot to assassinate him, both of which he quickly put down. In order to distract the English from domestic concerns he renewed the Hundred Years' War against France. Many of the early gains made by Edward III and the Black Prince had been lost and Henry demanded the return of Aquitaine and the other lands ceded by the Treaty of Calais in 1360. Then, in 1415, he proposed marriage to Catherine of Valois, daughter of Charles VI of France, demanding the old Plantagenet lands of Normandy and Anjou as his dowry. Charles refused and Henry declared war but this time he was pursuing a claim to the French throne.

Henry landed 11,000 men in Normandy in August 1415 and he captured Harfleur in the following month. By then, however, he had lost nearly half his troops, largely because of disease. Henry's army headed for Calais in the hope that they could sail back to England, but their retreat was blocked by a huge force under Charles I d'Albret, constable of France. At first, the English tried to outmanoeuvre the French, but the superior numbers of mounted troops fielded by the French made this impossible.

The weather was terrible and many of Henry's men were suffering from dysentery. Consequently they marched without hose, much to the amusement of the French. The state of the English army and the overwhelming superiority in numbers of the French made them overconfident. They had not learnt the lesson of Crécy. Certain of victory, the French stopped the English near a village called Agincourt (now Azincourt) in the Pas-de-Calais.

On 25 October 1415 the two armies rose before dawn and assembled for battle. Henry had some 5,000 archers and 900 men-at-arms at his disposal and the French fielded between 20,000 and 30,000 men. According to the rules of chivalry the field of battle should favour neither side, but the French had freely chosen a battlefield that was disadvantageous to them. It was flanked by two woods 1,000 yards apart. This would prevent the larger French force from manoeuvring freely and would stop them outflanking the smaller English force.

The battle lines formed up around 1,000 yards apart, between Agincourt and Tramecourt. They were separated by a recently ploughed field which was muddy after days of rain. It dipped slightly giving the armies a good view of one another.

Henry only had command of enough men-at-arms to form a single line. They were drawn up into three groups – the advance, the main body and the rearguard. Each group was around four men deep. The left was commanded by Lord Camous, the right by the Duke of York, and Henry himself took personal command of the centre. There was no reserve. The archers were formed up in wedge shapes on the wings, angled forward so that they could provide flanking fire. They were protected by thickets of eight-feet-long pointed stakes, which were hammered into the ground in front of them and angled forward so that they would impale the charging French horsemen.

It has been suggested that a small formation of English archers found their way through the Tramecourt woods to the rear of the French lines. From there they would have been able to cause confusion in the French ranks and it would have been necessary to divert troops from the main battle to deal with them. The deployment of such a force would contravene the rules of chivalry and its existence was vehemently denied by the English chroniclers.

To the north, the French men-at-arms formed three lines. The two front lines were dismounted and they carried lances that had been cut down for fighting on foot. The rear line remained mounted. The French archers and crossbowmen should have been deployed between the first and the second rows, but every French nobleman wanted to be in the front rank so that his banner was prominently displayed. Consequently there was much jostling for position, which pushed the archers and the crossbowmen out to the flanks so that the first two lines of men-at-arms merged into one large chaotic mass.

The cavalry was placed on the flanks – 800 on the right, commanded by Cligent de Breband, and 1,600 on the left under the Count of Vendôme. The French also had some artillery on the flanks, but they never contributed more than a few shots during the whole battle.

The two sides were assembled by around seven a.m. – and then they waited. D'Albret wanted the English to attack first, because their inferior numbers would place them at a greater disadvantage. Some of the French even argued that they should not join battle at all; now that they had the English trapped, they should keep them there and let them starve. This did not suit the men-at-arms, however, because they wanted to win honour on the battlefield. For the next five hours they stood waiting, spending the time jostling for position, settling scores and throwing insults at the English. Most refused to sit down because they were afraid to muddy their armour.

Henry waited too, because he knew that an attack would be costly. He also knew that he had to fight that day. The English had no food and they would only get weaker, so he gave the order to advance to within 300 yards of the French position. There the archers hammered in their stakes again. This advance would have taken at least ten minutes. If the French had attacked at that point, they could have destroyed the English. But instead they kept their position, leaving Henry with the initiative.

The French were at the limit of the English archers' range, but Henry ordered that they fire off a volley. Even though a flight of arrows is not very effective at that distance, it produced a thunderous noise when it hit the French armour. Trained English archers would loose off up to ten flights a minute, so by the time the first flight had struck home a second would be in the air.

Casualties were slight, but both men and horses had been wounded. It was enough to goad the cavalry on the flanks into charging. D'Albret followed suit and led a charge of dismounted knights across the muddy field.

Some of the cavalry had wandered off because of the delay, leaving the charge undermanned. The archers would have been able to loose off another six flights of arrows in the forty seconds it would have taken the French horse to reach the English lines, each flight becoming more accurate and more deadly as the French advanced. With the woods preventing a flanking attack, the French horse had to make a frontal assault, with the riders behind pushing those in front onto the English stakes.

The pride of the French aristocracy rode into battle at Agincourt, only to be cut down by English longbowmen. The day of the mounted knight was finally over.

Shying from the storm of arrows that had been released by the English archers, the French cavalry turned inwards. They were now directly facing d'Albret and his dismounted men-at-arms and they were making slow progress over the muddy ground that had been further broken up by the cavalry charge. As they closed, the English archers were able to fire into their flanks and their arrows were fixed with 'Bodkin points' – a specially-designed device that penetrated armour.

The French men-at-arms had no defence against the English arrows. They saw archers as inferior in social standing and, consequently, not worthy opponents. Also, the archers offered no prospect of the ransom that a French knight could expect if he captured an English noble. As the French advanced on the English position, the field narrowed by 150 yards, compressing the French line. The hail of arrows from English archers on the flanks compressed it further. By the time d'Albret's men arrived at the English line, they did not have enough room to wield their weapons.

The French rushed the last few yards in order to maximize the shock of impact. More men crashed in behind them and the weight of numbers pushed the English back. But this caused the French more problems. As men slipped in the crush or were cut down, others tripped over them. In these muddy conditions those wearing full armour found it difficult to get back on their feet again.

With the battle joined, the French artillery, archers and crossbowmen could provide no assistance because they had no clear line of fire. However, the English archers on the flanks could pour arrows into the crush of French knights. More piled in and many of the French were crushed to death. As one English chronicler wrote: 'More were dead through press than our men could have slain.'

At Henry's signal, the English archers dropped their bows and fell on the French knights with swords and axes. Many armed themselves with discarded French weapons. The heavily armoured French men-at-arms found it hard to keep their footing in the mud so they were vulnerable to attack by lightly-armed troops, who could knock them down or unfoot them by stabbing them behind the knee. Once the French men-at-arms were on the ground, they could be killed by a thrust from a sword or a misericord – a small archer's knife – through the visor or a joint in the armour.

The English line buckled in the centre, but it soon rallied. Neither side was willing to give way and Henry was in the thick of it. Many French knights had vowed to kill Henry so two English soldiers dressed as the king. The threat had been real because both were killed and the helmet that Henry wore at Agincourt, now on display in Westminster Abbey, bears a dent caused by a French battle-axe.

The first two French lines were almost totally destroyed. The troops had either been killed or had been taken prisoner. The third line of mounted men refused to attack, despite the urgings of the Duke of Alençon who rode up and down the line exhorting his men to charge. Eventually, he rode into the thick of battle and reached Henry. Upon recognizing him he offered to surrender, but as he held out his hand an English soldier despatched him with the blow of an axe.

The English were handed a problem when the scale of their victory mounted. By early afternoon their prisoners outnumbered the entire English army and the battlefield was far from secure. Three knights and a band of peasants under the command of the Lord of Agincourt attacked the English baggage train to the rear. It was protected by no more than a token guard who were quickly overwhelmed and the attackers made off with their plunder, which included one of Henry's crowns.

At the same time, the Counts of Marle and Fauquemberghes rallied 600 mounted knights for a new charge. Fearing that the prisoners were a threat to his rear in the renewed fighting, Henry ordered

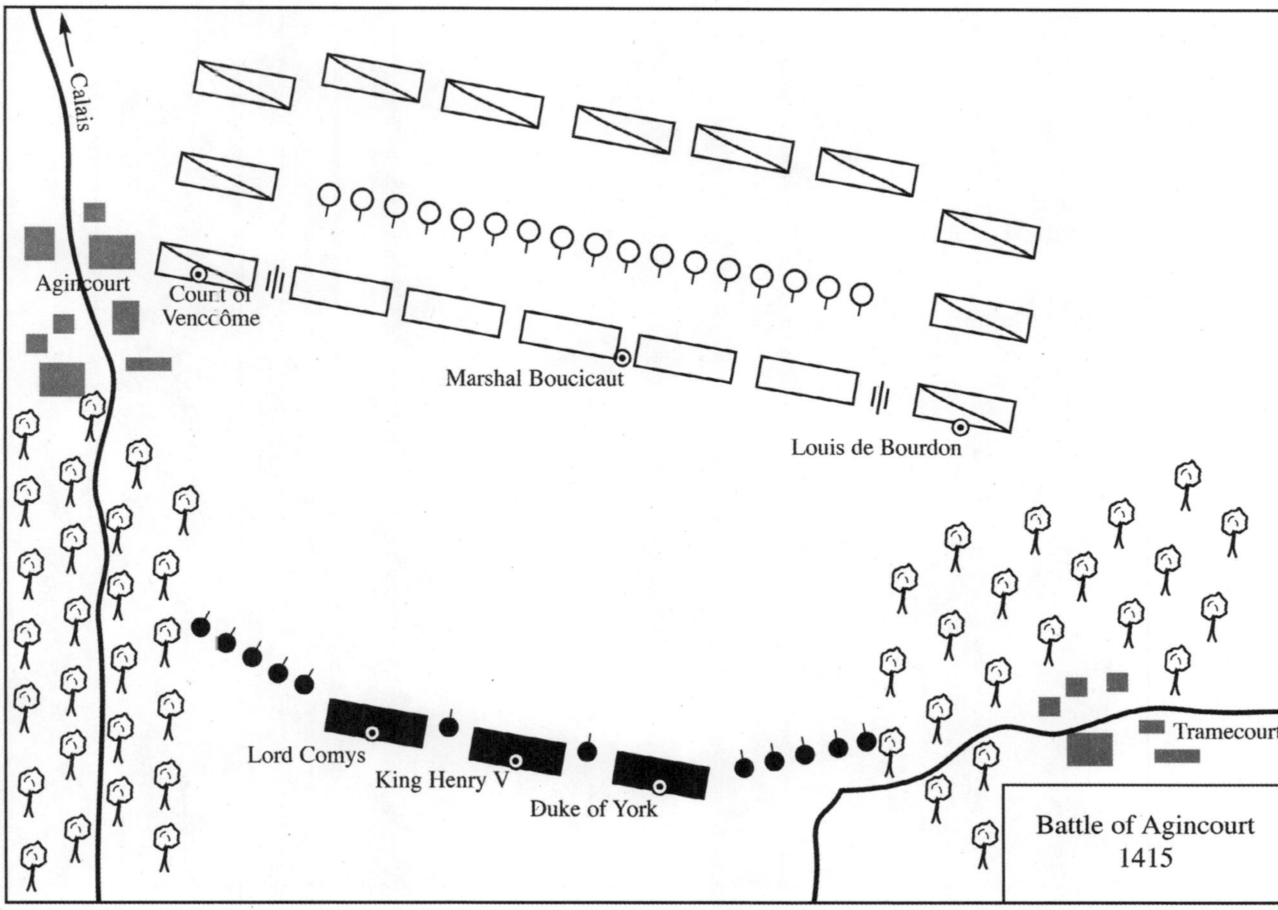

that they be killed. This was not a popular order. The English men-at-arms refused, because killing a man of equal rank after he had surrendered was dishonourable. Also, the archers had hoped to get rich with their share of the ransoms that the French nobles would attract. Henry picked out 200 of his archers – tough, professional soldiers – and threatened to hang them if they did not obey his order. Within minutes thousands of French men-at-arms were dead. Some of the wounded were burnt to death when Henry ordered the houses they were in to be set on fire. Modern scholars have attacked Henry for this, but at the time French chroniclers were more critical of their own knights for putting Henry in a position where this seemed necessary.

As it was, the French did not launch another attack, but some 2,000 prisoners were already dead, and around 10,000 French had been lost in the fighting. D'Albert was dead, along with Alençon and ten members of the highest nobility, while Marshal Boucicaut, the Dukes of Bourbon and Orléans and the Counts of Eu, Richemont and Vendôme survived captivity. The English lost fewer than 450 soldiers.

After Agincourt, Henry went from strength to strength. He gained mastery over the English Channel at the Battle of the Seine in August 1416 and by 1419 he had captured Normandy, Picardy and much of the Capetian stronghold of the Ile-de-France.

In May 1420 Charles VI was forced to sign the Treaty of Troyes. Henry won Catherine under its terms, whom he married on 2 June. Henry became both Charles' son-in-law and his regent and Charles passed over his own son to make Henry heir to the French crown. But Henry died of dysentery at the château of Vincennes on 31 August 1422. Had he lived just two months longer, he would have been king of both England and France.

Constantinople

The End of the Byzantine Empire

1453

Constantinople was founded as a Christian city by the Roman Emperor Constantine on 11 May 330. Over 1,100 years later it fell to Islam and the Christians were expelled. Only in 1930 did it become, officially, Istanbul.

THE EASTERN EMPIRE flourished long after the Roman Empire in the West had fallen. Based on Constantinople (formerly Byzantium) it was known as the Byzantine Empire. However, in the 1300s, while Europe fell victim to the Black Death or tore itself apart in internecine war, a new power emerged in the region. A Turkish chief named Osman assembled a highly-trained army and went on a campaign of conquest. The resulting Ottoman Empire took its name from him.

After a century of fighting, the Ottomans held most of Asia Minor and the Balkans. Tantalisingly, the Christian enclave of Constantinople was almost at the centre of their Islamic empire. When Mehmed II (known in Turkish as Mehmed the Conqueror) came to the throne in 1444, his dream was to put the crescent of Islam on top of the gleaming spires and domes of the great city at the entrance to the Bosporus.

The fall of Constantinople marked the end of the Byzantine Empire, which itself was the last vestige of the old Roman Empire. The artists expelled by its fall fled to Italy where they laid the foundations of the Italian Renaissance.

He laid his plans carefully. First he signed peace treaties with Hungary and Venice on terms that were so favourable to them that they were effectively kept out of the fighting. Then he spent the year of 1452 in building the Fortress of Bogazkesen (now Runeli Hisari), which overlooked the Bosporus to the north. He covered the south by assembling a fleet of thirty-one galleys in the Sea of Marmara. They were equipped with cannon of the largest calibre yet seen in Europe. The city was surrounded.

When Constantine XI came to power in Constantinople in 1449, he found the city shockingly ill-prepared for war. The fortifications were dilapidated and only 5,000 out of the population of 40,000 were willing to rally to the flag. They had no allies to speak of. The Pope in Rome was unwilling to come to the aid of the Eastern Orthodox Church that was based there and the King of France was only prepared to offer asylum to Constantine in the event of defeat. The only support that Constantine could count on was that of a small bunch of Venetian and Genoese mercenaries under the command of the brave and resourceful Giovanni Giustiniani.

Mehmed arrived with an army of 200,000 men, eager for booty from the city. He sent envoys urging Constantine to surrender and he laid siege to the city when these were rebuffed. However, the Ottoman ships were obstructed by chains thrown across the mouth of the Golden Horn, so they were dragged overland to attack the city from the north. Some guns from the ships were used to bombard the walls of the city from the landward side and each needed forty pairs of oxen to move them. One of them blew up, killing many of the Turks.

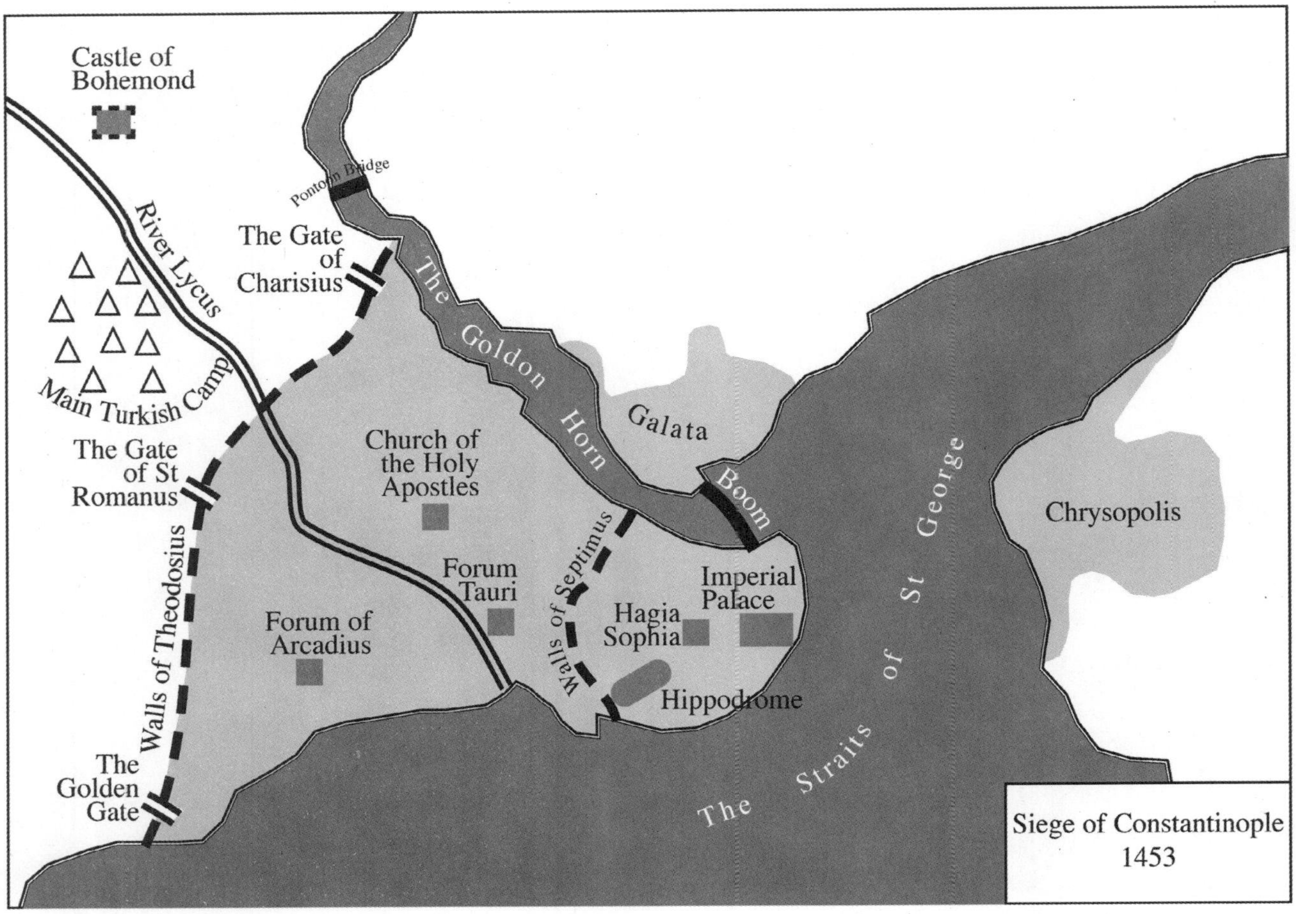

Constantine sent out agents in an attempt to spread defeatism among the Turkish troops. They failed. Morale within the city was the problem, combined with poor discipline and a lack of a coordinated defences.

Mehmed II began his assault on 29 May 1453 and soon discovered that the city was not going to be as easy to take as he had first thought. Giustiniani had deployed his men between the inner ramparts and the massive outer wall and the gates of the city were shut behind them so that no one could go in or out. They had no choice but to stand and fight.

The mercenaries acquitted themselves well. They threw back the ladders that had been hurled across the moat and up the side of the walls and they hastily repaired the damage that had been done by the Turkish artillery. Numerous attacks were repulsed, but then Giustiniani was hit by an arrow or a stone bullet and was mortally wounded. This robbed his men of their fighting spirit. When the city gates were opened to admit the wounded, the mercenaries ran into the city.

The Turks quickly crossed the moat and scaled the walls, which were now defenceless. The gates were breached and contingents of Turkish janissaries – highly trained infantry selected from prisoners and slaves – marched in perfect order into the fallen city. Once the streets had been cleared and the last vestiges of resistance had been put down Mehmed II rode into the city on horseback.

Constantine had been killed, probably trampled to death in the general stampede, though there is a tale that he died in a heroic last stand. The city's population took refuge in the great basilica of Hagia Sophia – the Church of the Holy Wisdom begun by the first Christian Roman Emperor Constantine when he established his new capital, New Rome (which later took his name), at the old Greek port of

Byzantium. Turkish troops battered down the door and slaughtered those inside or sold them into slavery. The cathedral was then turned into a mosque.

Mehmed let his men loot the city for the traditional three days. After that, any remaining inhabitants were removed. Byzantine artists sought refuge in Italy, sparking the Renaissance and the city was repopulated by people from all over the Ottoman Empire. For over 1,000 years, Constantinople had been the capital of the Christian Byzantine Empire. Now it became the capital of the Islamic Ottoman Empire. It gradually changed its name to Istanbul, which came about when thirteenth-century Arab traders misheard the Greek *eis ten polin* ('in the city'). In 1923, after the fall of the Ottoman Empire, the capital of the new Turkish republic was moved to Ankara in Asia Minor, on the other side of the Bosporus, although the former Constantinople remains Turkey's largest city. It officially changed its name to Istanbul in 1930.

Bosworth

The Beginning of the Tudor Age

1485

The Battle of Bosworth Field finally put an end to the fighting between competing dynasties for the throne of England. It heralded the Tudor period where a united England rose to be a major power.

THE BATTLE OF BOSWORTH FIELD in 1485 marked the end of the Wars of the Roses. The houses of York and Lancaster, whose symbols were white and red roses, had been fighting for the throne of England over the thirty years that led up to the battle. The battle put an end to the Plantagenet dynasty that had ruled England since Henry II came to the throne in 1154 and it marked the end of the Middle Ages in England. No longer would the country be in the hands of competing war lords. Instead all its subjects would owe allegiance to a single crown.

The victor, Henry Tudor, Earl of Richmond, was a Welshman but he was a member of the Lancastrian faction through his mother. He had no great claim to be king, but the wars between Lancaster and York had killed off all the better candidates. Following the Lancastrian defeat at the Battle of Tewkesbury in May 1471, his uncle Jasper Tudor took the fourteen-year-old Henry into exile in Brittany for safekeeping. The Yorkists were now so securely on the throne that it looked as though he might remain there for the rest of his life.

However, Edward IV died in April 1483 and his twelve-year-old son Edward V succeeded with his uncle, Richard Plantagenet, Duke of Gloucester, as protector. Richard, who was already thought to have been responsible for the deaths of Henry VI, his son Prince Edward and his own brother the Duke of Clarence, took the boy from his mother. She was a member of the powerful Woodville family and a number of the Woodvilles were arrested and executed. Richard housed Edward in the Tower of London, which was then a royal palace. Edward's brother, Richard, Duke of York, was brought to join him. Richard then declared his brother's marriage to Elizabeth Woodville invalid, making the two princes bastards. The children then disappeared and many presume, under Shakespeare's influence, that they were murdered by Gloucester who then took the throne as Richard III on 6 July 1483. In 1674, when

Richard III and Henry Tudor, Earl of Richmond and future King Henry VII of England cross swords in the field at Bosworth.

building alterations were being made to the Tower, the skeletons of two children were found. Generally assumed to be those of the unfortunate princes, they were taken to Westminster Abbey where they were buried.

Richard was widely seen as a usurper. His former ally, Henry Stafford, Duke of Buckingham, raised a rebellion in southern England which, although quickly put down, further weakened the Yorkist cause. Exiled Lancastrians rallied to Henry Tudor and his advisers convinced him that his time had come.

On 1 August 1485 Henry's fleet left Harfleur in Normandy, carrying a force of 2,000 French mercenaries under the command of Philibert de Chaundé and a number of prominent Lancastrians, including Jasper Tudor, the Bishop of Ely and John de la Vere, Earl of Oxford. A 'soft southern wind' took them down the Channel and around Land's End. Six days after leaving France, they landed at Milford Haven in Pembrokeshire, which was part of Jasper Tudor's earldom. Henry had spent much of his childhood there and the local Welshmen rallied to his support.

As Henry's growing army marched across Wales without opposition, it became clear to Richard that his supporters could not be relied upon. One of them, William Stanley, made no effort to hamper the progress of the rebels. His brother Thomas, Lord Stanley, was at court and begged to be allowed to return to his estates in Lancashire on the grounds of ill health. Richard gave him permission to go only if he left his son, Lord Strange, as a hostage.

There was no shortage of support for Henry in England. At Shrewsbury, he was joined by 500 men under Sir Gilbert Talbot and at Atherstone in Warwickshire he met William and Thomas Stanley, who would remain neutral at this point. By the time he reached Leicestershire, Henry had gathered a force of 5,000 men.

Richard was in Nottingham and he feared that the rebels might make a dash for London. On 19 August, he headed south to Leicester with some 8,000 men.

Leading the column were 200 knights and 1,200 archers under John Howard, Duke of Norfolk. Richard himself commanded the main force of 3,000 men armed with pikes, halberts and bills – bills were pikes with a hook-shaped blade on the end, while halberts added a battle-axe blade to a straight pike blade on the end of a six-foot pole. Bringing up the rear, under the command of Henry Percy, Earl of Northumberland, were another 2,000 men carrying bills. And guarding the rear and flanks were 1,500 horsemen. They were a tough, professional force and their leaders – both Richard and Norfolk – had won their battle spurs under Edward IV.

The two armies met early on 22 August at the village of Sutton Cheney, twelve miles west of Leicester and three miles south of Market Bosworth. Some 4,000 men under the command of the Stanley brothers were also in the vicinity, ready to join whichever side seemed to be winning. Richard sent Lord Stanley a message which said that if he did not join the king's forces his son Lord Strange would be killed. Stanley replied that he had other sons but Richard did not kill the boy, which is strange in the light of his reputation.

Richard took up position on Ambien Hill, giving him the advantage of the high ground. The Earl of Oxford, leading the vanguard of Henry's army, began the attack but the Tudor formations were broken up by the swampy ground at the foot of the ridge. Had Richard attacked then, taking advantage of the disorder in the enemy's ranks, he would probably have won the day. As it was, he held back. This may have been because Richard could not count on

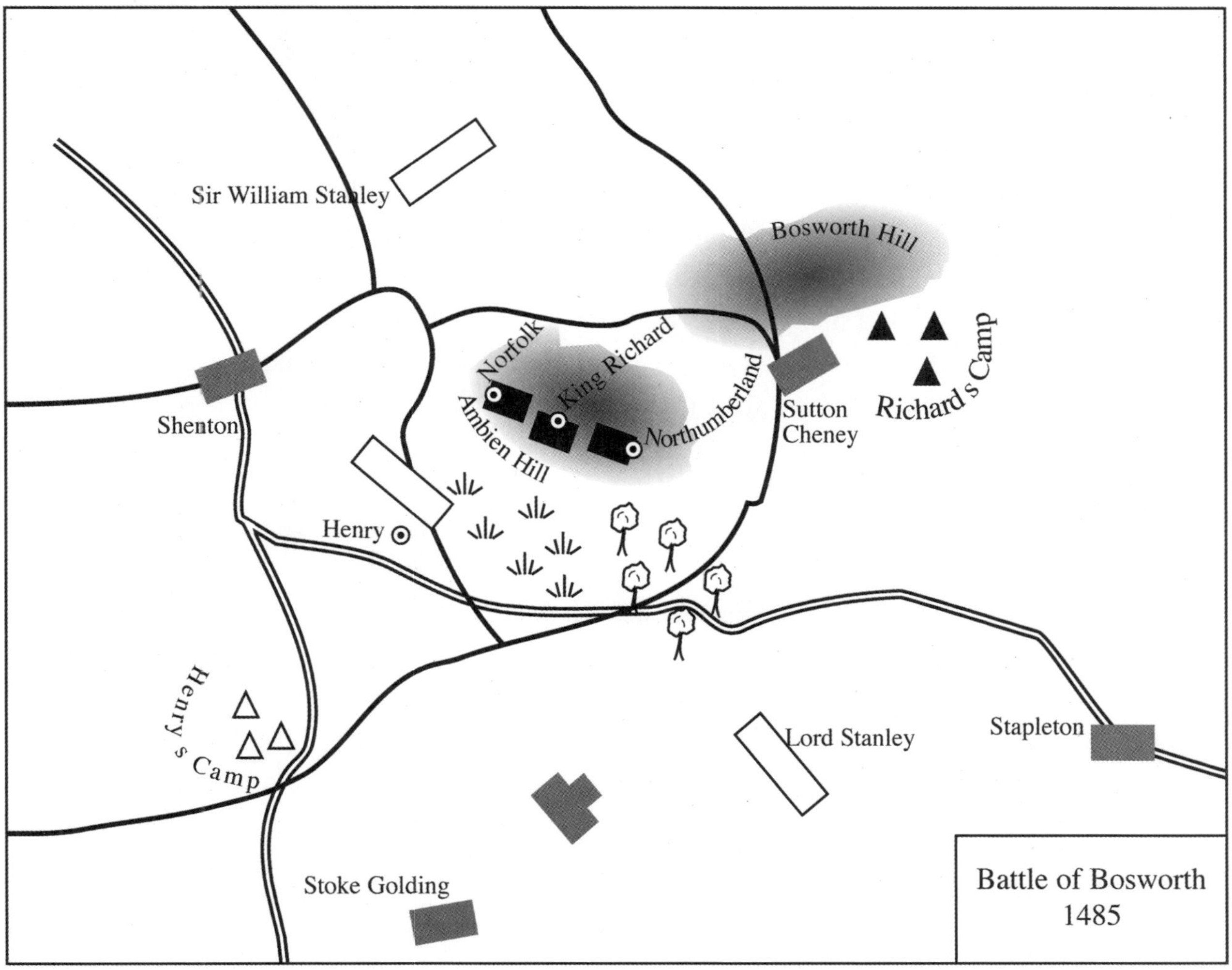

Battle of Bosworth
1485

his men. A chronicler recorded that there were many among them 'who rather coveted the king dead than alive, and therefore fought faintly'.

Oxford restored order and brought up artillery to pound Richard's army massed on the hills above. The bombardment produced few casualties, but it had a psychological effect on troops whose morale was already low. Oxford then gathered his men around his personal standard and led them up the hill into two hours of hand-to-hand fighting.

Norfolk was killed early in the battle – it is said by Oxford himself – and his son, the Earl of Surrey, was captured. This further demoralized Richard's men. A messenger was seen riding off to carry the news to the Stanleys, who promptly joined the battle on Henry's side. Perceiving which way the wind was blowing, Northumberland refused to commit his reserves and the Yorkist forces began to melt away.

For Richard there was still one slim chance that the day could be won – that is, if Henry were killed. Clutching a battle-axe, he mounted his white charger and rode directly to Henry, accompanied by his personal bodyguard of eighty knights. He hacked his way through the ranks of Welsh footsoldiers and then struck down Sir John Cheney, a man considerably bigger and stronger than himself. Next he cut down Henry's personal standard-bearer, Sir William Brandon. The odds he faced were overwhelming. He was pulled off his horse and killed in a bog before he could even reach Henry, only the second English king to be killed in battle at the head of his troops.

It is said that Richard's crown was found in a thorn bush. Lord Stanley, whose treachery had won the day, then crowned Henry Tudor king of England on the battlefield.

With Richard dead, the fighting was over. Richard's army had lost around 1,000 men; Henry's just 200. The casualties were thought to be light at the time. Richard's naked body was slung across the back of a horse and taken to Leicester where it was held up to public ridicule for two days before being buried in Greyfriars Church.

The year after Bosworth, the new Henry VII married Elizabeth of York, reuniting the two rival branches of the now defunct Plantagenet family. Henry's victory at Bosworth ushered in 118 years of Tudor rule, during which time England rose to become a major European power.

That Richard III has gone down as one of the worst villains in English history is largely due to Shakespeare's portrayal of him in the eponymous play. Shakespeare was writing in Tudor times, so he had good reason to blacken the character of Richard. In those days, it was thought that physical deformities were matched by moral deformities, hence the play's portrayal of Richard as an ugly hunchback with a club foot. However it seems unlikely that he was as ugly as Shakespeare made him because he left seven illegitimate children.

It took the combined sea power of Spain and the maritime states of Venice and Genoa to inflict a decisive defeat on the powerful Turkish navy.

Lepanto

The Defeat of the Turkish Navy

1571

The great sea battle at Lepanto thwarted the plans of Turkish sultan Selim II to expel the Christian fleets from the western end of the Mediterranean.

WITH EUROPE TORN by the Reformation and the religious wars that followed in its wake, the Turkish sultan Selim II aimed to crown the capture of Constantinople by expelling Christian fleets from the eastern Mediterranean, leaving the way open for an invasion of Italy and perhaps the capture of Rome itself.

He began by invading Cyprus, then under Venetian control. He took Nicosia on 9 September 1570 and then besieged Famagusta. Venice turned to Pope Pius V for help who turned to Spain, the staunchest Catholic country in Europe. In his letter to Philip II of Spain, he warned: 'Our enemy, the Turks, have constructed with immense care and energy a fleet of unprecedented size, and an army hardly less considerable.' The Turkish fleet was thought to have been the largest in the world at the time.

The Pope and Spain formed the Holy League with Venice and the Italian state of Genoa. Like Venice, Genoa was a maritime power and it had a lot to lose if it were denied the sea lanes to the east so Philip of Spain sent his half-brother Don Juan of Austria to command its fleet. Although only twenty-five, Don Juan had proved himself by fighting against Moorish pirates in the Mediterranean and the Moriscos, or Christians of Moorish ancestry, in Granada. He prepared a fleet that would match that of Selim ship-for-ship. It included some fast Venetian galleasses which would prove to be a decisive addition. Equipped with both oars and sail, galleasses had batteries of guns that pivoted so that they could fire both forward and to the sides. In addition, the allied fleet had fast frigates and brigantines that were used for reconnaissance and heavy galleys propelled by tiers of oarsmen.

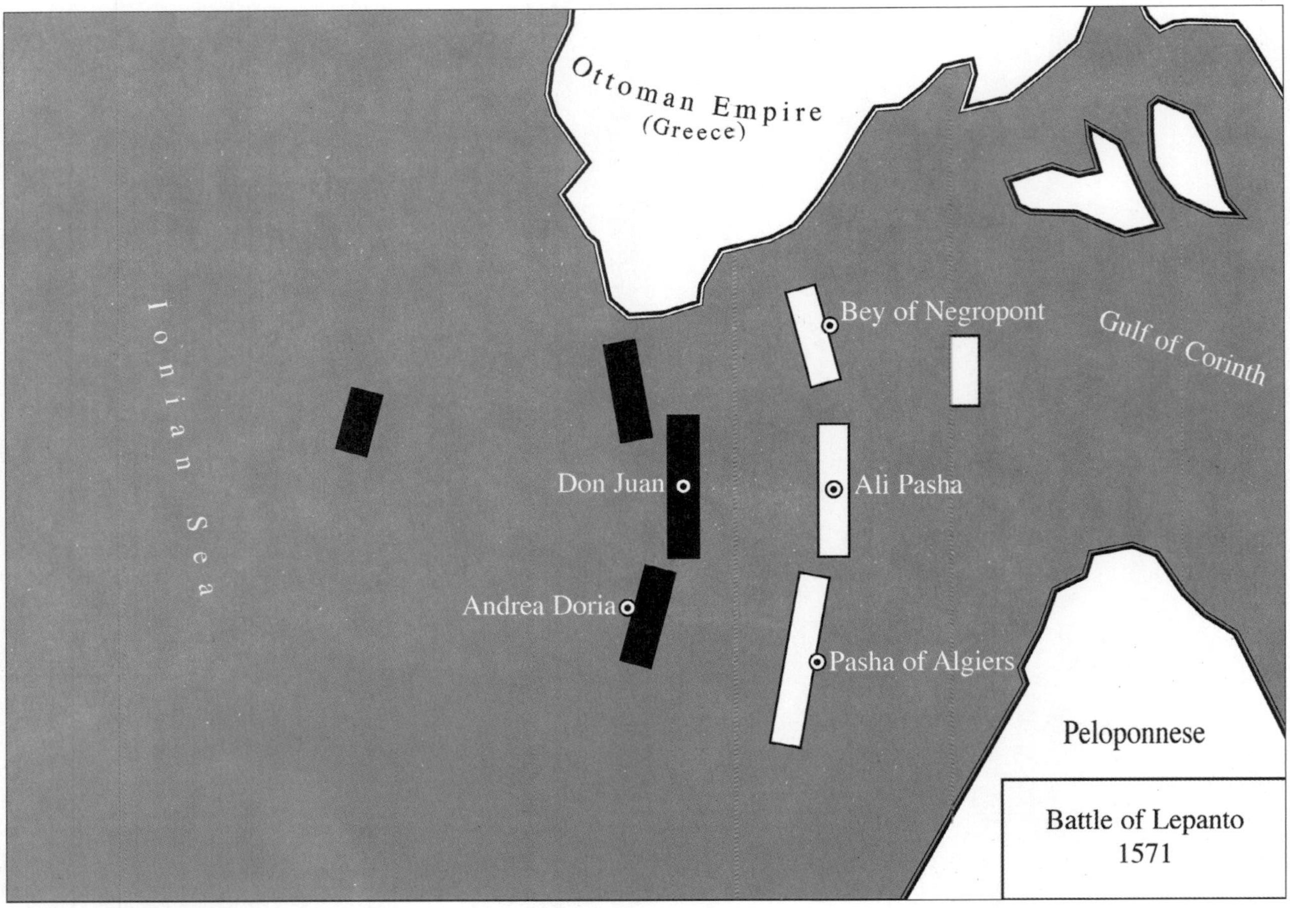

The Turkish fleet was commanded by the governor of Alexandria, Mohammed Saulak, also known as Sirocco, the great strategist Ali Pasha and the dey of Algiers, Uluj Ali. Uluj was an Italian adventurer who had formerly been a monk and a fisherman. When he converted to Islam, he took command of a band of North African corsairs.

After the invasion of Cyprus, the Turks entered the Adriatic and tried to take Corfu. When they failed, they retreated to the sheltered waters between the Gulf of Patras and the Gulf of Corinth, and lay at anchor near Lepanto (now Návpaktos) in Greece. Don Juan's fleet sailed to secure Corfu on 15 September 1571. Soon afterwards, four squadrons were despatched to attack the Turkish fleet.

Morale on the Christian ships was high. One oarsman wrote: 'We, the fighters of the Pope, are filled with joy now the decision has been taken. Everyone is prepared to give his life for his Holiness and for the Faith. We are sailing into combat and we shall claim victory.' The author was a convict who had been condemned to the galleys.

On the morning of 7 October 1571, Don Juan reviewed his fleet. He sailed past them holding up an ivory crucifix, saying: 'Sharpen your claws. This [the Turkish] carcass is tough. The day will be hard.'

The Turkish were equally confident of victory. Ali Pasha told his men to show no mercy. 'These Christians have come to be eaten alive,' he said.

Although the Turkish fleet seemed to be a match for anything that the Christians could throw at them, it had several disadvantages. While Don Juan's soldiers had armour, the Turks had little protection. They had few cannon compared with those that bristled from the Christian ships, and they had a weakness concealed deep within their ships: many of their toiling galley-slaves were in fact captured Christians, with no reason to wish a Turkish victory.

The Christian fleet formed up in a north–south line. At the northern end, closest to the coast were fifty-three Venetian galleys under the command of Barbaringo. There were sixty-two galleys in the centre under Don Juan himself and to the right, at the southern end of the line, there were another fifty-three galleys under Gian Andrea Doria. Leading the Christian line were the Venetian galleasses. Thirty-eight galleys were held in reserve behind the main line, while eight galleys formed up into a scouting party. However, they were investigating some small offshore islands and failed to spot the advance of the Muslim fleet.

Details of how the Turks were drawn up are more sketchy. Under Sirocco there were fifty-four galleys and two light galliots to the right of the north end of their line. There was a larger force in the centre under Ali Pasha and a third to the south under Uluj Ali. In reserve were eight galleys, twenty-two galliots and sixty-four smaller fustas.

As the two fleets approached each other, Doria saw that Uluj Ali's line extended further to the south so, to prevent being outflanked, he sailed southwards. Uluj took advantage of this by attacking the south end of Don Juan's central division before Doria could turn and join the battle.

However the Christian galleasses had done the damage. They had charged through the Turkish line with their guns blazing. To the north, Sirocco had managed to turn the allies' flank but this put him between the Christian fleet and the shore. Outgunned, the Turks depended on ramming the allied fleet and manoeuvring close enough to board. In this, they were hampered by their Christian oarsmen. During an intense battle which lasted about four hours, the Sirocco and Ali Pasha managed to get boarding parties onto the Christian flagships. However, none were lost although a Venetian admiral was killed and Sirocco was mortally wounded.

While bloody actions continued on both flanks, the battle was decided in the centre, where men in heavy armour leapt onto the ships of Ali Pasha's squadron. Ali Pasha's own ship was boarded and, against Don Juan's orders, Ali Pasha was beheaded. His head was displayed on top of the mast of the Spanish flagship. The Turks then became demoralized and took flight. As a trophy, Don Juan also took the Sacred Tent, covered with 29,000 inscriptions bearing the name of Allah, that had adorned Ali Pasha's flagship.

In all the Turks lost 180 galleys and sixty galliots while 117 galleys and six galliots were in good enough condition to keep. Eleven Christian galleys had been destroyed or were so badly damaged that they had to be scuttled and one Venetian galley had been captured. The Turks lost some 30,000 men and the Christians around 9,000, although they freed twice as many Christian prisoners. Among the 16,000 Christian wounded was Miguel de Cervantes, who later wrote Don Quixote. He was a soldier on board the Marquesa. Although stricken with a fever, he refused to stay below and joined the thick of the fighting. He suffered two gunshot wounds to the chest and a third rendered his left hand useless for the rest of his life.

After the battle, the Turks made a huge effort to rebuild their navy and within six months the Ottomans were able to reassert their naval supremacy. Lepanto was the first European victory over the Ottomans and it proved to be a great psychological boost. However, because the Europeans remained divided they failed to push the Ottomans back. They went on to complete the capture of Cyprus and they took Tunis but they never managed to dominate the sea lanes of the Mediterranean.

The Ottomans continued their efforts to conquer Europe but by land, through the Balkans, not by sea. However, Barbary pirates, who were nominally Muslim, continued to menace European shipping until the French occupied Algeria in 1830.

Blenheim

British Arms in Europe

1704

Britain was already a major sea power, but the Battle of Blenheim demonstrated that a well-trained British army could be supplied far from the Channel and win a major victory deep inside the Continent.

THE WAR OF THE SPANISH SUCCESSION broke out in 1701, after Charles II of Spain, a Habsburg, died childless and Louis XIV of France, the most powerful monarch in Europe, proclaimed his grandson king, as Philip V. Because Spain occupied part of the Netherlands and parts of Italy at the time, as well as its colonies in the Americas and the Pacific, war quickly engulfed Europe. Britain allied itself with the United Provinces (the part of The Netherlands that was not under Spanish control) and Austria. These were not strong allies. Meanwhile Bavaria, whose elector had his eye on the Habsburg throne of Austria, allied itself with France.

Queen Anne came to the throne when the king of England, William of Orange, died in 1702 but Louis XIV refused to recognize her. Instead he supported the Jacobite candidate James Stuart, the Old Pretender, as the rightful King of Great Britain. However, John Churchill, the Duke of Marlborough, marched an army 300 miles from the English Channel and defeated a Franco-Bavarian army that was threatening Vienna. His victory shifted the balance of power away from France and towards Britain for the next one hundred years.

William of Orange had been one of the great opponents of the French on the Continent. When he died, Marlborough became both Captain-General of the British army and Commander-in-Chief of the Grand Alliance. Greeted with joy by the Dutch, he suggested that the Dutch commander, General Auverquerque, should stay in The Netherlands and fight a defensive war while he took British troops and auxiliaries into Germany to defend Austria.

Marlborough assembled an army at Bedburg near Maastricht on the Meuse. It included 16,000 English troops, with fifty-one battalions of foot and ninety-two squadrons of horse. The famous march began on 19 May and along the way Marlborough picked up troops from the German states of Prussia, Luneberg and Hesse that were stationed along the Rhine and eleven Dutch battalions that were stationed at Rothweil in Germany.

His men marched a steady ten miles every day, with a full day's rest every fifth day. They travelled down roads that turned into quagmires if it rained. Forward parties prepared camps for the troops each night and Marlborough also made sure that there were dry clothes and shoes waiting at each stop as well as plenty of food. It was a masterpiece of logistics. In the 300 miles of the march only 900 stragglers dropped out.

'Surely never was such a march carried out with more regularity and with less fatigue to man and horse,' said one participant. In military terms this was as considerable a feat as victory in the battle itself.

Marlborough's manoeuvres fooled both his enemies and his friends. Marshal Tallard held back 45,000 French troops at Strasbourg, in the belief that Marlborough was going to attack in Alsace. Other French allies thought he planned to besiege Manheim or march into Hungary. They held back to maintain communication with France so when Marlborough quit the Rhine and struck out for the Danube, there was no one to oppose him.

A superior French army took up defensive positions at Blenheim and did not expect the smaller Anglo-Dutch force under the Duke of Marlborough to attack, but repeated assaults left them separated and surrounded.

When Marlborough met up with his ally Prince Eugène of Savoy at Mundelsheim, his army was still in excellent condition. An attack on the entrenched Franco-Bavarian camp at the heights of Schullenberg, near Donauwörth, where he intended to cross the Danube, cost Marlborough 10,000 men. But he was now unopposed in Bavaria, except around the fortified cities of Munich and Augsburg.

With Marlborough far to the east, Marshal Tallard realized that Alsace was not in danger. He crossed the Rhine and marched through the Black Forest to join up with the Bavarians at Augsburg. Marlborough recrossed the Danube with the Austrian forces under Prince Eugène and sought out Tallard. He now commanded 56,000 men and fifty-two guns, while Tallard had 60,000 men and sixty-one artillery pieces. For Marlborough it was vital to attack before more reinforcements could arrive from France.

Tallard's forces were drawn up between the village

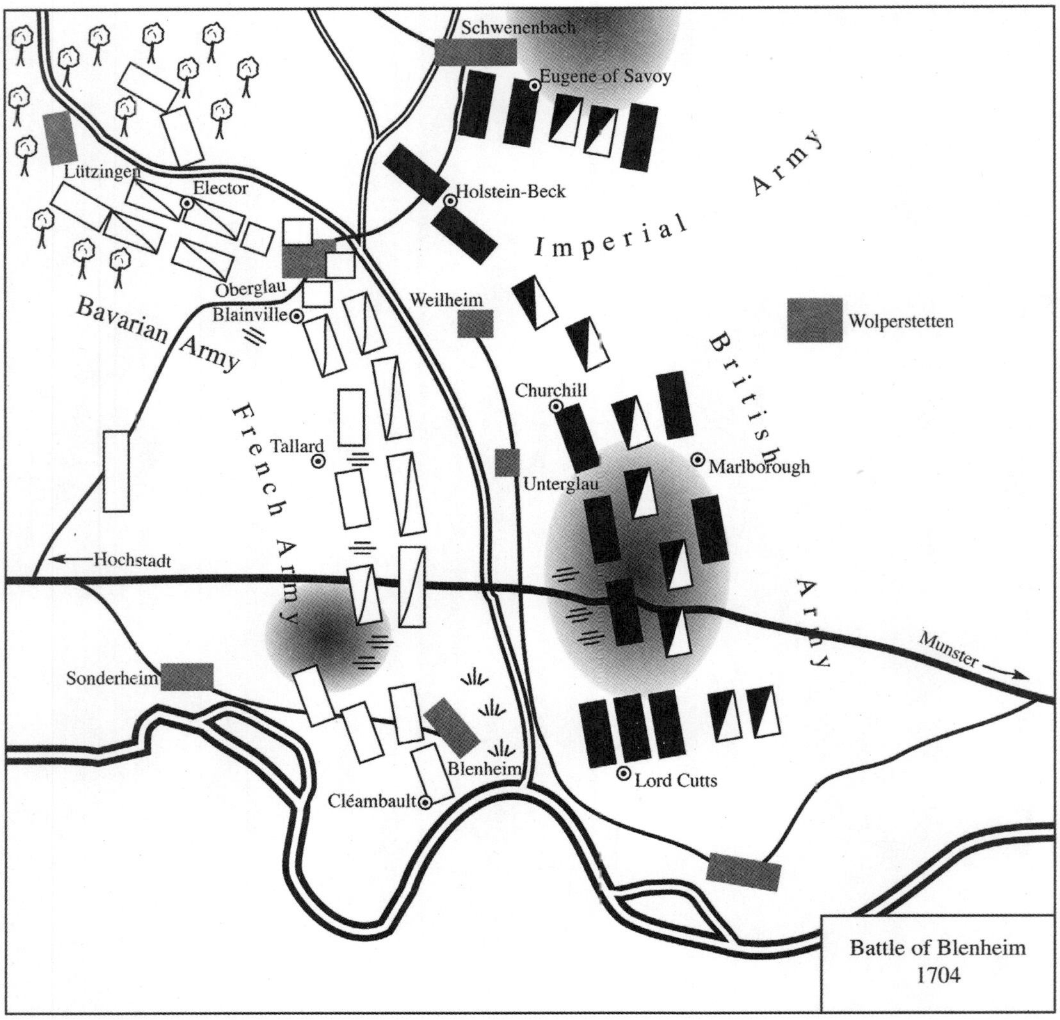

Battle of Blenheim
1704

of Blindheim (Blenheim) on the Danube and the wooded slopes around Lützingen to Marlborough's right. They had fortified the villages of Blenheim and Oberglau. Between the river and the woods was a flat plain, some four miles wide, with a small stream, the Nebel, running across it. The cornfield there had recently been harvested and all that was left was a short stubble. Observing this with a telescope from a church tower, Marlborough and Prince Eugène agreed this would make a good battlefield.

Once again, the French were surprised by Marlborough's rapid advance. They did not think that he would attack a numerically superior army that occupied fortified positions. The French had another advantage because the bulk of their forces were French, and had trained together and spoke the same language. Marlborough's army was made up of numerous nationalities – Austrians, Danes, Hanoverians, Dutch, Brandenburgers, British – who had no common language. They would also have to attack first and the initial loss of life would perhaps fatally damage their morale. But on 12 August 1704 Marlborough gave the order that they would attack on the following day. He told his council of war: 'I know the danger, yet a battle is absolutely necessary, and I rely on the bravery and discipline of the troops, which will make amends for our disadvantages.'

The French and the Baravians took up positions along the rising ground to the west of the little valley that was cut by the Nebel. Blenheim was to the extreme right of their position and the flank there was secured by the Danube. To their left was

Lützingen, three miles north of Blenheim. Beyond it, detachments were posted on the rugged high ground so that the left could not be approached. Their position could only be attacked by a frontal assault.

Blenheim and Lützingen were surrounded by trenches and palisades. Tallard's command post was in Blenheim, which was garrisoned by twenty-six battalions of French infantry and twelve squadrons of French cavalry. Marshal Marsin and the Elector of Bavaria were in command on the left. They had twenty-two battalions of infantry and thirty-six squadrons of cavalry in front of the village of Lützingen. The centre was occupied by fourteen battalions of infantry, including the celebrated Irish brigade that fought for the French against the British. They were posted in the little hamlet of Oberglau, which lay a little closer to Lützingen than to Blenheim. Eight squadrons of cavalry and seven battalions of foot were ranged between Oberglau and Blenheim. This meant that the Franco-Bavarian position was strong on the wings but relatively weak in the centre.

Marlborough's army was formed into two great divisions. The largest was to be commanded by Marlborough himself, who aimed to take on Tallard. The other division was under the command of Prince Eugène. It consisted largely of cavalry and it would attack the forces under Marsin and the Elector.

Early in the morning of 13 August, Marlborough's entire force left camp and marched out towards the enemy. There was a thick fog that morning and it was not until the right and the centre had advanced to within a cannon's shot of the French lines that Tallard was aware of their approach. There was chaos in the French camp as men rushed to their posts. At eight a.m. the French artillery began a heaving bombardment of the advancing left wing of the British. Marlborough ordered some of his batteries up to reply to it. During the ensuring artillery duel, Marlborough formed up his columns to the left and the centre.

To the right the terrain was softer and Prince Eugène found difficulty in bringing his artillery up. It was nearly midday before he could get his troops into line opposite Lützingen. In the meantime, Marlborough ordered the chaplains from each regiment to perform a service. Then he rode along the lines and found both officers and men in high spirits, waiting impatiently for the signal to attack.

When a messenger arrived from Prince Eugène confirming his readiness, Marlborough ordered Lord Cutts, who commanded the left, to attack Blenheim. He advanced with a strong brigade of infantry. They clambered over barricades hastily erected by the French and fought with sword, musket and bayonet, but the French fire was overwhelming. A third of Cutts's men were cut down and his brigade was repulsed. Another five battalions under Lord Ockney, including the Royal Scots, tried to force their way into the village, but they were repulsed with heavy losses. After that Marlborough made no further attempt to take Blenheim and he concentrated on trying to break the centre of the French line between Blenheim and Oberglau.

But the failed attack on Blenheim caused the French to make a fatal mistake. Tallard was away at the time. He had ridden over to see Marsin in order to enquire whether he could hold the left. While he was away, the commander in Blenheim, the Marquis de Cléambault, had grown alarmed at the Allied onslaught. First of all he ordered seven battalions from the centre to defend the village and then he called another eleven battalions from the reserve. Some 12,000 men were packed into Blenheim. They were barely able to move. As Marlborough had given up on taking Blenheim they were effectively out of the battle. This move fatally weakened the centre. When the Marquis de Cléambault realized the enormity of his error, he rode into the Danube and drowned himself.

Marlborough's brother, Charles Churchill, led the Allied forces across the Nebel, which was shallower than Marlborough anticipated. Some temporary bridges had been prepared and men also carried planks. They took the little stone bridge across the stream that lay in the centre of the valley near a hamlet called Unterglau.

Several cavalry squadrons crossed the Nebel but found difficulty in forming up on the swampy ground on the other side, which was little better than marsh in places. They were raked by French artillery and attacked by repeated French cavalry charges. The situation was critical and it looked as though the squadrons might have been thrown back, but Marlborough sent more troops across and the steady fire of the Allied infantry halted the advance of the enemy horse. Even so, by the time Marlborough got his left across the Nebel and formed up on the other side the stream ran red with blood. And now the Allied formation suffered flanking fire from Blenheim itself.

Watching from the centre, Tallard seized the opportunity to attack with his heavy cavalry. He sent squadrons of the scarlet-coated King's Household and Gendarmes, said to be the finest cavalry in Europe, galloping down the slope at a line of English dragoons. They should have forced the English from the battlefield by their sheer weight of numbers. Instead of fleeing, however, the dragoons, under Colonel Palmes, charged; meeting the Gendarmes head on, they sent them reeling.

'What! The Gendarmerie fleeing!' cried the Elector of Bavaria as a groan of disbelief echoed down the line. French morale plummeted.

At this point Marlborough was called away to an emergency. In the centre of the field, the Prince of Holstein-Beck and eleven Hanoverian battalions had crossed the Nebel opposite Oberglau. The Irish brigade that held the village charged and routed them, completely breaking the line. Marlborough arrived in the nick of time with some squadrons of British cavalry. On his white charger, with the insignia of the Order of the Garter glinting in the sunlight, he led a charge into the flank of the Irish. The Irish reeled back. As they retreated towards Oberglau, they were raked by the fire of three battalions of infantry that Marlborough had brought up from the reserve. Then the duke returned to the left.

On the right, Prince Eugène had made three attacks on the enemy and had been driven back three times. It was only the steadfastness of a regiment of Prussian infantry that prevented the right wing from being routed. However, when Marsin sent sixty squadrons against Marlborough's flank Prince Eugène counter-charged with his Austrian cuirassiers and scattered them.

The battle was not going the way Marlborough had expected. He had aimed to take the strong points of Blenheim and Oberglau. But they were neutralized, for the moment, so he put a plan into action to break through the centre with his cavalry. Marlborough drew up 8,000 horsemen into two lines. 15,000 infantry were drawn up in battalions to the rear to give support if the cavalry were repulsed and to keep in check the large French force that still occupied the village of Blenheim.

Tallard also drew up his cavalry opposite, but he interlaced then with infantry. To counter this, Marlborough brought up some of his own infantry and artillery and deployed it at intervals along the front of the line.

It was a little after five o'clock when Marlborough slowly advanced his cavalry, supported by foot and artillery, from the lower ground on the banks of the Nebel up the slope to where 10,000 French cavalrymen awaited them. When they reached the top of the slope they were greeted by withering artillery and small arms fire. At first the cavalry recoiled, but then they held their ground. The artillery and the infantry they had brought with them fired back and the French fire began to slacken. Then, at 5.30 p.m., Marlborough sounded the trumpet charge.

Victory at Blenheim secured the reputation of Marlborough, not least for organizing the supply of an army so far from home. He was rewarded with the gift of Blenheim Palace, near Woodstock in Oxfordshire.

As the Allied cavalry thundered forward, the courage of the French horsemen seemed to fail. They discarded their carbines at a distance and then wheeled around and spurred their horses from the field, leaving nine infantry battalions to be ridden down by the Allied charge. The French infantry tried to hold back the torrent but they were swept away. Nine battalions of raw recruits were slaughtered almost to a man.

The French line was now broken and the forces of Tallard and Marsin were separated. Tallard tried to re-form his cavalry in a line to the right, leading down to Blenheim, and sent orders for the infantry in the village to come out and join him. But before they had a chance, Marlborough's cavalry wheeled to the right driving Tallard's cavalry into the Danube. Tallard himself fled to the village of Sonderheim where he was surrounded and forced to surrender, along with the cream of Louis XIV's army.

With Tallard gone, Marsin and the Elector of Bavaria withdrew to Dillingen, leaving what remained of the centre to its fate. The massacre was terrible. A French officer recorded: 'We were borne back on top of one another. So tight was the press that my horse was carried along some three hundred paces without putting its hoof on the ground, right to the edge of a deep ravine.'

Marlborough then surrounded the remaining French forces in Blenheim. He brought up his artillery and began bombarding them. The French made several attempts to break out but these were unsuccessful. Lord Cutts then set fire to the thatched roofs of some nearby cottages before dowsing the flames with water. The resulting smoke filled the village, confusing the French, so much so that some 11,000 men surrendered to a far smaller British force.

The Allies had lost some 5,000 troops and 8,000 more were wounded. Of the opposing forces, 12,000 French soldiers had been killed, 10,000 wounded and 14,000 Frenchmen had been captured, along with all their cannon.

That night Marlborough sent his personal carriage to fetch Marshal Tallard from captivity. Over dinner, Tallard said: 'I hope your Grace is aware that you have had the honour to defeat the best troops in the world?'

Marlborough replied in fluent French: 'Your Lordship, I presume, excepts those who have had the honour to defeat them?'

The defeat of Louis's army at Blenheim put paid to his ambition to gain control over Europe. The French would have to wait another hundred years to see that ambition revived by Napoleon.

Culloden

The Jacobites Crushed

1746

The Scots had always found the 'Highland charge' to be effective against the English. But at Culloden, the Duke of Cumberland used the latest military disciplines from Europe to cut down the charging Scotsmen.

AFTER JAMES II OF ENGLAND and VII of Scotland was removed from the throne by the Glorious Revolution in 1688, there were several attempts to restore the Stuart dynasty. The fifth and final attempt sparked the Jacobite Rebellion of 1745. In the previous year, Charles Edward

Defeat on the battlefield led to a massacre. The followers of Bonny Prince Charlie and the Stuart dynasty were slaughtered.

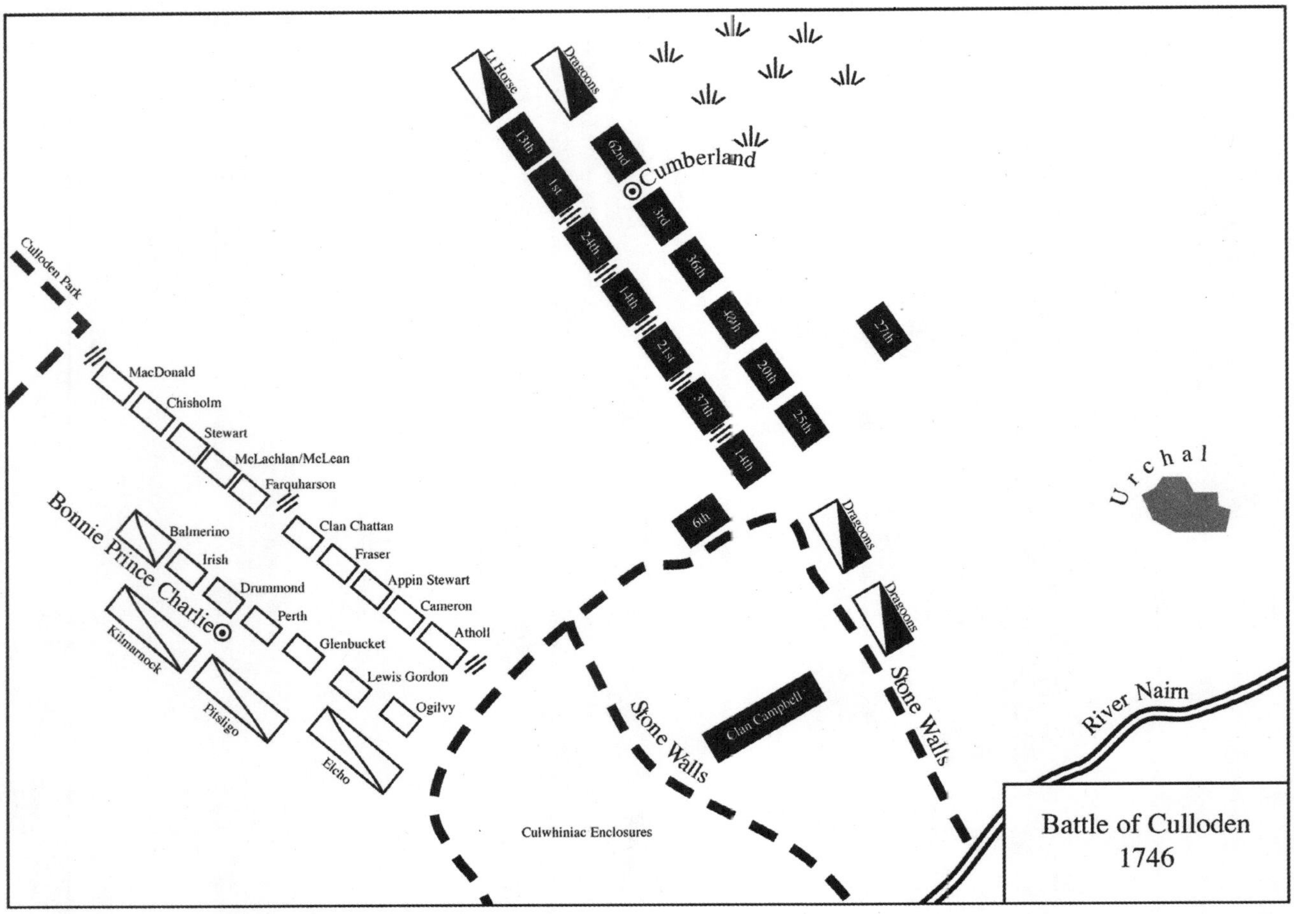

Stuart, the grandson of James II, was part of a huge French fleet that aimed to invade England. However, the fleet was torn apart by a storm before it could land. In 1745, he set out to regain the crown for his father James Edward Stuart, the Old Pretender.

In July 1745, Bonnie Prince Charlie, later known as the Young Pretender, landed on the west coast of Scotland with about a dozen men and raised a rebellion. Although the rising was smaller than the unsuccessful rebellion of 1715, there was little resistance because the British army was on the Continent at the time, fighting in the War of the Austrian Succession. On 17 September, Charles and some 2,400 men entered Edinburgh. Four days later they routed a superior force under Sir John Cope at Prestonpans, employing the blood-curdling 'Highland charge' that the Scots had been using since Bannockburn in 1314. It is said that the redcoats ran 'like rabets'.

The Scots rallied to the Young Pretender's cause and in early November he crossed the border with 5,500 men. However, before they could reach Derby, just 115 miles away, they had to face two powerful Hanoverian forces. The first was commanded by General Wade at Newcastle and the second was led in the west by William Augustus, Duke of Cumberland, the third son of George II. Between them they mustered 30,000 men. Although Cumberland was an incompetent general and a pretty unpleasant man, he had recently returned from the Continent where he had learnt a new way of fighting, introduced by the Swedish, that would make short work of the Highland charge.

Receiving no help from the French and no support from the English Catholics, Charles grew discouraged and retreated to Scotland. There more Scots rallied to him and he put an army, led by General Hawley, to flight at Falkirk. But when Cumberland's highly trained troops crossed the border, the Scots fell back before him. Some resorted to guerrilla warfare, but shortage of money meant that they could not buy food. Stealing supplies from local farms soon lost them support.

Charles realized that his only hope was to win a quick victory over Cumberland. He sent his quartermaster General O'Sullivan out to scout for an advantageous battlefield. The general found Drummoissie Muir outside Inverness, a boggy moorland that would neutralize the English cavalry. But Cumberland would not be lured onto the moor, so Charles planned an attack on his camp at night. From the beginning the raid was poorly organized. A quarter of Charles's men were away foraging and others refused to fight until they had been fed.

Eventually, Charles set out with some 4,000 men. The terrain worked against them and they got split up in the darkness. In the end they had to turn back to Drummoissie. However, the leader of the Jacobite vanguard, Lord George Murray, had reached the Hanoverian camp. This alerted Cumberland and he set off after the retreating Jacobites. Charles would now get the battle he had yearned for.

The Jacobites drew up on that part of Drummossie Muir that was known as Culloden Moor. The Macdonalds were on the left flank; in the centre were the Farquharsons under Lord John Drummond; and the right was under the command of Lord Murray, with the Athol Brigade, who were mainly Camerons, along with Mackintoshes, Frasers and Stewarts. There were some 5,000 men in all.

Cumberland commanded 8,000 redcoats. They were drawn up into two lines, with artillery in the front line while cavalry defended the flanks.

The battle began with a brief artillery duel when Cumberland was almost killed. Weighing eighteen stones and sitting on a huge grey charger, he was an easy target. Then Charles ordered a Highland charge.

The Macdonalds on the left refused to move. They were upset because they had not been given the place of honour on the right. But the rest of the Jacobites charged at the enemy. It was raining and the boggy conditions slowed their advance, but they hoped that the rain would dampen the redcoats' powder and prevent them from firing. However Cumberland had ordered his infantrymen to keep their cartridges under their lapels so that the powder would be kept dry.

He also had his artillery pieces reloaded with grapeshot – clusters of small iron balls that cut the charging Jacobites down. He put the infantry into three ranks. The front rank were ordered not to fire until the Highlanders were only twelve yards away. While the front rank reloaded the second rank fired their guns so, by the time the third rank had fired their guns, the first rank were ready to fire again. This system had been developed a hundred years earlier by the Swedish king Gustavus II Adolphus, often known as the 'Father of Modern Warfare'. However, Cumberland's infantry now used firelocks which were faster to reload than the old matchlocks. The new guns were also fitted with bayonets, so if the enemy were able to reach the Hanoverian front lines they would be able to defend themselves against the broadswords of the Highlanders, some of whom even resorted to throwing stones.

At Culloden, the English did not run away when the Highlanders charged. Their disciplined volleys brought the Jacobites down before they reached the Hanoverian lines. The gallant Highlanders did not abandon their tactic, but few were able to get close enough to use their broadswords.

When they did so, they were slaughtered by Cumberland's disciplined forces. A soldier in a front line regiment recorded how the English fought: 'Some [officers] cutting with their swords, others pushing with the spontoons, the sergeants running their halberds into the throats of the enemy, while soldiers mutually defended each other, ramming their bayonets up to their sockets.'

Perceiving that the position was now hopeless, the Macdonalds threw down their weapons and took flight. They were pursued and cut down by the English cavalry. Some 1,000 Jacobites were killed but Cumberland lost only fifty troops with 260 wounded.

After the battle Cumberland was asked for orders, so he wrote 'No quarter' on the back of a playing card. It was the nine of diamonds, which is still known as the 'curse of Scotland' today. The English were determined to ensure that the highland clans did not rebel again. George II then gave instructions that the Scots should be punished for supporting Charles. The Duke of Cumberland remained in Scotland for three months, rounding up some 3,500 men and executing about 120. The land of those he had executed was given to Scotsmen who had remained loyal. Meanwhile his soldiers killed anyone whom they thought retained Jacobite sympathies, including women and children. As a result Cumberland was given the epithet 'Butcher'. A flower was named after him to commemorate his success against the Jacobites at Culloden. In England it is known as the Sweet William but Scots know it as the Stinking Billy.

The English army also destroyed the Highlanders' homes and took away their cattle, and passed laws making it illegal for Highlanders to carry weapons, wear tartan or play the bagpipes. As a result some 40,000 Highlanders emigrated to America.

Charles Stuart fled back to France, where the major Catholic powers repudiated his title to the British throne. He died in Rome in 1788, a drunken and broken man. Although he is still remembered as a romantic hero in Scotland, his defeat at Culloden spelled the end of the Stuart hopes of a Restoration, and paved the way for the union of Scotland and England in 1707. Although Great Britain had been ruled by one monarch since James VI of Scotland became James I of England in 1603, its legislation would now emanate from one parliament in Westminster.

Plassey

Establishing the British Raj

1757

Clive of India's victory at Plassey put the East India Company in control in Bengal. This led to the eventual British take-over of the whole of India, while the Bengali treasuries funded the Industrial Revolution.

INDIA WAS THE JEWEL in the crown of the British Empire and its conquest began with a small action outside a village in Bengal called Palashi. The historic battle that took place there became known – in British history books at least – as the Battle of Plassey.

When the Nawab of Bengal, Ali Vardi Khan, died in 1756, he was succeeded by his great-nephew Siraj-ud-Dawlah. There was considerable opposition to his succession, even from within his own family. At the time, the British East India Company was fortifying Calcutta, ostensibly against the threat of attack by the French, but Siraj believed that the real intention of the British was to take over his territory. He told the British governor to raze the fortifications or he would expel the East India Company. The governor refused, so on 20 June the Nawab attacked and, after some weak resistance, took Calcutta. A number of prisoners were then held in a small jail, known as the Black Hole. It is not known how many people were held there and how many died in the overcrowded conditions that night.

On paper, the British stood no chance against the huge Bengali army. But the rains came, soaking the powder of the French artillery that was with the Nawab's army, while the British kept their powder dry under tarpaulins.

It was later claimed that 146 people had been confined and only twenty-three had survived. The 'Black Hole of Calcutta' incident was subsequently used to justify the British takeover of Bengal, although it was not mentioned at the time.

News of the fall of Calcutta reached Madras in August 1756 and Lieutenant-Colonel Robert Clive, with a force of 900 British soldiers and 1,500 sepoys (Indian colonial troops) was sent to take it back. The troops were transported around the Bay of Bengal to Calcutta by Admiral Watson. On 2 January 1757, Clive's small force dislodged a garrison of 3,000 and retook the trading post. Clive forced the Nawab to restore the East India Company's trading privileges and also pay compensation.

By this time the Seven Years' War had broken out, which once again pitted Britain against France in Europe, the Americas and India. The French had artillery and 300 troops at nearby Chandernagore and, on 14 March, Clive attacked and overwhelmed them. This led Siraj to fear Britain's growing strength in the region, so he allied himself with the French. Clive and Watson then decided to remove Siraj.

A cruel and debauched man, Siraj was not a popular ruler and there were numerous rivals to the throne. A number of the Nawab's principal officers approached Clive and asked for his help in dethroning Siraj. Their leader was Mir Jafar so Clive agreed to put the crown upon his head. In return, Mir Jafar promised to keep the French out of Bengal and pay £500,000 to the East India Company and £250,000 to the European residents of Calcutta in further compensation for the loss of their city the year before.

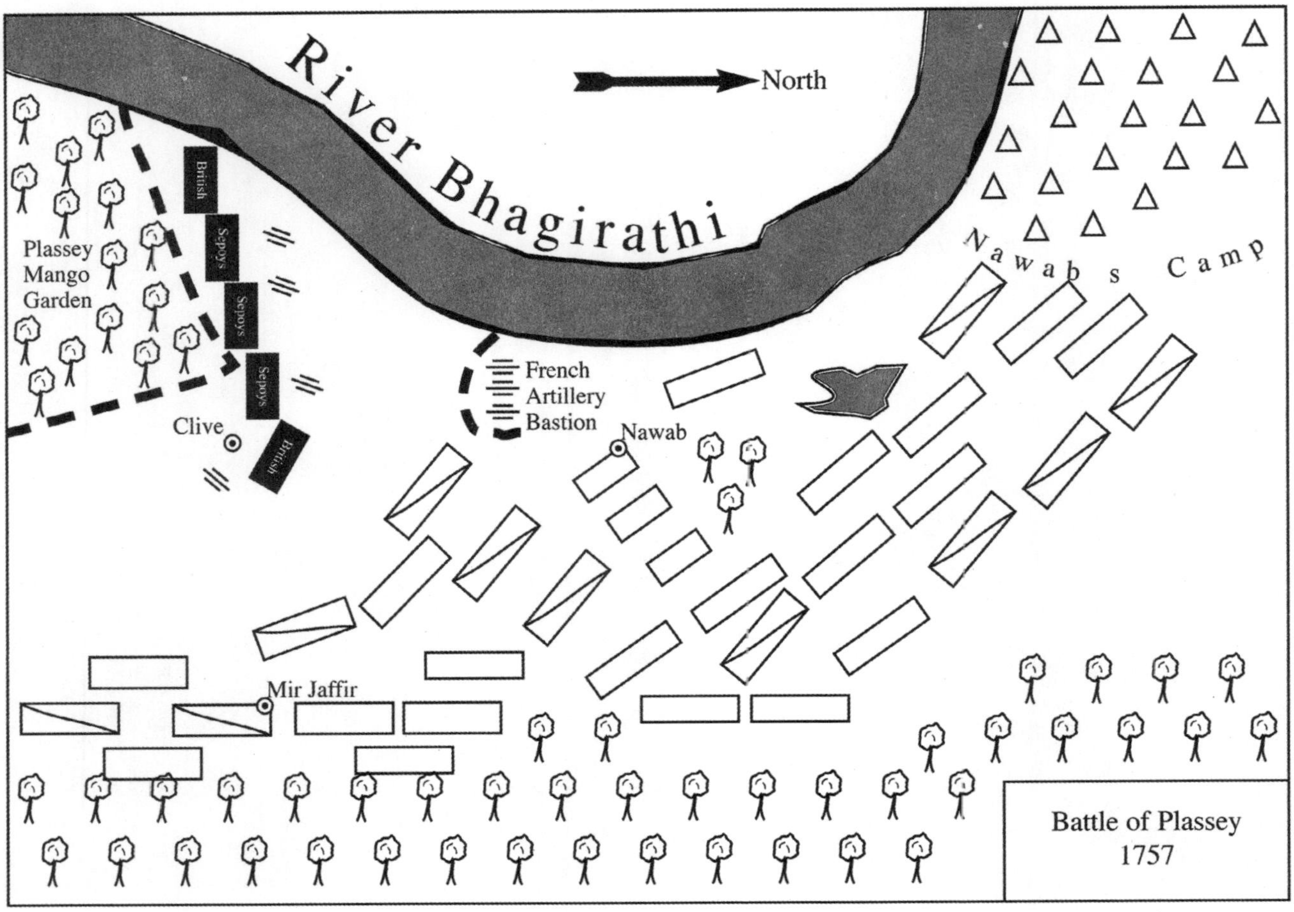

Clive left Chandernagore and marched on Siraj's capital Murshidabad with a force of 1,000 Europeans, 2,000 sepoys and eight cannon. They reached the village that Clive called Plassey on the night of 22 March and camped in a grove of mango trees.

At daybreak the British awoke to find the Nawab's army moving towards them. Siraj had raised an army of 15,000 horse and 35,000 foot, with upwards of forty cannon. A small detachment of French soldiers had joined them, bringing with them another four field guns.

Although he was outnumbered by more than ten to one, Clive decided that he had nothing to lose by being bold. Accordingly, he marched his entire force out towards Mir Muddin, the only one of Siraj's officers that he knew to be loyal. If Clive could defeat him, the rest would come over to his side.

The French artillery opened up, but were quickly silenced. The nawab's army, which was formed up into a huge arc around the British, then started to fire and, as Clive put it, 'continued to play on us very briskly for several hours'. The nawab kept his artillery at a distance, and widely spread out, so there was no way the British could attack it. Instead they fell back behind the mud banks that surrounded the mango grove and kept their heads down. An artillery duel developed, but the British guns were protected by the bank, while the nawab left his men exposed. Many were killed.

Then a miracle happened. A rainstorm appeared out of a cloudless sky. The British erected tarpaulins to keep their powder dry but out in the open the Bengalis' materials were soaked and their artillery ceased firing. Mir Mudden chose this moment to charge, but his men were cut down with musket fire and grapeshot. Those not killed took flight.

Siraj did not know what to do next and asked Mir Jafar for his advice. Scarcely believing his luck, Mir Jafar told Siraj that the British were defeated. The nawab should return to Murshidabad while he concluded the operation.

Clive attacked as Siraj left the field. He sent a detachment, accompanied by two field-pieces, to take raised ground about 300 yards from the grove where they had been fired on by the French. They seized more high ground near the Bengali camp and when the Bengalis tried to bring out their artillery they were fired on by the field guns that Clive's men had brought with them.

When the cavalry came out they were racked with artillery fire and many of the horses were killed. Although Clive credited the Bengalis with 'four or five officers of the first distinction', their army was 'visibly dispirited and thrown into some confusion' by the British advance. Clive's men then stormed the Bengali camp and took it with little or no loss. A general rout ensued. The British pursued the enemy for six miles, passing upwards of forty cannon that had been abandoned, along with a huge number of carriages that were filled with baggage of all kinds. Clive estimated that the enemy had lost about 500 men. 'Our loss amounted to only twenty-two killed and fifty wounded, and those chiefly sepoys,' he said.

Siraj was pursued by Mir Jafar's son, who captured him before executing him in cold blood. Clive reached Murshidabad on 29 June and, keeping to his word, installed Mir Jafar as nawab. However, Clive and his successors were never very far from his side.

Not only did the Battle of Plassey begin the British occupation of India but it also gave Britain access to the treasurers of Bengal. The industrial revolution was just getting under way. James Watt, the steam-engine pioneer; Edmund Cartwright, the inventor of the power loom; and James Hargreaves, the inventor of the spinning jenny were all backed by Bengali money, which was invested in their inventions by the East India Company.

Quebec

Deciding the Future of Canada

1759

Britain and France struggled for control of North America, but in an astonishing outflanking movement General Wolfe scaled the Heights of Abraham and took Quebec, establishing British title and driving out the French.

WITH THE SEVEN YEARS' WAR raging in Europe, France could do little to protect its colonies in North America and the British were determined to seize them. In February 1759 thirty-two-year-old General James Wolfe returned from sick leave in England to command the attack on the Quebec and the St Lawrence.

First he assembled a force at Louisburg, Nova Scotia, which the British had captured in 1757. Then, in the first week of June 1759, he set sail for the St Lawrence. This took the French by surprise. They had been expecting attacks from Lake Champlain to the south and Lake Ontario to the west, where the British had organized diversionary actions.

The French commander-in-chief in Canada was the Marquis de Montcalm. He was one of their most able generals. He had forced the British to surrender at Oswego in 1756, returning control of Lake Ontario to the French. In the following year he defeated the 2,500-man garrison at Fort William Henry. Then at Ticonderoga, in 1758, he repulsed a

Built on top a cliff that rose 200 feet above the St Lawrence river, Quebec seemed impregnable. But to the rear, the Plains of Abraham ran right up to the city walls.

force of 15,000 men under General James Abercombie with just 3,800 troops.

Montcalm assembled five regular French battalions, militia and 1,000 Indians at Quebec, which sits on a rocky headland that rises hundreds of feet above the confluence of the St Lawrence and the St Charles rivers. The city was heavily fortified. Montcalm was convinced that any attack would need to come from the east because the French navy maintained that the St Lawrence was not navigable beyond Quebec. So he built trenches and gun emplacements to the east, which ran along the northern back of the St Lawrence between the St Charles and Montmorency rivers.

Montcalm had 14,000 men and 106 guns to defend his position. Wolfe arrived with 8,500 soldiers and occupied the Île d'Orleans on the south of the river opposite Montcalm's riverside entrenchments. Also, a battery was deployed opposite the city.

On 31 July 1759 Wolfe attempted an assault across the river. It was repulsed, producing around 500 casualties. Plainly, this was no way to defeat Montcalm. However, the Royal Navy came to the rescue. Among the naval contingency were some talented navigators, including James Cook who later found fame in the South Seas. Over the next few weeks British ships managed to pass the batteries, proving that the river above the city was navigable. The Navy could now prevent supplies from reaching the French. Montcalm now feared a landing to the west of the city and he sent Louis Antoine de Bougainville to patrol the area.

If Wolfe was to defeat the French, he had to draw

them out from behind their defences so that they would face him on a wide, flat battlefield. The only place available was the Plains of Abraham which ran right up to the city walls of Quebec from the west. The only problem was that it stood on top of a cliff that rose 200 feet from the St Lawrence. However, it was then discovered that a path ran up to the top of the cliff from a small bay called Anse de Foulon.

While a feint attack was made on Montcalm's fortifications east of the city, those of Wolfe's men that were camped along the Montmorency were carried at night by longboat past the besieged city. A sentry on the banks noticed the dark shapes of the boats moving up the river and cried out: '*Que vive?*'

Captain Donald McDonald answered in faultless French: '*La France*'.

'*Quel régiment?*' asked the sentry.

'*De Reine*', said McDonald. It was one of Bougainville's units.

In the boats, Wolfe recited Thomas Gray's *Elegy Written in a Country Church- Yard*, published eight years earlier, and said that he would rather have written that poem than take Quebec. However, his final speech to the assault troops put iron into their souls.

'A vigorous blow struck at this juncture may determine the fate of Canada,' he said. 'The officers and men will remember what their country expects from them, and what a determined body of soldiers inured to war are capable of doing.'

Arriving at Anse de Foulon they found the beach unguarded. The French commander had been so confident that the British would not land there that he had sent the forty men who should have been guarding the beach to a nearby village to help with the harvest. Wolfe himself landed from the first boat. His men then cleared away the felled trees and bracken that the French had used to hide the track.

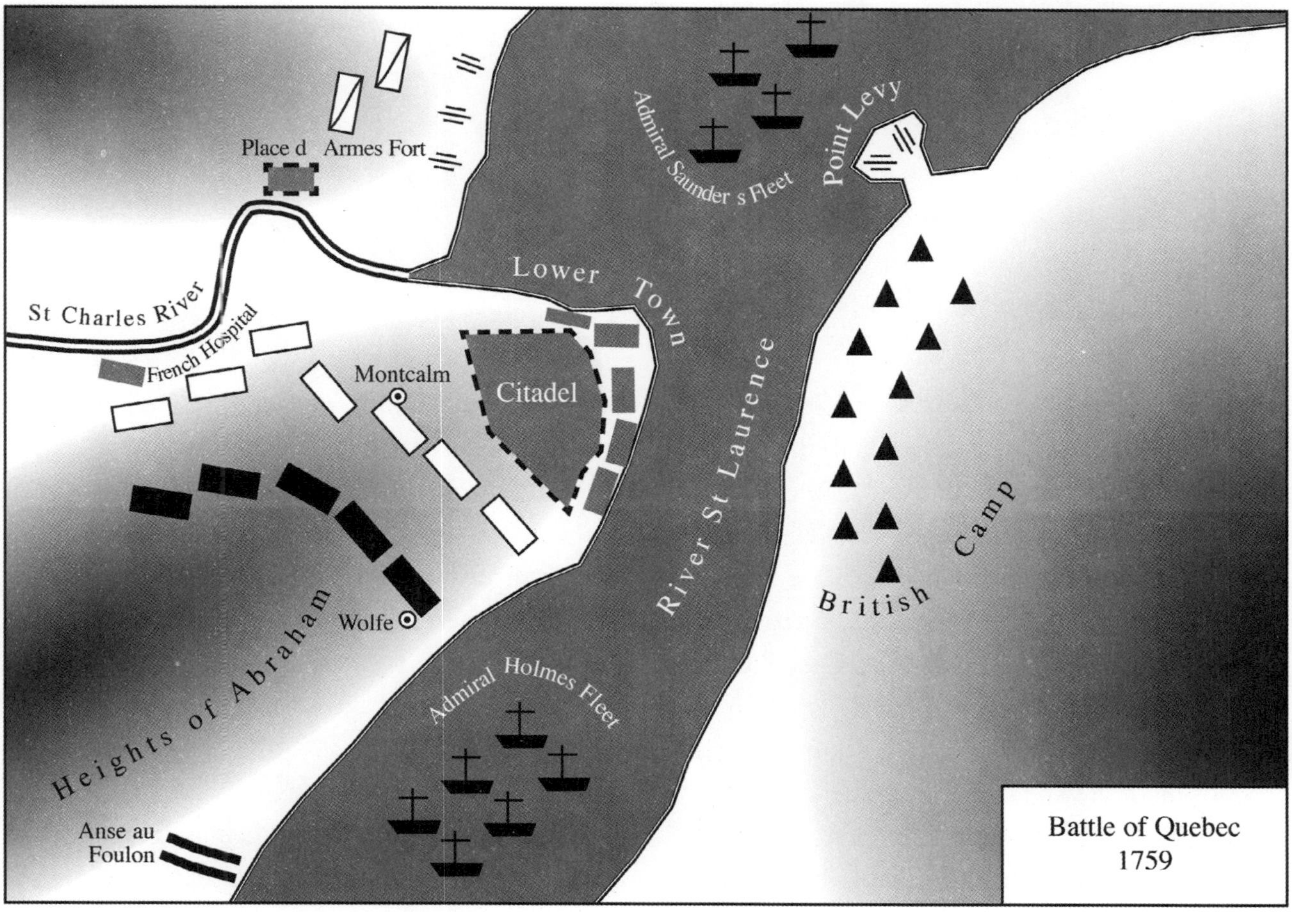

Battle of Quebec
1759

The hero of the Battle of Quebec, General James Wolfe, died during the battle. He was just thirty-two, leaving historians to speculate how differently the American War of Independence might have turned out had he lived.

Then Wolfe and a party of twenty-four light infantry scaled the Heights. By dawn 4,500 British and American troops were assembled on the cliff top.

Wolfe formed his army up on the plains into a single line of battalions with two battalions in reserve and two companies forming a rear guard against Bougainville, who was dangerously to their rear. They possessed just one light gun that they had managed to hurl up the hill. He positioned himself on the right of the line with the 28th Foot.

When Montcalm saw the British formed up in battle order on the plains behind him that morning, he sent out 5,000 of his garrison to give battle. The governor of Quebec only allowed him to take three of the guns from the city's ramparts. He did not even wait for Bougainville and his 3,000 men to be recalled but instead he decided to attack the British line. He formed up his army with regular French regiments in the centre, battalions of Canadian militia on either side and Canadian skirmishers and Indians on the flanks.

The battle began on Wolfe's left with a savage fight between the skirmishers and the force composed of the British Light Infantry and the reserve regiments under Brigadier Townsend. Meanwhile the limited artillery pounded the centre of the opposing lines. The French regulars advanced and the British regiments, who had been lying down to avoid the fire, rose up. The French fired at too great a distance and their fusillade was ineffective, although one stray bullet hit Wolfe on the wrist. As the French advanced, the British withheld their fire until the range was thirty-five yards, then they stopped and fired. Sir John Fortescue said that it was the 'most perfect [fusillade] ever fired on any battlefield, which burst forth as if from a single monstrous weapon, from end to end of the British line'. A second volley destroyed the French line. The Highlanders and the redcoats then charged at the French and drove them from the field.

Wolfe was at the head of the 28th Foot when he was first shot in the groin and then in the chest. An officer supported him so that his men would not see him fall. Then a group of soldiers carried him to the rear. He was lying there mortally wounded when he heard a soldier shout: 'See how they run!'

'Who run?' asked Wolfe.

'The enemy, sir', said the soldier.

'Now God be praised, I will die in peace,' said Wolfe.

It was clear that Quebec had fallen. Wolfe ordered the 28th to march to the bridge across the St Charles in order to cut off the French retreat, then he died.

Montcalm had also been hit while attempting to rally his troops. He rode back to the city, so that no one could see that he was wounded. Then he was carried away with the retreating throng and into a house, where he died. He was buried in a shell hole in the Ursuline convent in Quebec

Brigadier Townsend took command of the British forces and rallied them to fight off an attack from Bougainville to his rear. He went on to take the city. On the afternoon of 17 September, the Union Jack flew above the citadel in Quebec and the French formally surrendered on the following day. The casualties were light compared to other battles between the British and the French in North America. The British had lost just 630 men and the French 830.

In the following year General Sir Jeffery Amherst received the French surrender of Montreal and, in the Treaty of Paris of 1763, the French ceded all their North American colonies to the British.

Yorktown

US Independence Achieved

1781

At Yorktown, the French helped the rebellious American colonists deal a decisive defeat on Britain, which was already on its way to becoming the world's first superpower. This victory led to the founding of the United States.

DURING THE AMERICAN WAR of Independence, the colonists turned for help to the French who were still smarting from being ejected from Canada by the British. In 1780, 6,000 men were sent under the command of the Comte de Rochambeau.

In order to determine their next move, Rochambeau met up with George Washington in White Plains, New York in 1781. Washington wanted to attack the British stronghold of New York City but Rochambeau convinced him that it would be wiser to make his move in the south.

General Cornwallis marches his troops out of Yorktown, flanked by French and American forces.

The British commander in the southern colonies, General Lord Cornwallis, had suffered a number of reverses and had pulled back from Wilmington, North Carolina to Petersburg, Virginia before retreating to Richmond and then Williamsburg. He finally ended up in Yorktown and the adjacent promontory of Gloucester, where his force of 7,500 men made a fortified camp.

In many ways, Yorktown was an excellent position for a fort. It was protected on two sides by impassable swamps, so all sixty-five of Cornwallis's guns could be trained on the single approach route.

Some 4,500 American troops under General Anthony Wayne, Baron von Steuben and the Marquis de Lafayette were in pursuit. When they arrived outside Yorktown, the Franco-American force to the north left a screen facing the British main force under General Henry Clinton in New York City, while 2,500 Continental troops under Washington and 4,000 French troops under Rochambeau hurried south.

Cornwallis's only hope lay in a seaward direction.

The Royal Navy were holding Chesapeake Bay and the British fleet there, under Admiral Thomas Graves, comprised nineteen ships. However, on 5 September the French Admiral, the Comte de Grasse, arrived from the West Indies with twenty-four ships. The leading squadrons of the two fleets engaged in battle for around two and a half hours. Although the British suffered heavier losses, the battle was undecided when they became becalmed. For three days the two fleets drifted along on parallel courses without incident. The French were reinforced with more ships and siege guns from Newport, Rhode Island. They then sailed back into Chesapeake Bay and secured the mouth of the York River, while the British fleet made for New York. Cornwallis was now cut off to landward and to seaward.

On 28 September 1781, Washington and

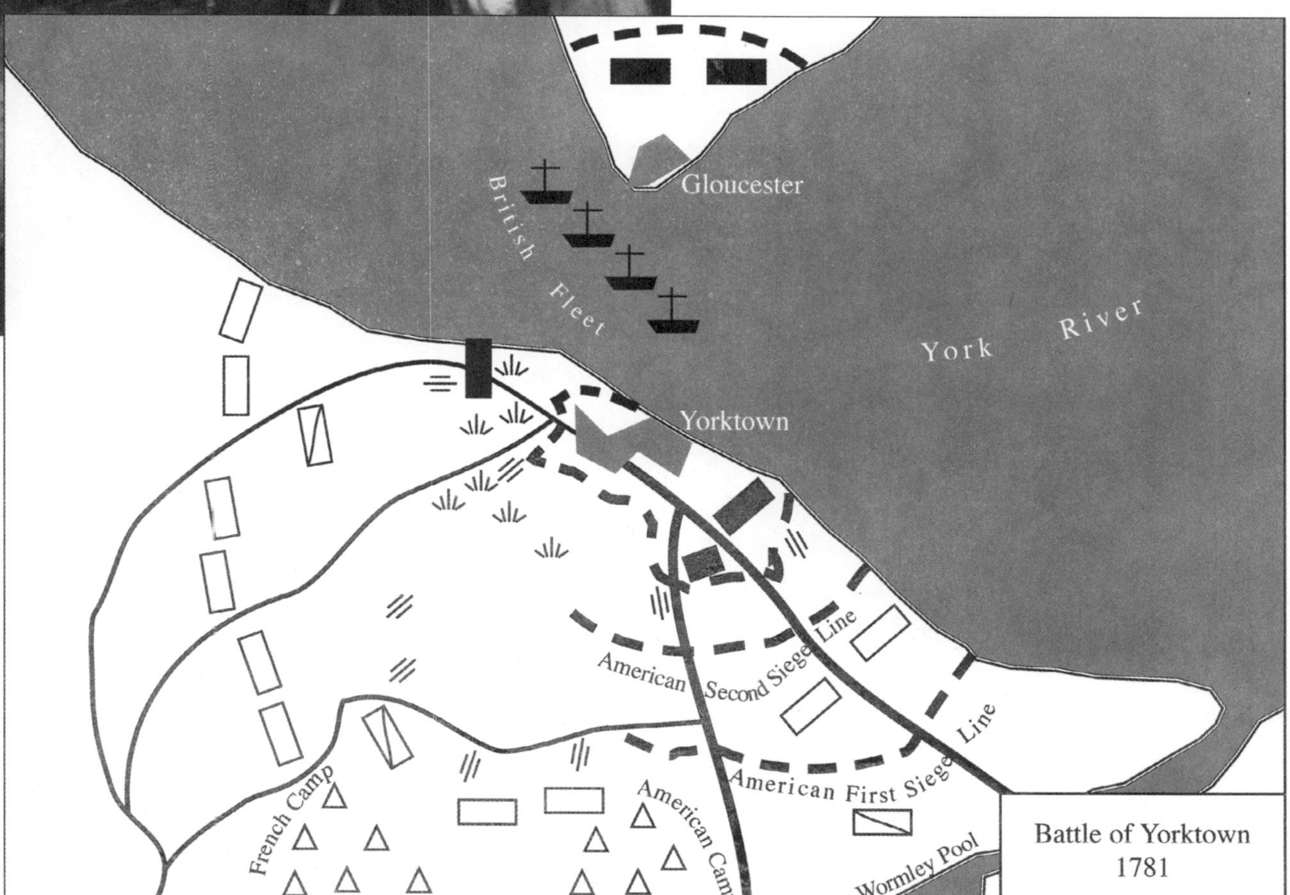

Battle of Yorktown 1781

Rochambeau arrived at Yorktown. Together with de Grasse's 3,000 men some 17,000 troops were now besieging Cornwallis's camp. The remaining British ships in the York River were bombarded. On the night of 10 October, the largest of Cornwallis's warships, HMS *Charon*, was hit by red-hot shot from a French cannon and she caught fire. She drifted across the river, setting fire to several other ships on the way and then sank. Numerous other British ships were sunk. Some were scuttled to make shore defences, although several were later refloated by the French.

Cornwallis was surrounded and raked by heavy fire. On 14 October, the Franco-American forces captured two major British redoubts at bayonet point. Cornwallis then grew so desperate that he even tried sending African slaves infected with smallpox over enemy lines in an attempt to disable the enemy troops. A counterattack proved futile. Cornwallis was outgunned and was running low on food. On 17 October, he sent a message to Washington, declaring that he was ready to surrender. Two days later, the papers were signed. The British were then marched out, their standards furled, and paraded between the ranks of American and French troops. Cornwallis was not present. He could not stand the humiliation of the occasion. A subordinate symbolically surrendered his sword to the French commander, who signalled that Washington should receive it.

A strong relief force was already on its way to Yorktown, but the British public, many of whom supported the colonists, were tired of the war. The British merchants and bankers who had been cut off from the American trade for six years were particularly keen to see the conflict over with.

Lord North, the British prime minister whose insensitivity to the colonists' grievances had started the war, resigned and his successor declared that it was not in Britain's interest to continue the war. A peace treaty was signed at Versailles on 3 September 1783, making the United States an independent country.

Trafalgar

Napoleon Defeated at Sea

1805

The British fleet defeats the combined French and Spanish navies at Trafalgar. This put an end to Napoleon's plan to invade Britain and put the Royal Navy in command of the world's oceans for the next one hundred years.

Recently Admiral Lord Nelson's hastily sketched battle plan has been discovered. In a revolutionary ploy, Nelson sent two columns directly into the enemy's broadside. These succeeded in cutting the French line and scattering their ships.

IN 1805, NAPOLEON WAS MASTER of the Continent, but still harboured ambitions to invade Britain. In order to get his invasion force across the English Channel, though, he needed to become master of the sea. The Royal Navy blockaded French and Spanish ports in an effort to hinder him.

In September it became clear that a large fleet under Admiral Pierre de Villeneuve was refitting in Cádiz, southern Spain. On 16 September Admiral Lord Horatio Nelson set sail from Portsmouth in his flagship HMS *Victory* and arrived off Cádiz on the 29 September.

On 19 October, HMS *Mars* reported that the French and Spanish fleet was leaving port so Nelson gave the order to give chase. That night, the British sailed southeast on the assumption that the enemy was making for the safety of the Mediterranean. On the following morning they were nowhere to be seen, so Nelson turned back to the north.

At sunset, however, Captain Blackwood on HMS *Euryalus* spotted Villeneuve's fleet heading westwards and he shadowed them during the night. On the morning of 21 October, as the weather worsened, Nelson caught up with them off Cape Trafalgar, as they were making a run back into Cádiz.

Villeneuve ordered his fleet to make a single line heading northwards. Typically, naval engagements involved huge broadsides. This would give Villeneuve a tremendous advantage because he had thirty-three ships, including seven large frigates, while Nelson only had twenty-seven ships. Not only were Villeneuve's ships bigger but he also had 4,000 troops on board, many of them trained marksmen.

Nelson died at Trafalgar, shot by a sniper in the rigging of an enemy ship. His body was returned to England, where he was given a majestic funeral in St Paul's Cathedral.

In a pre-arranged plan, Nelson ordered his ships to break into two squadrons and attack Villeneuve's line at right angles. This was a revolutionary tactic as the British ships, sailing bow-on to the sides of the enemy, would risk numerous broadsides before they could bring their own guns to bear.

At 11.50 a.m. Nelson raised the famous signal: 'England expects that every man will do his duty.' By noon, Admiral Cuthbert Collingwood on HMS *Royal Sovereign* was attacking the sixteen ships at the rear of the Spanish line with his squadron of fifteen ships.

While *Victory* was leading the other squadron in the middle of the line, the French and Spanish tried to shoot away her rigging. Next came raking fire that killed Nelson's secretary while he stood talking to Captain Hardy. When eight marines who were standing together on the poop deck were killed by a single cannon shot, Nelson ordered that the men be dispersed around the ship. A few minutes later a shot struck the rail of the quarterdeck and passed between Nelson and Hardy, showering Hardy with splinters. The two men looked at one another, each expecting the other to be wounded. Nelson smiled and said: 'This is too warm work, Hardy, to last long.'

By this time *Victory* had not fired a single shot, but fifty men were dead or wounded and her main topmast and several of her sails had been blown away. At 12.04 a.m. *Victory*'s guns opened up on both sides, but they needed to ram an enemy ship in order to break through the French line.

'Take your choice, Hardy,' said Nelson. 'It does not signify much.'

Hardy ordered the helm to port and ran into the *Redoubtable*, who greeted the *Victory* with a broadside. Another two ships surrounded the *Redoubtable*, whose guns fell silent as she closed her gunports to prevent boarders from entering her through them.

Although *Victory* kept up her fire on Villeneuve's flagship *Bucentaure* and the huge Spanish ship *Santissima Trinidad*, Hardy twice gave orders to stop firing on the *Redoubtable* because she had no flag showing and he thought she had struck – that is, surrendered. But then at 1.15 p.m., in the heat of the action, a musket ball fired from the *Redoubtable*'s mizzen top struck the epaulette on Nelson's left shoulder. He fell on his face on the deck, where it was still stained with his secretary's blood. Three men rushed to his assistance and picked him up.

'They have done for me at last, Hardy,' said

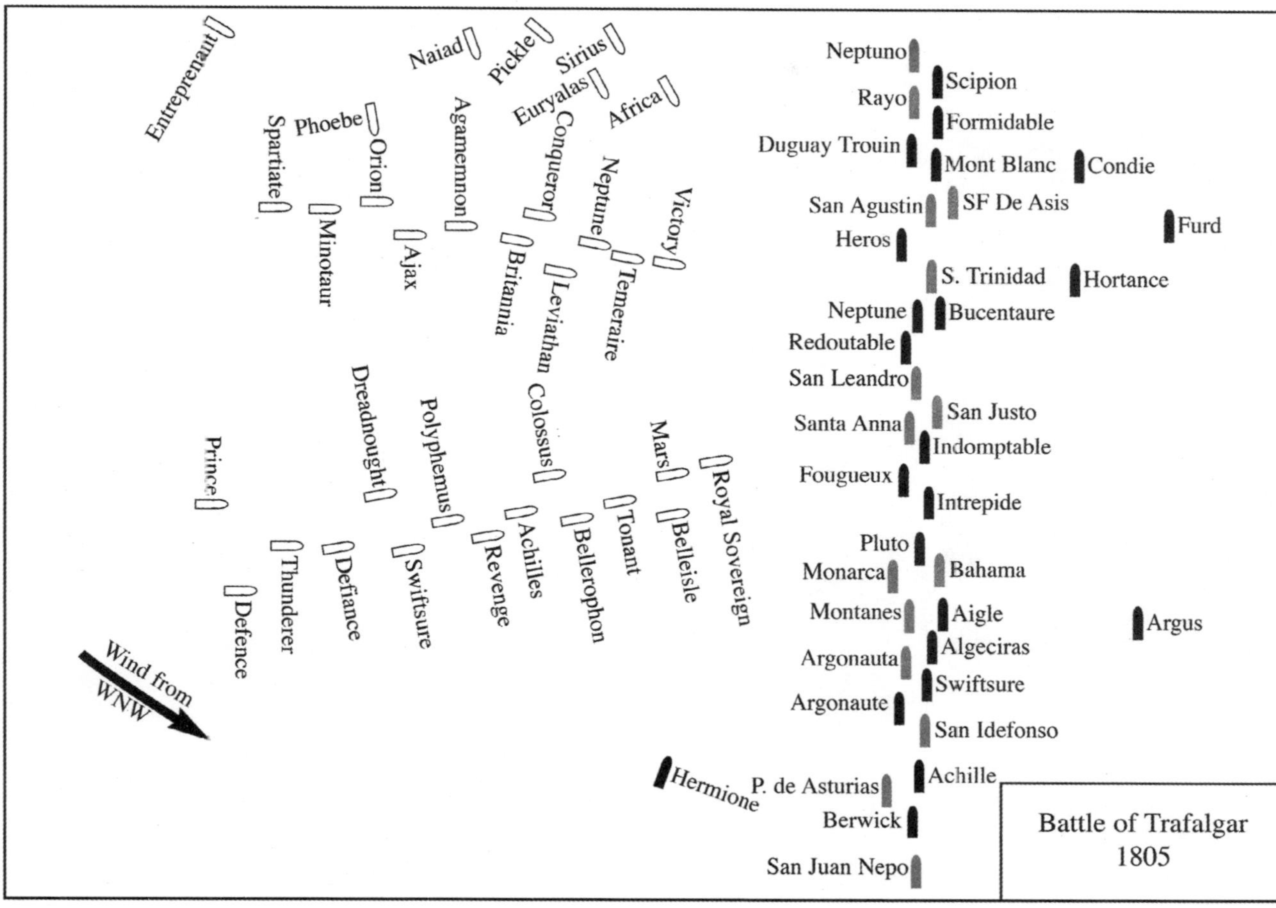

Battle of Trafalgar
1805

Nelson, a veteran of eight previous battles.

'I hope not', said Hardy.

'Yes', said Nelson, 'my backbone is shot through.'

He was carried below where he took out his handkerchief and covered his face and insignia so that the crew would not recognize him. Although it was clear that he was dying, Nelson was still concerned about how the battle was progressing and he asked for Hardy to be sent to him.

Nelson's tactic had worked brilliantly, for Villeneuve's line had been smashed. The six leading ships under Admiral Pierre Dumanoir had been missed in the first attack. At 3.30 p.m. they turned around and counterattacked. Hardy chose this moment to visit Nelson below decks.

'Well, Hardy. How goes the day with us?' he asked.

'Very well', replied Hardy. 'Ten ships have struck, but five of the van have tacked and show an intention of bearing down on the Victory. I have called two or three of our fresh ships, and have no doubt of giving them a drubbing.'

Nelson asked how many ships they had taken. Hardy told him fourteen or fifteen. Nelson said: 'That's well, but I had bargained for twenty.'

Dumanoir's counterattack was effectively repelled and the French and Spanish lost nineteen or twenty ships in total.

Nelson asked that his mistress Lady Hamilton and his daughter Horatia be cared for. Then he said famously, 'Kiss me, Hardy', before he died at about 4:30 pm.

The snipers in the rigging of the Redoubtable killed another fifty of the Victory's crew before all of them were shot in their turn – including the man who had fatally wounded Nelson. The quartermaster had recognized him as he fell. The battle ended at around five p.m. when Villeneuve himself was captured along with 7,000 of his men. The

French had lost a further 7,000 sailors, while 1,500 British seamen were killed or wounded. No British ships were lost.

The British victory at Trafalgar put an end to Napoleon's plans to invade Britain and it meant that Britain would be the world's greatest naval power for the next one hundred years, allowing it to build a huge empire.

Austerlitz

Napoleon gains control of Europe

1805

Although the French at lost at Trafalgar, Napoleon was nearing the height of his power in Europe. Two months later he beat the combined Austrian and Russian forces at Austerlitz in what became known as the Battle of Three Emperors.

IN 1805, BRITAIN, AUSTRIA and Russia had formed a new alliance against France. At the time, most of Napoleon's forces were deployed along the coast of the English Channel but the French and Spanish fleets under his control failed to take control of the seaways, making an invasion of Britain out of the question. So Napoleon turned his attention to the east.

He had long wanted to seize Vienna and force the Austro-Hungarian Emperor out of the alliance. Accordingly, on 25 September the French Grand Army crossed the Rhine and marched across the Black Forest, with the aim of attacking a smaller Austrian force under Field Marshal Karl von Mack at Ulm in Bavaria. He was waiting for the slow-moving Russia army to meet him there. Two weeks later the Grand Army crossed the Danube, thereby preventing Mack from retreating to the east. Sporadic battles broke out, scattering the Austrian troops. On 16 October, French artillery began firing on the city of Ulm. Mack saw that his men were in

Fleeing Allied troops escaping across the frozen Lake Satschen. The French fired red-hot cannon balls to melt the ice.

no condition to withstand a siege and the Russians were still a hundred miles away. He surrendered on 20 October, causing an army of some 80,000 men to be shrugged aside.

The French lost the Battle of Trafalgar on the following day, but that did not affect the situation in central Europe. Napoleon still marched on towards Vienna. Circling north through Moravia, he stopped at Brünn (now Brno in the Czech Republic) for eleven days in order to allow the slower units to catch up. When Czar Alexander met the Austrian Emperor Francis I, forty miles to the northeast at Olmütz (now Olomouc in the Czech Republic), they interpreted Napoleon's hesitation as weakness. He now faced a large Russian army, with Austrian forces under the Archduke Charles on his flanks. To the rear the Prussians were massing an army of 180,000 men. The Prussians had so far remained neutral in the Napoleonic Wars, but they were now incensed that Napoleon had marched across their territory.

Napoleon used his time at Brünn to negotiate a

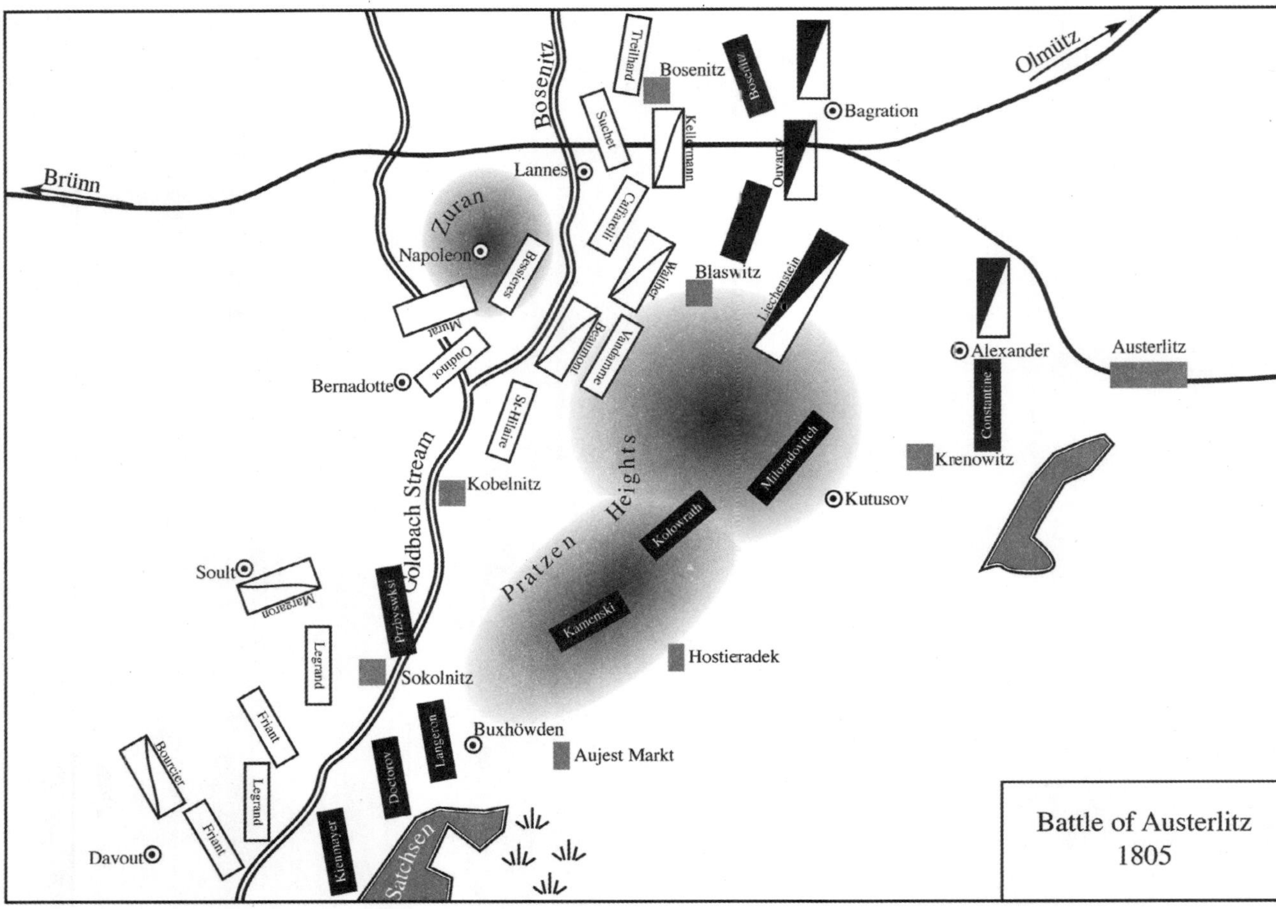

Battle of Austerlitz
1805

generous settlement with Prussia. He also tried, unsuccessfully, to buy off the Czar. Meanwhile he studied the ground around Brünn and decided that the battle should take place twelve miles to the east at a Moravian village called Austerlitz (now Slavkov u Brna in the Czech Republic).

By 2 December Napoleon had amassed 68,000 men around Brünn while the Austro-Russian force, under the nominal command of the Russian general Prince Mikhail Illarionovich Kutuzov, numbered 90,000. December 2 was also the first anniversary of Napoleon's coronation as Emperor and the Battle of Austerlitz is sometimes known as the Battle of Three Emperors.

The allies occupied the Pratzen Heights to the west of Austerlitz on the night before the battle. Their aim was to stand between Napoleon and Vienna and also push the French back from the south. That night, Napoleon addressed his men, sometimes personally, telling them how to manoeuvre or when to fire their guns. Morale was high and some men set fire to the palliasses in order to light Napoleon's way. To the Russians and Austrians on the heights, it looked as though the French were preparing a retreat. At least, that is what they hoped!

Before daybreak, the allies formed themselves up into four columns. At dawn, the vanguard of the first allied column attacked the French positions at the southwest corner of the battlefield. Soon after seven a.m. the whole of the exclusively Russian first, second and third columns marched down from the heights. While one division of Napoleon's IV Corps resisted stoutly, the French faced a much superior force and were forced back. By ten a.m. the allies had nearly broken through the French lines and the situation was only saved by the arrival of III Corps, just in the nick of time. Nevertheless the tactic had succeeded in drawing the allied forces to the right.

At about 7.45 a.m. Napoleon struck back with a manoeuvre known as the 'lion leap'. He sent the rest of IV Corps, which had been hidden in the morning fog, to move forward against the right flank of the allied advance. The French emerged from the haze as the sun rose over Austerlitz, taking the allies by surprise. Improvising a defence, the allies' fourth column marched down from the heights, but it was hit by a flanking action mounted by the French Imperial Guard. It seemed that Napoleon had anticipated every allied move.

Three allied columns were now trapped in the valley at the foot of the Pratzen heights. By noon the French had the heights to themselves. The Russian Imperial Guard, who had been held in reserve, charged up the heights but were turned back. In order to avoid being utterly destroyed, the allied columns were forced to retreat to the south.

They tried to escape across the frozen Lake Satschen but the French, who now held the heights, fired red-hot cannon balls, melting the ice. Soon 4,000 men were in the water. The water was not deep but the bottom was muddy. Many of those who were not killed by the cannon balls were drowned when they became entangled in their equipment and those who struggled to the shore were in no condition to continue fighting.

The guns fell silent at five p.m. The allies had lost 12,200 men, who were either dead or wounded, and 15,000 others had been taken prisoner – nearly a third of the combined force had been lost. The French had lost 6,800 soldiers. The Russians were forced to withdraw, while the Prussians recognized that it was best to maintain their neutrality. The Austrian Emperor was forced to sign the Treaty of Schönbrunn, which handed the eastern provinces of Dalmatia, Istria and Venice over to Napoleon, along with the Tyrol, one of the Habsburgs' most ancient possessions.

With Venice incorporated into Napoleon's Italian possessions, he sent a French force under Marshal André Masséna to expel the Bourbons from Naples. When the Pope objected, Napoleon announced that he was Emperor of Rome and temporal head of the Church. He occupied Italy for eight years after Austerlitz, plundering its art galleries and treasuries and taking its young men off to war.

Moscow

Napoleon's retreat through the Russian winter

1812

In invading Russia, Napoleon over-stretched himself. The Russians pulled back, evacuating Moscow. Then they let 'General Winter' do the rest. As a result, Napoleon no longer had the forces to hold back his enemies and fell from power.

In 1807, CZAR ALEXANDER I signed a peace treaty with Napoleon, which meant that Britain was now France's only serious foe. Unable to invade, Bonaparte decided to close Europe's ports to British merchandise in an attempt to destroy the British economy. However, the Czar became increasingly distrustful of Napoleon and refused to exclude British shipping.

In the spring of 1812, Napoleon took his Grand Army into Poland in an attempt to intimidate the Czar. When he could not reach an agreement with Alexander he crossed the Niemen River and marched into Russia. Instead of fighting, Prince

Kutuzov, who had learned his lesson at Austerlitz, pulled his forces back and adopted a 'scorched earth' policy. This did not stop the French, however, even though they were starved of supplies.

Eventually, the Russians halted at Borodino, seventy miles west of Moscow, where they built fortifications in an attempt to halt Napoleon's march on their capital. Unwilling to risk outflanking the Russians, thereby leaving their army intact, Napoleon made a frontal assault on 7 September. Unable to judge the situation due to smoke on the battlefield, he held back 30,000 of his best troops. As it was, the Russian army was badly mauled. It lost 45,000 men, substantially more than France's 30,000, but it

In its summer uniform, the Grand Army was in no way prepared for the Russian winter. For a second time in his military career Napoleon abandoned his army to their fate.

managed to escape the battlefield unbroken.

A week later, Napoleon entered Moscow to find it deserted. No delegation turned up from Alexander to surrender or to negotiate with Napoleon. Then a fire broke out that razed much of the city and Napoleon found that he had no alternative but to withdraw. This proved disastrous.

Kutuzov was watching as Napoleon marched out of Moscow. Napoleon's plan was to make his way back to Smolensk by a southerly route. He sent an advanced force of 15–20,000 men under Prince Eugène to secure the town of Maloyaroslavets, some seventy miles to the southwest, and also establish a bridgehead across the Luzha River. Prince Eugène arrived at Maloyaroslavets on the evening of 23 October and found it unoccupied.

The Russian General Docturov had been following the French down a parallel road with 12,000 infantry, three cavalry and eighty-four guns. He attacked two isolated battalions before sunrise on 24 October, who fled back towards the bridge over the Luzha. A counterattack under General Delzon resulted in the town being retaken, but when the French tried to force their way out of the other side they were stopped by the Russians. Eventually Napoleon turned up with the main force. The French now had sufficient men to broaden the bridgehead that would allow his army to cross.

On the following day, Napoleon went out to survey the situation but his small party was attacked by Cossacks. His escort was able to fight them off but some of the attackers got very close to the Emperor. After that experience he carried a bag of poison around his neck so that he could kill himself rather than be captured.

Kutuzov was shadowing the Grand Army with his main force of 110–120,000 men – he was coming up fast behind the French. Although the French were winning the Battle of Maloyaroslavets, their losses of 5,000 being less than the Russians' 6,000, they were forced to withdraw towards Mozhaysk rather than get caught between the two forces. This was ironic because Kutuzov had decided not to engage the French – he considered his raw recruits to be no

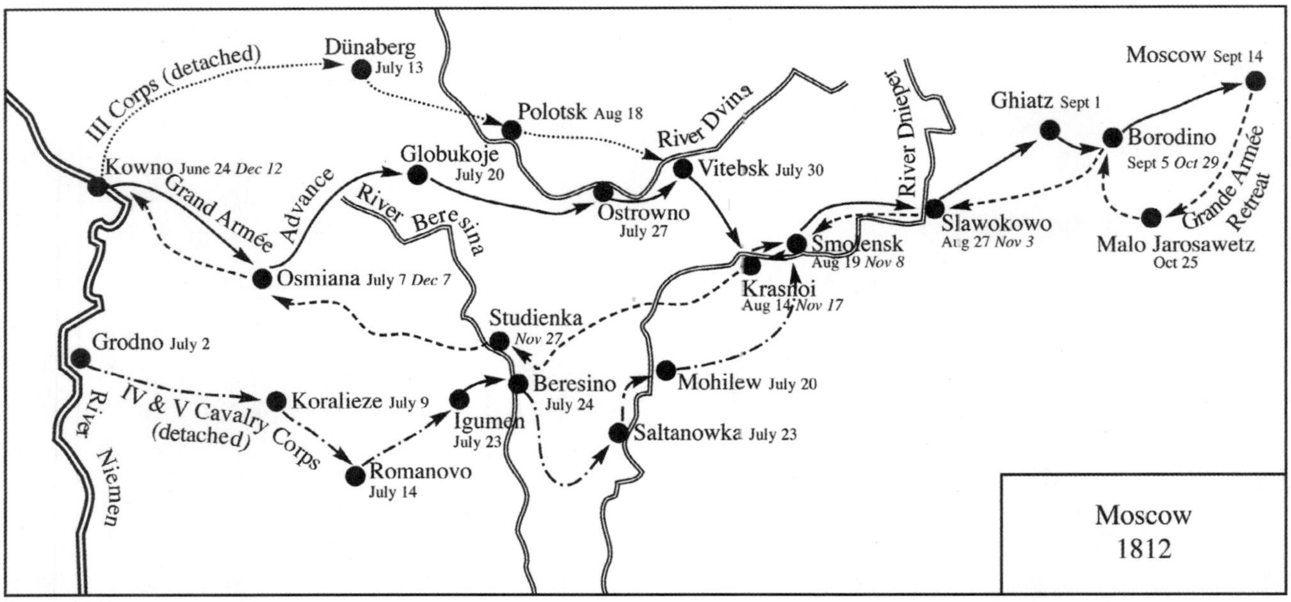

Moscow
1812

match for France's veterans. Nevertheless the Russians had secured an important strategic victory, forcing Napoleon to abandon his planned southerly exit route from Russia. He now had to head northwest, through the area that had been devastated by this advance.

With no food or provisions the French commissariat collapsed, leaving men and horses hungry. Artillery pieces had to be abandoned and the horses were eaten. Meanwhile Russian regular forces, Cossack regiments and partisans not only harassed the French flanks but also the rear. What was worse, the French now faced the onset of the Russian winter.

The French column now stretched for over forty miles. Soldiers were intermingled with the camp followers, which included a number of French actresses that had been picked up in Moscow, as well as carts carrying booty. To the rear was Marshal Davout, who tried to round up the stragglers. Kutuzov had already made it clear that any of his men who fell into Russian hands could expect no mercy. They had, after all, violated the soil of Mother Russia.

Kutuzov was well aware of the hardships that Napoleon's men were about to face and he sent cavalry ahead of the column to destroy the French outposts and depots. In response, Napoleon increased the pace and sent an advanced guard on to Vyaz'ma in the province of Smolensk to secure the depot there. This had the effect of stretching the column even further and on 31 October and 3 November the Russians attacked Napoleon's now weakened rear.

Then, on 4 November, it began to snow. As the weather worsened, malnourished soldiers had no way of coping with the cold and hundreds of Frenchmen froze to death each night. Setting villages on fire was the standard way of keeping warm. Disease was rife. When the organized distribution of supplies failed completely, men wandered off in search of food. Many did not return, falling victim to the cold or the Cossacks. Without horses, there was no defence against the Cossack cavalry who hacked to pieces an entire brigade under General Baraguay d'Hilliers. The very idea of the Cossacks struck fear in the hearts of the French, who now succumbed to fatalism.

Napoleon halted at Smolensk and tried to re-order his army but discipline had broken down. His men broke into food and clothing stores, causing immense waste. So the Grand Army continued its retreat. The army that had left Moscow had been double the present size and the amount of available troops was still falling fast.

The Russians attacked at Krasnoi, cutting the column in two. Napoleon sent his Imperial Guard and his artillery back to fight off the Russians and that night they attacked the Russian camp. The Russians had not imagined that the French would stage such a risky raid and they had not deployed proper pickets. They paid a terrible price.

This victory raised French morale. Soon they had more reason to cheer because Marshal Ney turned up. He had stayed behind in Smolensk in order to collect the stragglers and had been cut off. The Russians demanded that he surrender, but he refused. Having failed to fight his way out, Ney ordered fires to be lit one night. He then slipped out into the darkness and around the Russians' northern flank.

The next major obstacle Napoleon faced was the Beresina River, in what is now Belarus. Marshal Oudinot staged a surprise attack on the garrison at Beresino and took the depot there. However, a second Russian army of 60,000 men under Admiral Chichagov had marched up the western bank of the Beresina and burnt the bridge. After that there was a sudden thaw that left the river impassable. Meanwhile another 50,000 Russians under General Wittgenstein were approaching from the north.

Napoleon had to send a large force under Marshal Victor to slow Wittgenstein down. Then, on the night of 25 November, French army engineers began building three bridges at Studienka, ten miles north of Beresino. During the construction, men had to wade chest-deep in the freezing water. Many lost their lives.

In the late afternoon of the following day Ney and Oudinot crossed the river and took on Chichagov, while Victor's men formed a rearguard. The main force began crossing but, with hundreds of sick and wounded, this was a slow and disorganized process. By the night of 27 November, Victor was running low on ammunition. As more and more Russians arrived on the field, he withdrew his men to the west bank and oversaw the retreat for as long as it remained practicable. Eventually, though, he was forced to set fire to the bridges in order to prevent the Russians from using them, thereby abandoning thousands of French stragglers on the eastern bank.

Temperatures plummeted once they had crossed the river. The French column stretched out along the road to Vilnius and was constantly harassed by the Cossacks, who could operate freely off the road.

News came that General Malet had staged a coup d'etat in Paris. Claiming that Napoleon had died in Russia, he briefly seized the reins of power on 23 October 1812, before being arrested. Napoleon now abandoned his army in Russia – as he had previously abandoned his army in Egypt after the Battle of the Nile – and dashed back to Paris, where he tightened the screws of his dictatorship and began to levy new men.

At Vilnius, the French went on the rampage again. The only way to restore order was to resume the retreat, with Ney fighting valiant rearguard actions. When they crossed back over the Nieman, Ney stayed behind until the last moment, in the process famously making himself the last Frenchman to leave Russia.

Napoleon's Grand Army was now no more and the French, as a nation, had lost its taste for conquest. Austria, Russia, Prussia and Britain were now ranged against them. Napoleon fought on, but he could not hold the allies back. The British expelled the French from Spain and crossed the Pyrenees. On 16–19 October 1813, Napoleon lost to the combined forces of Austria, Russia, Prussia and Sweden at the Battle of Leipzig, also known as the Battle of the Nations. With the allies reaching Paris, Napoleon was forced to abdicate on 6 April 1814 and was exiled to the Isle of Elba, off the west coast of Italy.

Waterloo

'A Damned Near Thing'

1815

After a short exile on Elba, Napoleon escaped, returned to France and went on the rampage again. All Europe knew there was only one man who could stop him: Arthur Wellesley, the Duke of Wellington.

THE BATTLE OF WATERLOO was Napoleon Bonaparte's final defeat. It ended twenty-three years of war between France and the other European powers. After his catastrophic invasion of Russia in 1812 and his comprehensive defeat by the Duke of Wellington in the Peninsular War, Napoleon had been forced to abdicate and the Bourbon monarchy was restored. Although exiled to the Isle of Elba, he stayed there less than a year.

In 1815, Napoleon gave his guards the slip and returned to France, landing at Cannes on 1 March. As he crossed the Alps, republican peasants rallied to him. Louis XVIII sent Napoleon's old comrade-in-arms Marshal Ney, who had by now sworn an oath to the Bourbons, to capture him. Ney promised the king that he would bring Napoleon back to Paris in a

Scotland for Ever; the charge of the Scots Greys at Waterloo, 18 June 1815. The attack by the Royal Scots Greys cavalry regiment on the French 45th Infantry was immortalized in this famous painting of 1881 by Lady Elizabeth Butler.

cage. However, Ney changed his mind when his soldiers cheered Napoleon, and rejoined the Emperor.

At the time, the European powers were meeting at the Congress of Vienna. Their business was to re-organize the Continent after the devastation of the Napoleonic Wars. Hearing the news that Napoleon was marching on Paris at the head of an army, the Czar Alexander turned to Wellington and said: 'It is for you to save the world again.'

By the end of May, Napoleon had raised an army of 284,000 men and, with a force of 124,500, he moved north to the Belgian border. His aim was to manoeuvre his forces between the 93,000-strong Anglo-Dutch force under Wellington and a 115,000-

The 2nd and 3rd Battalions of First Guards, under Lieutenant-Colonel Lord Saltoun, defend Hougoumont.

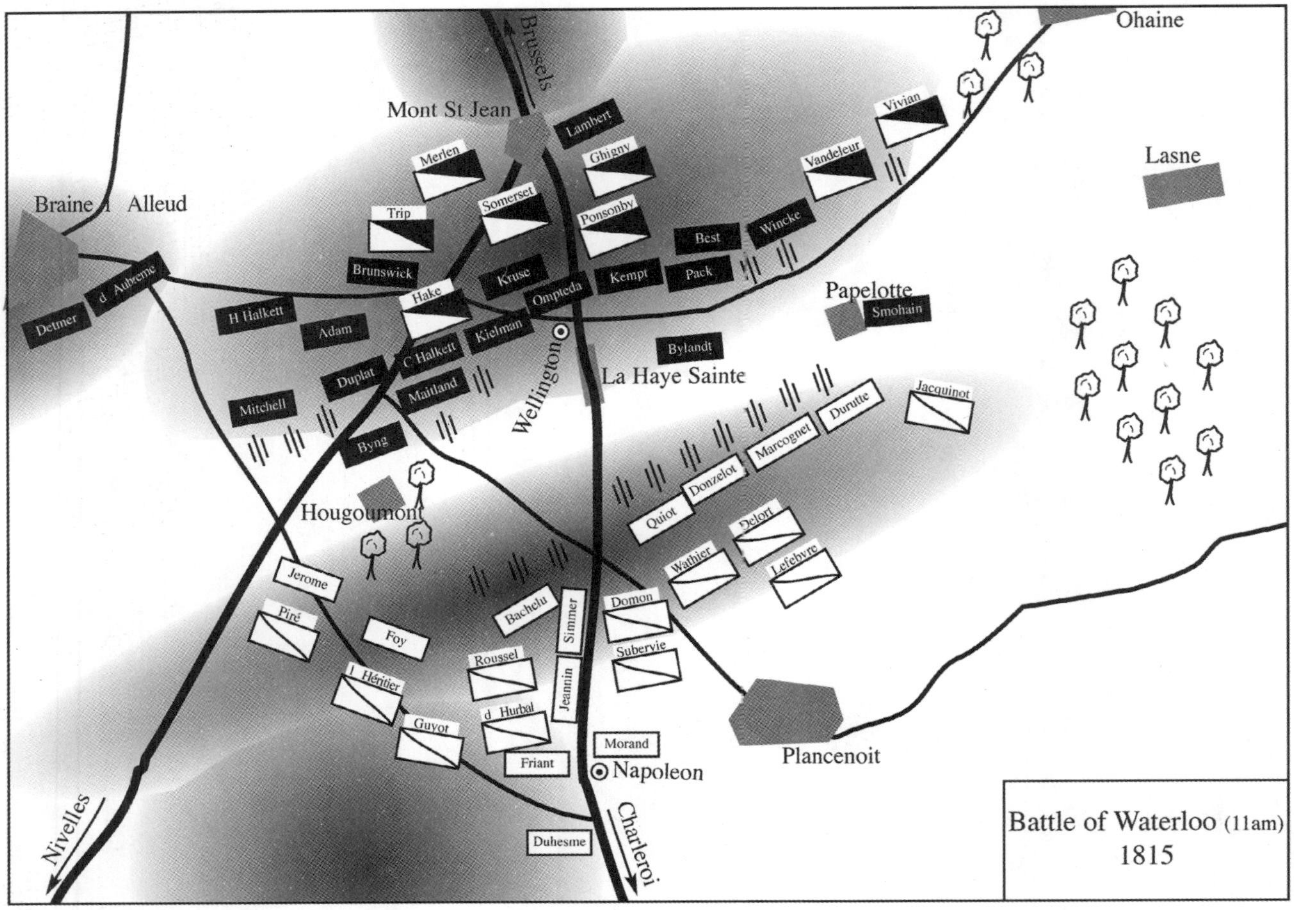

Battle of Waterloo (11am)
1815

man Prussian army under Field Marshal Gebhard Leberecht von Blücher. He then hoped to defeat the two armies separately, pushing Wellington up towards the Belgian coast and Blücher back into Prussia.

Napoleon ordered Ney to cross the border and march to Les Quatre Bras, an important crossroads on the way to Brussels. There, on 16 June, he engaged Wellington. Although the French had overwhelming superiority, Wellington managed to withdraw in good order and regroup at Mont St Jean, just south of Waterloo.

That same day, Napoleon inflicted a serious defeat on Blücher at Ligny but the Prussian army was not completely destroyed. Napoleon sent Marshal Grouchy to pursue the remnants. Napoleon had succeeded in his plan of keeping the two armies apart, but he mistakenly thought that the Prussians were finished and so he set off after Wellington.

Vastly outnumbered, Wellington's only chance was to hold his ground until the Prussians sent reinforcements. He chose his battlefield carefully, picking a place where he could fight the kind of defensive battle that he had mastered. The ridge at Mont St Jean ran for just three miles. He put most of his men out of sight behind it, while others garrisoned the farmhouses at Hougoumont, Le Haye Sainte and Papelotte.

The French drew up on an opposing ridge just 1,300 yards away. Some 140,000 men and 400 guns would be squeezed into a battlefield of little more than three square miles, which gave Napoleon little chance to employ the complex manoeuvres he excelled at. He would need to attack Wellington's position straight on.

Wellington concentrated most of his strength on his right flank, where the ridges were closer. He left the flank lightly manned in the hope that it would be reinforced by the Prussians. The forward positions, such as Hougoumont and Le Haye Sainte, were designed to act as breakers in a French attack. Under Wellington's command were 13,253 British troops, 6,387 men of the King's German Legion, 15,935 Hanoverians, 29,214 Dutch and Belgians, 6,808 Brunswickers and 2,880 Nassauers. This gave him 12,408 cavalry, 49,608 infantry and 5,645 gunners with 156 artillery pieces.

The French fielded 15,765 cavalry, 48,950 infantry and 7,232 gunners with 246 guns. Napoleon would have had an overwhelming superiority if he had recalled Grouchy's corps of some 33,000 men. As it was, they were held down by 17,000 men of Blücher's rear guard at Wavre, some eight miles to the east, while Blücher's main force of around 28,000 was on its way to reinforce Wellington. It would save the day.

Napoleon was unwell. The piles that plagued him in his later years were playing up and he was testy. He pooh-poohed the idea that Blücher might relieve Wellington and refused to recall Grouchy. Dismissing Wellington as a 'sepoy general' – Wellington's early military experience had been in India – he claimed he could overwhelm him with a frontal assault. When it was pointed out that Wellington had not suffered a single defeat during the Peninsular War, Napoleon exploded with rage.

Not only did Napoleon underestimate his opponent but he made another fatal blunder. It had been raining for the last few days, making the going heavy for cavalry and infantry assaults. Instead of attacking at the first opportunity on the morning of 18 June, he delayed until midday in order to allow the field to dry. This gave Blücher's Prussians the time they needed to reach the battlefield.

The battle began with a diversionary attack on Hougoumont under the command of Napoleon's

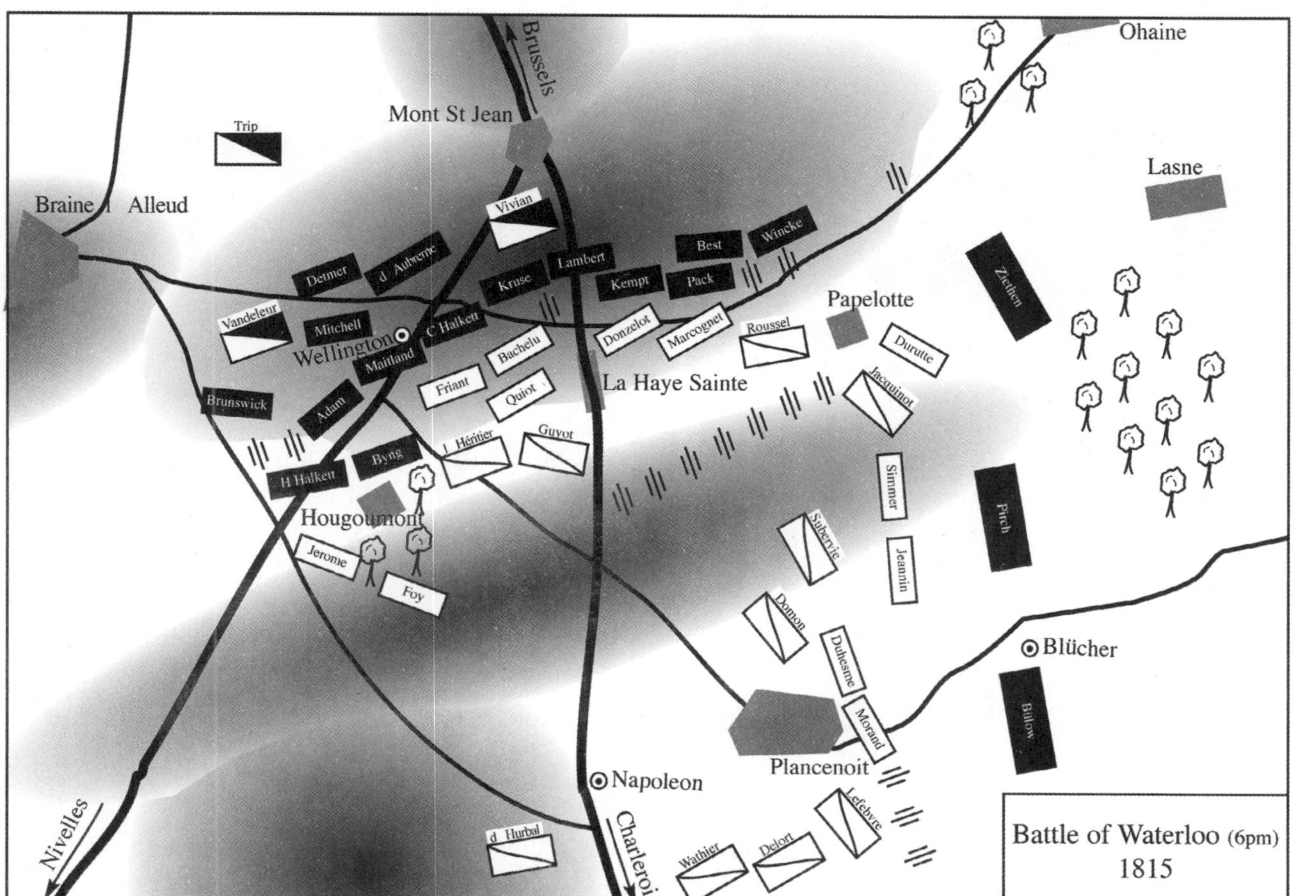

Battle of Waterloo (6pm) 1815

Arthur Wellesley, the first Duke of Wellington, urges his men on. He famously once remarked of his troops: 'I don't know what effect these men will have upon the enemy, but, by God, they terrify me.'

brother Jerome. The idea was to lure Wellington away in order to weaken his centre. But Jerome was jealous of his brother's military record and so he tried to take the château in earnest. Soon his entire division was involved in a full-scale battle. As heavy fire from prepared positions took its toll on the attackers, Jerome had to call for reinforcements which weakened the French centre. He had achieved the opposite of Napoleon's intentions.

For Wellington, it was vital that Hougoumont be held, otherwise his right would have been turned and his position on the ridge would have been untenable. However, just thirteen companies of Coldstream Guards were sent to support Hougoumont, while the position held down a quarter of Napoleon's infantry. Napoleon underestimated the resilience of the British guardsmen.

At one p.m. Napoleon received an intercepted message from General Bülow, who was leading the Prussian advance guard. It was addressed to Wellington, and it informed him that Bülow was in the area of St Lambert. Napoleon sent cavalry and infantry units to hold off Bülow and dispatched an order to Grouchy recalling him. But it was too late. The order did not reach Grouchy until five p.m., when it was too late to help.

With Blücher on his way, it now became even more urgent to dislodge Wellington from his ridge. Napoleon ordered the troops on the right – General d'Erlon's Corps, some 20,000 men – to move forward in formation. They came under attack from the garrison at La Haye Sainte and suffered heavy casualties. Nevertheless, they succeeded in capturing Papelotte and La Haye Sainte. But a terrible mistake had been made. The French did not advance up the ridge in narrow battalion columns but in broad divisional columns, 200 men wide and twenty-four to twenty-seven men deep. This presented the British gunners with an unmissable target.

D'Erlon's men had little artillery or cavalry support. The British guns were drawn up behind a thick hedge and could rain fire down on them with impunity. When the depleted French ranks reached the top of the ridge, they were met with a volley of musket fire. A bayonet charge was then made by 3,000 redcoats. Two British cavalry brigades moved in for the kill. Papelotte was retaken and 3,000 Frenchmen were taken prisoner. In all the excitement, the cavalry charged the French guns. French lancers counterattacked and over 1,000 British cavalrymen were lost. But even that could not disguise the fact that Napoleon's knock-out blow had failed.

By three p.m. Napoleon knew that he could expect no help from Grouchy. He decided that the lynchpin of the whole battle was La Haye Sainte and he ordered Ney to take it. As he prepared the assault, Ney could see wounded British soldiers making their way down the road to Brussels. This put it into his head that Wellington was retreating. Without artillery or infantry support, Ney ordered his 5,000 cavalrymen to charge up the ridge in what he believed would be a decisive attack. When they saw the French approaching, Wellington's infantry formed themselves into squares behind the ridge. Because of this, the French cavalry made little impact when they reached them, and Wellington counterattacked with his own cavalry.

Another 10,000 French horsemen were sent in. They made little impression on the infantry squares, but the French managed to take La Haye Sainte. The French artillery also began to take its toll on Wellington's centre, leaving it weak and vulnerable. Ney was convinced that with one more push he would break through and so he sent a message to Napoleon asking for more troops.

'More troops!' yelled Napoleon. 'Where does he expect me to get them from? Make them?'

His reserves had been sent to hold off the Prussians who had captured nearby Plancenoit.

Wellington then took personal command of a brigade of Brunswickers and mounted on his favourite grey, Copenhagen, he rode to fill the hole that Ney had punched in his line. The Prussians were now arriving on the battlefield. Napoleon spread the word among his troops that these were Grouchy's men coming to support them. When they discover that this was a lie their morale plummeted.

Napoleon could have saved his army at this point, if he had withdrawn. But his Imperial Guard had held the Prussians on the left and at seven p.m. he withdrew several battalions in the belief that one more charge up the centre by the veterans of the Imperial Guard would break the British on the ridge.

To the beat of the drum, the Imperial Guard marched up the ridge, magnificently attired in their tall bearskin caps decorated with long red feathers. Wellington ordered his men to lie down so that shot from the French artillery would fly harmlessly over their heads. When the Imperial Guard reached the top of the ridge they were met with a fusillade of musket fire and grapeshot. With the Imperial Guard just twenty yards away, Wellington is reputed to have given the order: 'Up Guards and at 'em.'

They leapt to their feet, let off a volley of fire at close range, then charged with fixed bayonets. The Imperial Guard were Napoleon's elite and the guardsmen pushed them back. Seeing this, the cry went up among the French: 'La Garde recule' ('The Guard is retreating'). This was the first retreat in their history. With it, French morale collapsed completely.

As the Imperial Guard were pushed back, they were ambushed by a reserve brigade hiding in the cornfields. Some turned and fled, while others screened Napoleon's retreat by forming a square in the middle of the battlefield. Meanwhile, Wellington raised his hat and ordered a general advance that swept the French from the field.

At nine o'clock that night Wellington and Blücher met up at La Belle Alliance, which Blücher thought would make a good name for the battle. But Wellington insisted on an old tradition he had built up – naming his battles after the place in which he had slept the night before. So the battle was called Waterloo.

The French lost 25,000 men, who had either been killed or wounded, and 9,000 more had been captured, along with 220 guns. Wellington's army lost 15,000 troops and Blücher's about 8,000. The Duke of Wellington declared the Battle of Waterloo 'a damned serious business – the nearest run thing you ever saw in your life.' With the Prussians in pursuit, Napoleon tried to rally his men at Genappe, seven miles to the south. But it was an impossible task because his units had lost all cohesion. He returned to Paris and, four days later, he abdicated for a second time.

Hoping to take ship for the United States Napoleon headed for Rochefort, but the port was blockaded by the Royal Navy. He appealed to the British for protection, and, on 15 July, he boarded HMS *Bellerophon*. This time he was exiled to the remote island of St Helena off Africa in the south Atlantic where he died in 1821 at the age of 51.

Sebastopol

Siege ending the Crimean War

1854–55

In the Crimean War, Turkey, Britain and France tried to put a stop to Russia's expansion to the south. Key to victory was the capture of the home port of the Russian Black Sea port – Sebastopol.

SINCE THE 1600s, RUSSIA had tried to expand southwards at the expense of the Ottoman Empire. This had caused a series of wars with Turkey. In 1853, Russia was in expan-

The Crimean War was characterized by cavalry charges. The catastrophic Charge of the Light Brigade has become legend, while the largely successful Heavy Brigade charge has largely been forgotten.

sionist mood again. The Czar demanded the right to protect those Orthodox Christians who were subjects of the Ottoman Empire. He came in conflict with France over the rights of the Russian Orthodox and Roman Catholic churches in the holy places of Palestine.

In July 1853 Russia seized the Ottoman Empire's provinces on the Danube (which now make up modern Romania). The British backed the Turks because of Britain's fear of Russian expansion into Afghanistan and India and so they sent a fleet to Constantinople (now Istanbul). On 4 October 1853, the Turks declared war on Russia and on 28 March 1854 the British and the French followed suit. The Russians promptly pulled out of the Danubian provinces, which Austria then occupied. But that appeared to be of no consequence. Another European war was now underway, with Turkey, Britain and France on one side and Russia on the other.

On 14 September 1854, 50,000 British and French troops landed on the Crimean peninsula, which had been held by Russia since 1783. Their aim was to take the city of Sebastopol, the home port of the Russian Black Sea Fleet.

The Russians occupied the heights above the Alma river, under the command of Prince Aleksandr Menshikov, thereby blocking the road to Sebastopol. On 20 September, they were attacked by British and French forces under Lord Raglan and Marshal Armand de Saint-Arnaud. The Russians repulsed the first assault, but then withdrew their artillery. When the allies attacked again, they were forced to retreat towards Sebastopol. Although the allies had won the field, they had lost 3,000 men in the action. They failed to pursue the Russians and take the city, which was poorly fortified at the time.

Instead the British took the port of Balaklava, some seven miles away, and the heights overlooking Sebastopol, while the French built a base in Kamish Bay. By this time, cholera was rife among the troops and Saint-Arnaud fell ill and returned to France.

On 10 October, the British troops began digging-in around Sebastopol, cutting off the small peninsula on which the city stood. The Russian artillery fired on them so, a week later, the allies brought up their own artillery. The idea that the city could be taken easily was now forgotten. The Russian military engineer Colonel Eduard Totleben had constructed huge earthworks and fortifications and an eleven-month siege began.

The Russians tried to break the siege on 25 October. They attacked along a line of hills called the Vorontsov Ridge, cutting off the approach to Sebastopol and threatening Balaklava itself. The Turks were forced to withdraw after stubborn resistance but the Russians were prevented from taking the town by General Sir James Scarlett's Heavy Brigade – who made one of the greatest cavalry charges of the nineteenth century – and Sir Colin Campbell's 93rd Highlanders, who formed the original, celebrated 'thin red line'. After the Turks had fled, just 550 of them held a front of 150 yards.

The 93rd did not form a square, the traditional defence against cavalry, as the Russian Hussars cantered towards them. They remained stretched out in their 'thin red line tipped with steel'. There were, in fact, two lines, both with muskets at the ready.

'There's no retreat from here, men,' Campbell told them. 'You must die where you stand.'

'Aye, aye, Sir Colin, and needs be we'll do that,' said Private John Scott.

In fact, rather than wait for the Russians to arrive, some of the Scots wanted to attack.

'Ninety-third! Ninety-third! Damn all this eagerness!' barked Campbell.

When the Hussars' canter turned into a charge, the 93rd fired a volley and calmly reloaded. A second volley at 250 yards sent the Hussars tumbling from their horses. The rest veered away, only to be hit by a third volley which scattered them and sent them into a hasty retreat.

Observing the action from the heights above Sebastopol, Lord Raglan saw the Russians removing the guns from the artillery positions they had captured on the Vorontsov Ridge. He then ordered the Light Brigade, under gentleman-adventurer Lord Cardigan, to stop them. But instead of attacking the isolated Russians on the heights, they charged down the valley towards the Russian batteries, with notoriously disastrous results. What actually happened has ever since been a source of controversy. It is usually assumed that there was a mix-up in the orders. Of the 673 men who charged down the valley at the Russian guns it is said that 387 were killed, as well as 520 horses. But those were the initial figures and they did not account for the survivors who returned to the British lines later.

General Bosquet, who was with a French observation party watching from the heights is quoted as saying: '*C'est magnifique mais ce n'est pas la guerre*...' ('It is magnificent but it is not war....'). However, the rest of the quotation is rarely given. It is: '*C'est de la folie*' ('It is madness').

The Russians simply assumed that the British were drunk. The Russian General Lipandi asked one of the men he had taken prisoner what they had been given to make them charge like that. The trooper replied: 'By God, if we had so much as smelt the barrel we would have taken half Russia by this time.'

In fact, the charge was a success. They overran the guns, cut down the gunners and charged on into the Russian cavalry that had formed up behind them. However, the infantry support they had been promised by Lord Raglan never appeared and there was little else to do but ride back down the valley again, pursued by the Russian cavalry. Bosquet sent the Fourth *Chasseurs d'Afrique* to head them off.

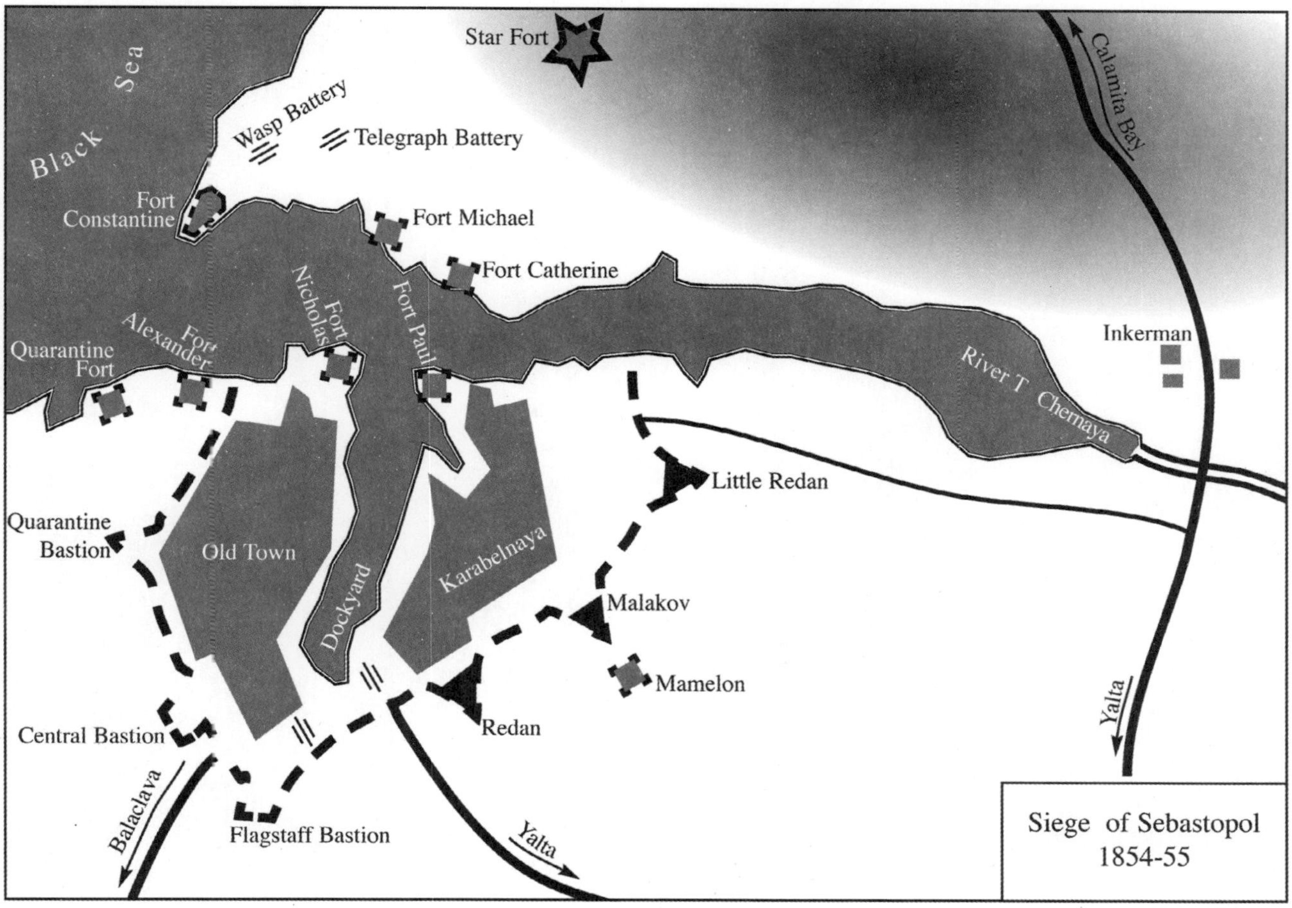

Raglan blamed Cardigan, claiming that he had 'lost his head'. Cardigan informed the survivors that it was not his fault, to which one of the troopers responded: 'Go again, my lord?'

Balaklava was a victory for the allies, but the charge of the Light Brigade went down in the annals of military folly. The poet laureate, Alfred, Lord Tennyson, wrote two poems about the battle: the first, 'Charge of the Heavy Brigade', was a success, and it was promptly forgotten; the second, 'Charge of the Light Brigade', has remained in the public imagination.

On the following day the Russians attacked the right flank of the British with 5,000 men. A division under Sir De Lacy Evans repulsed them with the loss of 500 men.

The British and the French continued digging trenches, despite the cold. They also found that their artillery did not stand up well to continual use, while the better-built Russian guns could stand more frequent firing. The Crimean War was also the first war in which rifles were employed to any extent and there were frequent exchanges of small arms fire.

While the allies besieged the Russians in Sebastopol, they were being besieged themselves by Russian forces to the east. Although they could receive supplies by sea there were soon shortages, however – particularly of firewood as the winter closed in. Troops were regularly put on half rations at short notice. On Christmas Day 1854, Colonel Bell's command got nothing to eat at all. When they complained they were eventually given some meat but with no fires they had no means of cooking it. Usually the troops survived on a diet of dried or salted meat and biscuit. Men succumbed to scurvy, although the Royal Navy ships in port in Balaklava had plenty of lime juice which would have prevented it. They were also give raw green coffee beans. Some

The French Zouaves from North Africa ride to the help of the British at the Battle of Inkerman.

assumed that this was an insult. Were they supposed to eat the raw beans like a horse eats barley? So they threw them into the mud. Others, however, were more resourceful. They cut their dried meat into strips to use as fuel for roasting the beans and they ground them using cannon balls.

The men were no better clothed than fed. Lord Cardigan took to wearing a woollen jacket that came to bear his name. Boots were a particular problem. When the 55th Regiment formed up in the sea of mud that the battlefield had become and tried to march away they all got stuck in the mud. All they could do was leave their boots behind them, so men were seen fighting in the snow without boots but wearing two pairs of socks.

The troops' suffering was brought home to readers of *The Times* in Britain by William Russell, the world's first war correspondent. As he pointed out:

> *A few guns judiciously placed when we first came here might have saved us incredible toil and labour, because they would have rendered it all but impossible for the Russians to cast up such entrenchments and works as the Russians have done before the open and perfectly unprotected entrance to Sebastopol. Here has been our great, our irremediable error.*

Russell was later joined by the world's first combat photographer, Roger Fenton, whom the British government sent in an effort to counter Russell's caustic reports. Meanwhile some of the suffering of the sick and wounded was relieved by the pioneering nurses Florence Nightingale and Jamaican-born Mary Seacole. However, as Russell put it in *The Times*: 'The authorities generally treat the medical officers with cool disrespect and indifference.'

On 5 November, Prince Menshikov collected together 60,000 men and 234 guns and attacked the Anglo-French force of less than 10,000 men on Cossack Hill. The Battle of Inkerman, a village at the mouth of the Chernaya (Black) River, was then enveloped in thick fog, which stopped the Russians from witnessing the overwhelming superiority they enjoyed.

It began with the pealing of the bells in Sebastopol, after which elements of the Tomsky Regiment scaled Shell Hill and captured the British pickets there. The Russians then attacked the British Second Division under Brigadier General Pennefather. When General Sir George Cathcart rode up and asked him where his Fourth Division was able to lend a hand, Pennefather replied: 'Everywhere'.

However, Cathcart himself and other British commanders refused Bosquet's offer of assistance because they were veterans of the Peninsular War and the French were still considered enemies.

Lost in the fog, the Coldstream Guards called out to Sir Charles Russell: 'If any officer will lead us, we will charge.'

His response was: 'Come on, my lads, who will follow me?'

Russell was nearly killed in the ensuing engagement. One of his men described the ferocity of the fighting in the following way:

> *I bayoneted the first Russian in the chest. He fell dead. I was then stabbed in the mouth with great force, which caused me to stagger back, where I shot this second Russian and shot a third through. A fourth and a fifth came at me and ran me through the right side. I fell but managed to run one through and brought him down. I stunned him by kicking him, whilst I was engaging my bayonet with another. Sergeant-Major Alger called out to me not to kick the man that was down, but not being dead he was very troublesome to my legs. I was fighting the other over his body. I returned to the battery and spat out my teeth. I found two only.*

At Sandbag Battery, a hundred guardsmen found themselves surrounded by three Russian battalions. With typical British understatement, General Cathcart said, just before he was killed: 'We are in a scrape'. A sergeant remarked that they would need the 'greatest miracle in the world' if they were going to escape – and they got it. Assistant-Surgeon Wolesley was returning from tending the wounded when he found his path blocked by Russians, so he gathered together a handful of guardsmen.

'I was the only officer in sight,' he said, 'and I gave the order, 'Fix bayonets, charge, and keep up the hill.' We charged through, losing I should think about half our number.'

The Russians assumed that this was the advanced guard of a major formation and fled. Captain Burnaby led twenty Grenadier Guards on a similar suicide mission and put to flight 700 Russians. The fighting back and forth over this useless piece of terrain was so ferocious that General Bosquet remarked: 'Quel abattoir'.

In this uneven battle, the British fell back on their regimental tradition. Officers of the 57th ('Diehards') told their men to 'remember Albuera' – in Spain, where they had beaten the French in 1811. And the 20th let out the 'Minden yell' – after the Battle of Minden, Westphalia, in 1759, during the Seven Years' War – as they forced the Iakousk Regiment back at bayonet point towards a ravine.

The battle raged for eight hours, the Russians finally turning back when General Bosquet sent 2,000 North African Zouaves to aid the British. *'Au nom d'Angleterre, je vous remercie'* ('In the name of England, I thank you'), said Raglan.

The Russians lost 11,000 of the 45,000 that were actively engaged in the battle. The allied losses were high too. Of the 1,300 guardsmen who fought at Sandbag Battery, only 200 survived.

For all his criticism of the army, William Russell was impressed by the spirit of the fighting men at Inkerman, writing

> *It is considered that the soldiers who met these furious columns of the Czar were the remnants of three British divisions, which scarcely numbered 8,500, that they were hungry and wet, and half-famished; that they were belonging to a force which was generally 'out of bed' for four nights out of seven; which had been enfeebled by sickness, by severe toil, sometimes for twenty-four hours at a time without relief of any kind; but among them were men who had within a short time previously lain out for forty-eight hours in the trenches at a stretch – it will be readily admitted that never was a more extraordinary contest maintained by our army since it acquired a reputation in the world's history.*

Or as General Pennefather said: 'We gave them one hell of a towelling.'

The siege dragged on half-heartedly. The troops only needed to defend their trenches at night and return shot for shot whenever the enemy fired. The Russians took advantage of the lull to build more fortifications around Sebastopol. Meanwhile artillery duels continued across the Chernaya River.

By 2 January 1856, there were 3,500 sick among the British. The Russians celebrated their New Year on 12 January – using the old Julian calendar – not by the ringing of bells, but by a huge cannonade. They then came rushing out led by the Cossacks. Though they were more than a match for the British cavalry, the infantry were driven back. With sufficient force the city might have fallen at that point.

Between 1 December and 20 January, over 8,000 sick and injured British soldiers had been evacuated, but the French – who had been regularly reinforced – still held the line. On 26 January, Sardinia-Piedmont joined the war, with 10,000 men.

The Russians continued to skirmish almost every night and seemed to have endless artillery and ammunition, while their earthworks withstood any sort of bombardment. And there were still 35,000 Russians behind the allies to the east. The British maintained morale that spring by organizing horse races and cricket matches.

On 22 May, the second attack was made on Kerch at the eastern end of the Crimea, the first assault having met with failure. This time the British took the fort. The Russians exploded the magazines, but the guns were taken intact, along with large quantities of provisions and ammunition. The fall of Kerch meant that the Royal Navy could move through the strait into the Sea of Azov, where it sank 245 ships that were carrying supplies and munitions.

On 18 June 1855, the allies decided to make their final assault on Sebastopol. It was repulsed. Ten days later Lord Raglan came down with cholera and was replaced by General James Simpson.

On 16 August, the Italian forces attacked along the Chernaya. Then on 8 September the Zouaves, under Patrice MacMahon, attacked the well-defended rifle pits at Fort Malakhov. The British attacked another strongpoint called the Grand Redan while, on the left, the Sardinians pushed forward. At the same time, despite heavy seas, the Royal Navy bombarded the fortifications from the rear.

The Russians counterattacked in places, but largely fought defensive actions. The French took Fort Malakhov and refused to be dislodged. The French commander Amable Pélissier announced, famously: *'J'y suis, j'y reste'* ('I am here, I stay here').

The Russians then gave up and the siege of Sebastopol ended on 11 September.

'Night had hardly descended,' wrote Pélissier. 'Fire arose on all sides. Mines exploded, powder reserves went up, and the spectacle of Sebastopol in flames, lit by the Russians themselves, appeared to the eyes of all the army as one of the most imposing and saddest spectacles in the history of warfare.'

The Russians blew up their fortifications, sank their own ships in the harbour and evacuated Sebastopol. Relieved to have taken the city in the end, the allies did not pursue them.

Early in 1856, the Austrians threatened to join the alliance against Russia. Peace talks began in Paris on 1 February and a peace treaty was signed on 30 March. Each side had lost around 250,000 men.

Gettysburg

Advantage to the Union

1863

Until Gettysburg, the Union and Confederate armies had been evenly matched. But after the slaughter there, the Confederacy no longer had the strength to fight off the invading Yankees and the war was lost.

DURING THE FIRST HALF of the nineteenth century, the northern states of the United States become increasingly industrialized, while the southern economy relied on agriculture, principally the production of cotton. This difference was underlined by what was called the 'peculiar institution' of slavery which provided cheap labour in the South. At the same time, improvements in transportation – canals, toll roads and railroads – and the distribution of newspapers was rapidly forging a collection of disparate states into one nation.

Into this boiling cauldron, in 1852, was thrown Harriet Beecher Stowe's novel *Uncle Tom's Cabin*, which stirred up anti-slavery feelings in the North. And it was not a problem that was going to go away. As the US fulfilled its 'manifest destiny' and expanded westwards new territories and states either had to be Free States or Slave States, altering the balance in Congress. In 1858, there was a series of debates between Illinois senator Stephen A. Douglas, who supported a territory's right to choose, and Abraham Lincoln who famously said: 'A house divided against itself cannot stand.'

With the election of Lincoln to the presidency in 1860, the southern states saw their way of life under threat. Accordingly, they broke away to form the Confederate States of America. Fort Sumter, a Federal military post in South Carolina, was besieged. Confederate guns in Charleston opened fire on the fort when a Federal supply ship was sent and it surrendered two days later. By then, the war had begun.

The war went badly for the North when it first began. The Federal government's objective was to take the Confederate capital, Richmond, Virginia, less than a hundred miles from Federal Washington, DC. A Union army was sent to invade the South but it was stopped at the first Battle of Bull Run near Manassas on 21 July 1861. The North managed to take Richmond in the following spring, but it was recaptured by the Confederate army under Robert E. Lee soon after. The Union army was defeated at the second Battle of Bull Run on August 30, 1862, and Lee then took the war to the North. He was under no illusion that he could defeat the Union, but he felt that an invasion might prompt recognition and aid from Britain or France. In early September, he crossed the Potomac to be met by the Union General McClelland at Sharpsburg, Maryland. Casualties at the resulting Battle of Antietam on 17 September exceeded 23,000 in one day and Lee was forced back into Virginia. General Burnside replaced

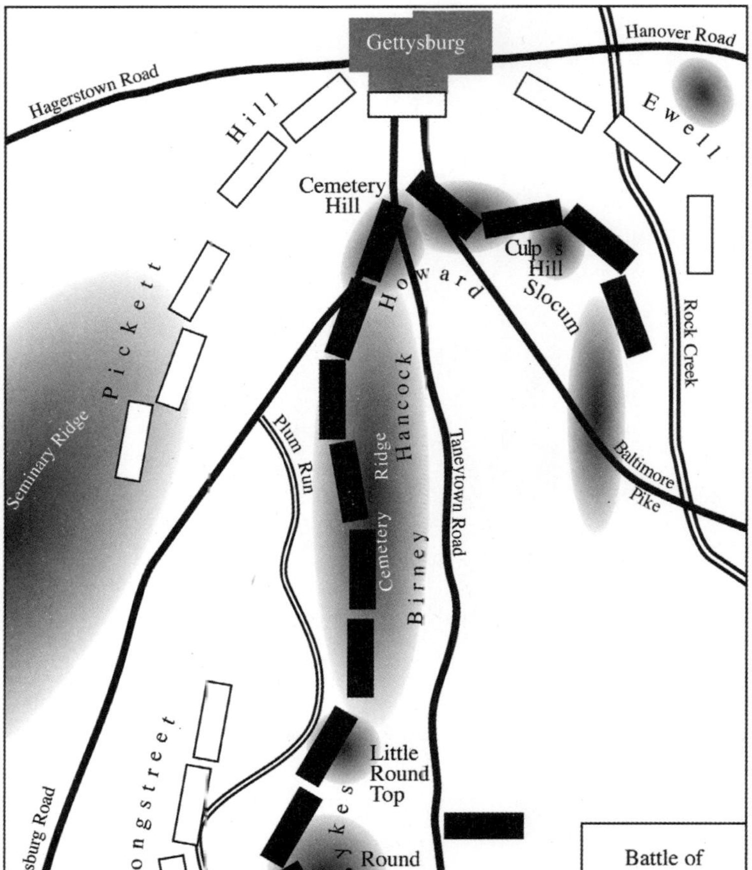

Battle of Gettysburg 3 July 1863

McClellan and pursued Lee back towards Richmond. Lee won a stunning victory at Fredericksburg on 13 December. He then defeated General Hooker at Chancellorsville on 5 May 1863.

In the following year, Lee invaded the North again, meeting the Union's Army of the Potomac at Gettysburg, Pennsylvania, on 1 July 1863. The Confederate army was made up of about 76,000 men who were organized into three corps commanded by Generals Longstreet, Ewell and Hill. The corps were subdivided into three divisions with approximately 8,500 men in each division. The Army of the Potomac, under its new commander General George G. Meade, had nineteen divisions, each around half the size of the South's divisions. These nineteen divisions were organized into seven corps – 95,000 men in all.

Confederate morale was high. After winning the Battle of Chancellorsville in May, they had taken the Federal garrison at Winchester on 15 June. Lee's army then moved into Pennsylvania's Cumberland Valley. By 28 June, the corps of Longstreet and Hill were at Chambersburg, while forward divisions of Ewell's corps were preparing to attack Harrisburg. However, Lee had learned that the Union army was far to the south at Frederick, Maryland. He decided to move his entire army to the east of the Appalachians and then head south to meet the Union forces in a decisive battle that would have ended the war had he been successful. Meanwhile, Meade turned north.

On 30 June one of Hill's battalions was approaching the small town of Gettysburg, where they hoped to find stocks of shoes – always in short supply among the Confederate army. They discovered that the town was occupied by a division of Union cavalry. The cavalry commander General John Buford had realized the strategic importance of Gettysburg as a road junction and was prepared to hold it until reinforcements arrived.

At dawn on 1 July, Hill's leading brigades advanced on Gettysburg with orders to reconnoitre but not to engage the enemy in battle. Having been alerted to the advancing Confederate forces, Buford dismounted his cavalry who took up positions astride the Chambersburg Road. They were supported by a battery of horse artillery. At around 5.30 a.m. shots were exchanged. Nevertheless, the reconnaissance force pushed on cautiously and took up positions about two miles west of Gettysburg.

At around nine a.m. two brigades of Ewell's infantry arrived and drove Burford's men from their positions. A lull then settled over the field as both

In the last action at Gettysburg, General Lee ordered a frontal assault across open ground. The courageous southern troops were cut down. Virginian troops under General George Pickett briefly held their objective, Cemetery Hill, but were forced back.

sides brought up reinforcements. The Union I Corps under General Hancock was deployed to defend the western approaches to Gettysburg, while General Howard's XI Corps formed up north of the town with Buford's cavalry covering the flanks. However, Howard had left one division in reserve on Cemetery Hill to the south. The aim was to delay the Confederates long enough for the rest of the Union army to arrive.

Lee arrived around noon. He had hoped to avoid a general engagement because the strength of the enemy was unknown and the terrain was unfamiliar. However, the two forces had collided at Gettysburg and it was now too late to withdraw. Soon after noon, the lead division of Ewell's Corps attacked the right flank of I Corps on Seminary Ridge. At three p.m. fighting broken out to the north of the town with another division of Ewell's Corps attacking down the Harrisburg Road. This crushed the flank of XI Corps. Confederate artillery firing from the high ground north of Gettysburg then opened the way for their infantry. By four p.m. both Union corps were forced back through the town to Cemetery Hill, the position held by Howard's reserve division. The hill and the hook-shaped ridge that ran from it formed an excellent defensive position where Meade's army, arriving from the south, quickly deployed. The Confederates took up an encircling position with their right flank on Seminary Ridge, which ran parallel to Cemetery Ridge.

The Confederates had definitely got the best of the first day with Union losses amounting to slightly over 9,000 troops, including some 3,000 prisoners. However, Confederate losses were also high, running at about 6,500 men, because the Union troops had just been issued with new Spencer repeating carbines. What is more, the Federal forces held onto the high ground south of Gettysburg, where their position continued to be strengthened by reinforcements.

The success of Lee's army on 1 July encouraged him to attack again on the following day. His aim was to envelop the Federal forces. An early morning reconnaissance of the Union's left revealed that its line did not extend as far south as a hill called Little Round Top. Lee directed Longstreet to take two divisions and march south until they reached the flank of the Union forces. They would attack from this point, supported by a division of Hill's corps – a total force of nearly 20,000 men. If they could take Little Round Top, Confederate artillery would be able to bombard the entire Union position.

While Longstreet was engaged in the main offensive, Ewell was ordered to make a diversionary attack against the Federal right. However, he was given permission to mount a full-scale assault if the opportunity presented itself.

The Union army was well prepared. Six of its seven corps had arrived and VI Corps was making a thirty-six-mile forced march to reach the battlefield. Meade's army was deployed in a fish-hook-shaped formation along Cemetery Ridge with its right on Culp's Hill. The left was held by General Daniel Sickles's III Corps. He was dissatisfied with the position to which he had been assigned and in the early afternoon, without orders, he advanced his men nearly half a mile west to a peach orchard. III Corps had just arrived there when Longstreet attacked. Sickles was hard pressed and Meade sent V Corps and part of II Corps to reinforce him. After furious fighting, however, Longstreet's forces broke through and the entire Union line collapsed. Sickles pulled back to Little Round Top where, with Union reinforcements, he halted the Confederate advance.

Further along Cemetery Ridge another Confederate attack was repulsed. Then, in the evening, after Longstreet's attack had been checked, Ewell attempted to storm Cemetery Hill. This was unsuccessful, but Ewell managed to establish a foothold in the captured Union trenches on Culp's Hill.

The second day's fighting had been more evenly matched. The Confederate forces had gained ground, but they had failed to dislodge the Union army from its strong position. Both sides had suffered some 9,000 casualties. It was clear that Meade was going to stand and fight.

Lee also was undaunted as Confederate reinforcements arrived, including cavalry units under General Stuart. On the following morning Longstreet was to renew his assault on the Union's left, while Ewell was to storm Culp's Hill. Stuart's cavalry was to move around to the east of Gettysburg and attack the Union rear, disrupting communications and distracting Meade from the main assault.

But Meade had a plan of his own. While his overall strategy was to hold position in the face of Lee's onslaught he ordered XII Corps, at dawn, to drive Ewell's forces out of their positions on Culp's Hill. After a concentrated Union artillery bombardment, the battle for the trenches developed into a tremendous small arms battle. Meanwhile, three miles east of Gettysburg, Stuart's cavalry was engaged by Union cavalry under General Gregg. The clash was indecisive, but Stuart was neutralized and posed no threat to Meade's rear.

Finally, by noon, Ewell's men were dislodged and an eerie silence fell on the battlefield. It seems that Longstreet had misunderstood his orders and the chance of a coordinated attack on both flanks was now lost. Lee rode to Longstreet's headquarters and ordered a full-scale attack on the Union centre along Cemetery Ridge. The action would be supported by 15,000 troops.

At one p.m. 172 Confederate guns opened up in what was intended to be a devastating bombardment of the Union line. But Meade's men were well dug in and it did little damage. The Union army fired back with around eighty cannon in a duel that lasted for nearly two hours. When the smoke cleared, Union soldiers saw three lines of Confederate grey approaching. Unbelievably, Lee had ordered a frontal assault across open country.

With fixed bayonets and flags flying, the Confederate infantry had to cover over half a mile of open ground between Seminary Ridge and Cemetery Ridge. They were less than halfway across when the

Union artillery on Round Top opened fire. Soon after the Union troops let loose with their carbines. The Confederate divisions under Generals Pettigrew and Trimble melted away under the withering fire, but the 4,800 troops under General George Edward Pickett continued in what has become known as 'Pickett's Charge'.

Despite the Union fire, Pickett's Virginian infantry reached the Union line and briefly broke through but at a terrible cost. Two of Pickett's brigade commanders were killed along with ten of his battalion commanders. The other five battalion commanders were wounded, as was Pickett himself. Over three-quarters of Pickett's division – some 3,393 men – were left on the battlefield. Their one moment of glory was when General Armistead, with his cap on the point of his sword, leapt over a stone wall into the Union lines. A hundred men followed him and, for a few minutes, the Confederate flag flew on the crest of Cemetery Hill. The Union counter-attacked and Armistead's men were either killed or captured.

With the repulse of Pickett's Charge, the battle of Gettysburg was practically over. It was the turning point of the war. The Confederate defeat caused such bitterness that Pickett was charged by some with cowardice, although Lee retained him as a divisional commander for the rest of the war.

As Pickett's men limped back to Seminary Ridge, the Confederates counted up some 5,600 casualties from that action alone. Meade refused to order an attack that would finish them off because Lee still commanded a formidable force. That evening Lee withdrew and headed back to Virginia, accompanied by his baggage train and a number of Union prisoners. Confederate losses added up to around 30,000 men and the Union side had sustained some 23,000 casualties.

Meade was given yet another chance to annihilate the Confederate army and end the war. The Potomac was in flood, halting Lee's retreat. Lincoln telegraphed Meade, saying: 'Act on your own judgement...do not let the enemy escape.' But Meade hesitated. Two days later the Potomac dropped and Lee's army escaped. Meade was sharply criticized, although he retained command of the Army of the Potomac until the end of the war, which lasted for two further years.

Vicksburg

The US Civil War Turns

1863

If the Union could take Vicksburg, they could control the Mississippi and cut the Confederacy in two. But attack from the north proved impossible, so a Union army had to cross the river and attack from the rear.

BOTH THE UNION and the Confederate sides in the American Civil War considered that the fortified city of Vicksburg, Mississippi held the key to victory or defeat. It lay on the east side of the river, halfway between Memphis, Tennessee to the north and New Orleans, Louisiana to the south. These two cities had fallen to the Union in the spring of 1862, along with Fort Henry and Fort Donelson, leaving Vicksburg as the Confederate's only stronghold on the river. If it fell, the entire Mississippi would be in Union hands, cutting the Confederacy in two.

However, Vicksburg was in a perfect defensive position. It was built on high bluffs along the river and

Even through Vicksburg was surrounded, the Confederate defenders fought on, repelling all attempts to break into the city. Eventually, though, they were reduced by hunger and disease, and, running out of ammunition, were forced to surrender.

its northern flank was protected by swampy bayous. Confederate batteries along the bluff could fire down on Union shipping on the river. Even an attack by Union ironclads in May–June 1862 was beaten off.

From mid-October 1862, Major-General Ulysses S. Grant, then commander of the Army of Tennessee, made several attempts to take Vicksburg. In December 1862 an attack through the bayous to the north proved a costly failure and in February–March 1863 he even tried to cut a canal around Vicksburg in order to divert the river. This too proved to be impracticable.

Grant decided that he needed to attack the city from the south and east in order to be successful. He would march his men down the west bank of the Mississippi, cross over the river and attack the city from the rear. However, Confederate batteries at Port Hudson, Louisiana to the south prevented Union shipping from sailing up the river from Baton Rouge and New Orleans. The ships that would be needed to ferry the troops across the river would have to come from the Union fleet north of Vicksburg which was under the command of Admiral David D. Porter. They would be forced to run the powerful Vicksburg batteries. Once the Union forces were on the east bank, they would face two Confederate forces. One was based near Jackson, Mississippi, under General Joseph E. Johnston and the other, commanded by General John C. Pemberton, was stationed at the Vicksburg garrison.

Grant re-organized his force into four corps under Generals John A. McClernand, William T. Sherman, James B. McPherson and Stephen A. Hurlbut, although Hurlbut's corps was transferred to New Orleans before the offensive began. At the same time, a small force under General Nathaniel P. Banks would commence manoeuvres along the Red River in Louisiana.

McClernand and McPherson had been standing by at Millikens Bend and Lake Providence to the northwest of Vicksburg. On the 29 and 30 March they began working their way south. The going was tough and they had to build a military road to New Carthage, Louisiana. From there they were to move on south to Hard Times, Louisiana, a village on the west bank opposite Bruinsburg, Mississippi. Grant had originally planned to land at Rodney, Mississippi, but a local slave advised him to attack at Bruinsburg instead.

On the night of 16 April Porter ran the Vicksburg batteries with twelve vessels, losing just one to Confederate fire. The following day a squadron of Union cavalry under Brigadier General Benjamin H. Grierson left La Grange, Tennessee on a sixteen-day ride across Mississippi to Baton Rouge. This pulled some large units away from Vicksburg, who set off to pursue them. Then, on the night of 22 April, Porter ran a large supply flotilla past the Vicksburg batteries, emboldened by his light losses in the previous week.

The troops that had been at work on the canal project at Duckport dropped their tools, picked up their rifles and joined in a fresh action along the Yazoo River to the northeast of Vicksburg. On 29 and 30 April they made diversionary attacks on Confederate positions on Drumgould's and Haynes's Bluffs, drawing Pemberton's forces away from Vicksburg's southern defences.

McClernand's and McPherson's troops reached Hard Times on 29 April. That same day Porter's fleet attacked the Confederate batteries at Grand Gulf, thirty miles downstream from Vicksburg and nine miles upstream from Bruinsburg. This drew more of Pemberton's troops away from Vicksburg.

On 30 April, Porter ferried McClernand's and McPherson's men across the river. Grant then sent word to Sherman in the north. On the next day the Union force engaged the Confederates ten miles inland at Port Gibson, Mississippi. Al-

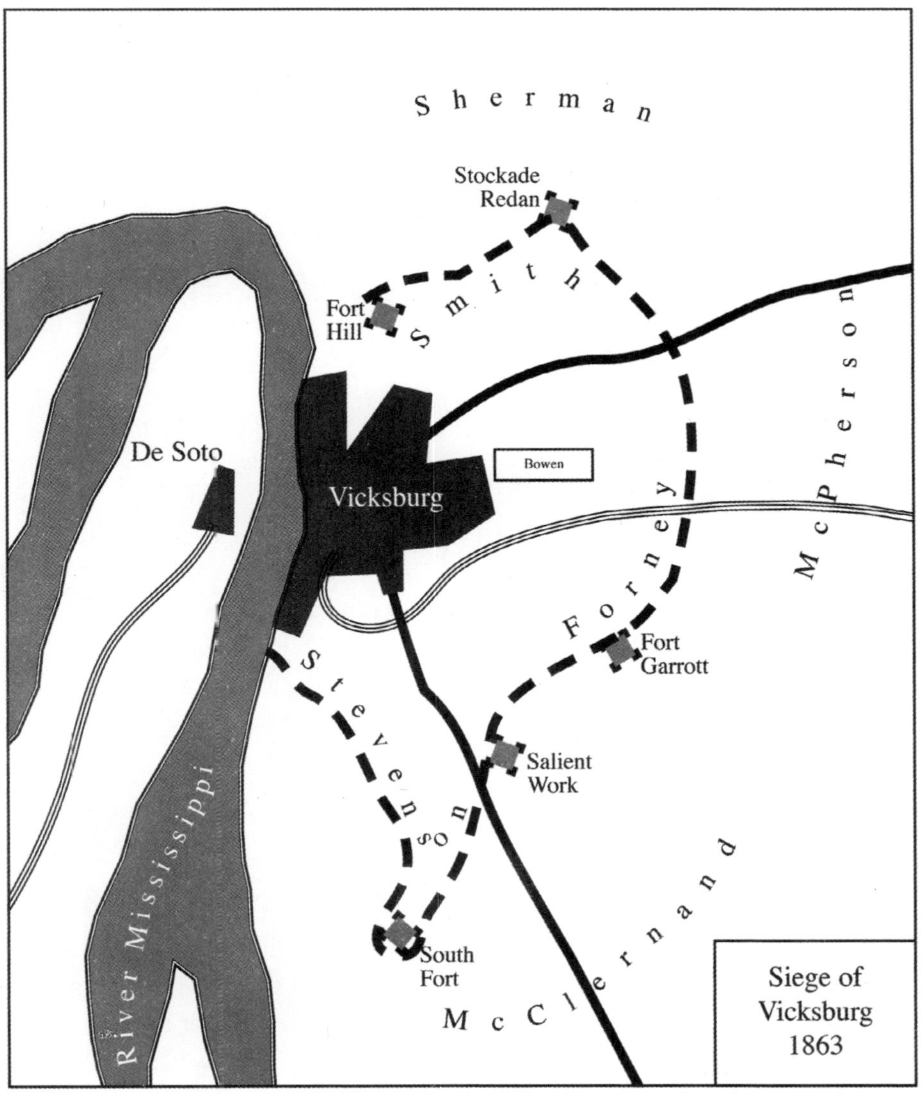

Siege of Vicksburg 1863

though Pemberton could command over 40,000 men for the defence of the Vicksburg area, they were now scattered across the region, some still chasing Grierson. Few could be concentrated at Port Gibson, which fell easily.

Grant then moved northeast and Sherman joined him on 8 May. On 12 May, they took Raymond, Mississippi, cutting Pemberton's force away from Johnston's. Two days later they took Jackson itself, thereby neutralizing Johnston. Grant ordered Sherman to destroy Jackson's railroad facilities and heavy industry while he turned west, where he beat Pemberton in a major action at Champion Hill on 16 May.

On the following day, the Confederates fought a delaying action at the Big Black River Bridge. They destroyed the bridge behind them after they had crossed it. The Union troops simply built a new bridge and by 18 May Grant's three corps were approaching Vicksburg's outer defences from the east and the northeast.

Sherman moved around to the north in order to take the height overlooking the Yazoo River. With these hills in their possession, the Union forces could bring in reinforcements and supplies from the North. Grant then attacked the city, with Porter providing artillery support from the river. The first assault failed and a second, all-out assault began at ten a.m. on 22 May. Although Grant's men broke through at first, the Confederates quickly restored their original line of defence. The Union suffered 3,199 casualties, while Pemberton lost less than 500 men. This was enough to convince Grant the miles of Confederate defensive works around the east of the city were too strong to be overcome by assault so he ordered his engineers to besiege the city.

During the protracted siege, Pemberton's 30,000-man garrison was reduced by disease and starvation, while the city's civilian residents were forced to seek shelter in caves and bomb shelters in the surrounding hills. Vicksburg suffered daily bombardments by Porter's gunboats and Grant's artillery, but eventually shortage of ammunition and hunger compelled Pemberton to ask for surrender terms on 3 July. Grant offered none. The following day Pemberton surrendered unconditionally. However, Grant magnanimously paroled the bulk of the garrison. He would face many of these men again at Chattanooga. With the fall of Vicksburg, and the Union victory at Gettysburg on the previous day, the South was finished as a fighting force.

Kut-al-Amara

A British Disaster

1916

The First World War battle of Kut-al-Amara was the greatest military disaster ever to befall the British Army. Some 25,000 were lost in the fighting and another 16,000 were taken prisoner, few of whom survived captivity.

WITHIN THREE MONTHS of the start of World War I, the British occupied Basra (now in Iraq), which was the Ottoman Empire's port at the head of the Persian Gulf. Turkey had allied itself with Germany so Britain, with its huge navy, needed to secure its oil supplies in the Middle East.

The British also sought to destabilize the Ottoman Empire, which had been in decline for centuries, and also add its eastern provinces to the British Empire.

In December 1914, an Anglo-Indian force advanced forty-six miles northwards from Basra. Then in May and June of the following year they advanced another ninety miles up the River Tigris. Although the oil supplies were now secure, the lure of the fabled city of Baghdad was too strong for Major-General Sir Charles Townshend, commander of the Sixth (Poona) Division. They were just eighteen miles outside Baghdad – and 300 miles from their base in Basra – when they met a strong Turkish force at the ancient city of Ctesiphon. After a fruitless battle, the British pulled back a hundred miles to Kut-al-Amara, arriving there on 3 December.

Kut-al-Amara lies on the River Tigris at its confluence with the Shatt-al-Hai canal. It was 120 miles upstream from the British positions at Amara, and 200 miles from Basra. The town lies in a loop of the river, with a small settlement on the opposite bank, and in 1915 it was a densely-populated, filthy place. The civilian population added up to around 7,000, many of whom were evicted when Townshend's army of 10,000 marched into the town. Aware that his men were exhausted, Townshend resolved to stop at Kut, a town of key importance if the British were to hold the region. As a market town, it had good supplies of grain and it offered his men some shelter and warmth in the freezing night temperatures.

Townshend's decision to stop at Kut was approved by the region commander-in-chief General Sir John Nixon, but the War Office in London wanted him to continue his retreat to the south because it would be impossible to get reinforcements to him there, given the other demands on manpower at the beginning of the war. Unfortunately it was already too late. By 7 December, Townshend's 10,000 men were under siege by a Turkish force of 10,500 and eight more

After Turkey sided with Germany in the First World War, the British seized an opportunity to finish off the Ottoman Empire, only to find that there was still fight left in the Ottoman army.

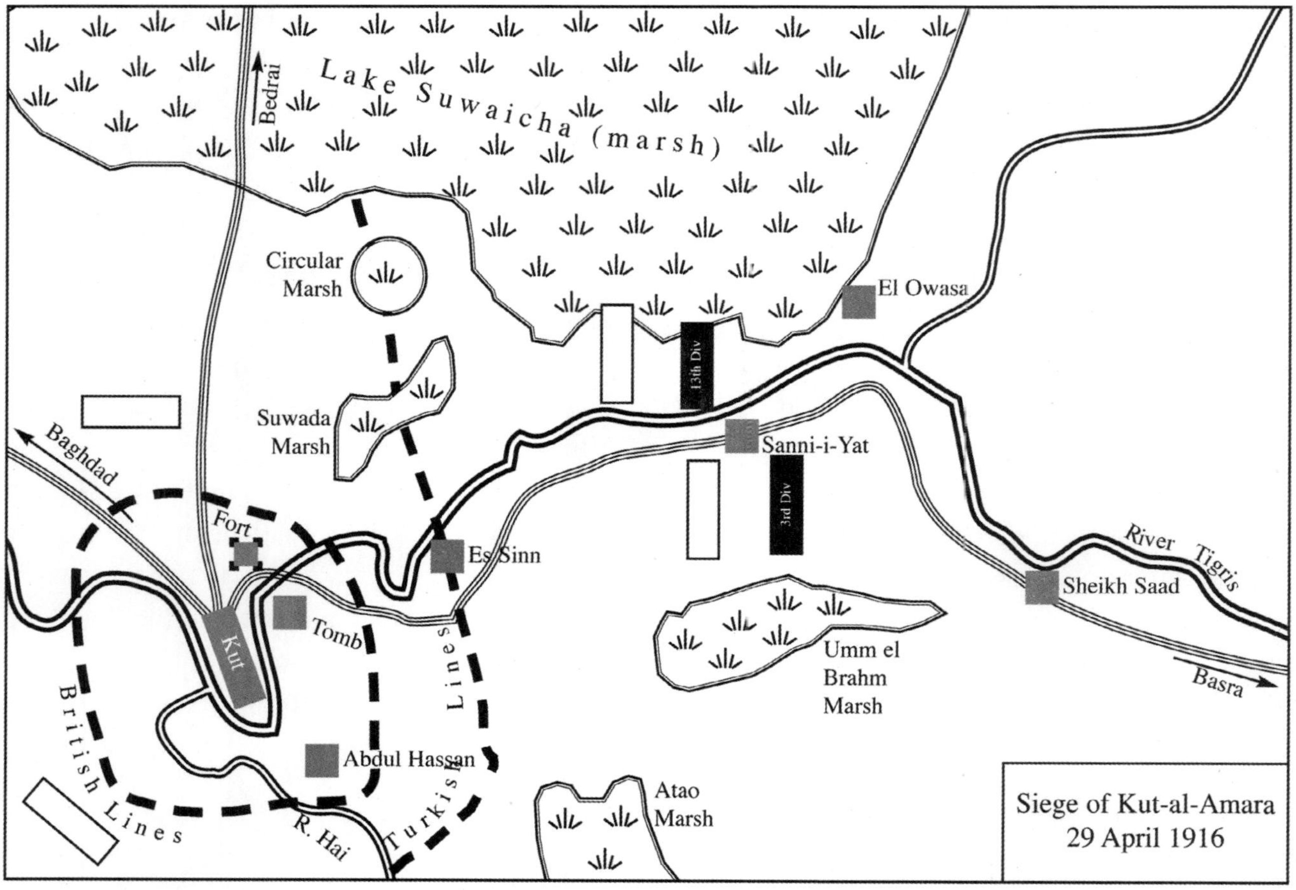

Siege of Kut-al-Amara
29 April 1916

Turkish divisions, recently released from Gallipoli, were massing near Baghdad.

Townshend calculated that there were enough supplies in Kut to last a month. Fortunately he had evacuated the cavalry on the day before the Turks arrived because there was little forage. However, Townshend was told that it might take two months for a relief force to arrive. Even so, he kept his men on the full daily ration because he planned to break out. General Nixon, on the other hand, ordered him to remain and hold as many Turkish troops around Kut as possible.

The Turkish commander, Nur-Ud-Din, and his German counterpart, Baron von der Goltz, were given straightforward instructions. They were to drive the British out of Mesopotamia. In December they made three large-scale attacks on Townshend's position. These were beaten off with high losses on both sides so the Turks then set about blockading the town. At the same time, Turkish forces were dispatched south to prevent any British relief columns reaching Kut.

In the following January a British expeditionary force led by Sir Fenton Aylmer set out for Basra. However, their efforts w ere repeatedly repulsed at Sheikh Sa'ad, the Wadi and Hanna, involving them in heavy losses. They met similar resistance in March, this time at Dujaila.

A second relief operation began in April under Sir George Gorringe. He managed to get far enough to meet up with Baron von der Goltz and the Turkish Sixth Army, piercing their line some twenty miles south of Kut. The expedition then ran out of steam and it was abandoned on 22 April. A final attempt to reach the town on the paddle steamer Julnar also failed, although small quantities of supplies were dropped by air. By this time, sickness in the town had reached epidemic proportions.

On 26 April 1916 Townshend was given permission to ask the Turks for a six-day armistice. They also agreed that ten days' food could be sent to the garrison while the talks were underway. If he were allowed to withdraw, said Townshend, he would give the Turks £1 million sterling and all the guns in the town, along with a guarantee that his men would never again engage with the Ottoman Empire. Khalil Pasha, the military governor of Baghdad, wanted to accept, but the Minister of War Enver Pasha demanded unconditional surrender. He wanted a spectacular victory so that British prestige was damaged as much as possible.

During the armistice period Townshend destroyed everything that was useful in the town and on the 29 April the British garrison surrendered. It was the greatest military disaster ever to have befallen the British Army. There were 227 British officers, 204 Indian officers and 12,828 other ranks – of whom 2,592 were British. All of them were marched into captivity.

While Townshend himself was treated as an honoured guest, his undernourished men were force-marched to prison camps where they were savagely beaten, many being killed in acts of wanton cruelty. More than 3,000 men perished in captivity and those who were released two years later were little more than walking skeletons.

Approximately 2,000 British losses were sustained during the fighting at Kut-al-Amara and another 23,000 troops were lost in the attempts to relieve the trapped army. The Turks lost 10,000 men.

It was a grave error to have made a stand at Kut. Until then the British had the initiative in the fighting in Mestopotamia. The loss of Kut and the Poona Division stunned the British and their Allies and it provided a huge morale boost for both the Turks and the Germans, particularly because it came so soon after Britain's ignominious withdrawal from Gallipoli.

Baron von der Goltz did not live to witness the triumph. He died of typhus ten days before the surrender, although there were persistent rumours that he had been poisoned by a group of young Turkish officers. Townshend was released in October 1918, in time to assist in the armistice negotiations with the Ottoman Empire.

Baghdad

The Ottoman Death Knell

1917

After the disaster of Kut-al-Amara, the British struck back. They marched up the River Tigris and took Baghdad, where they were greeted as liberators by the Iraqis. The Ottoman Empire was doomed from that moment on.

THE BRITISH REVERSED the humiliation of their surrender at Kut-al-Amara in February 1917 by retaking the town. The Anglo-Indian Mesopotamian Expeditionary Force then advanced another fifty miles up the River Tigris to al-Aziziyeh where the regional commander-in-chief Sir Frederick Stanley Maude ordered them to wait until he had received confirmation from London that a march on Baghdad was in order. Their target lay another fifty miles up the river.

This hiatus gave the regional Turkish commander-in-chief Khalil Pasha a chance to plan his defence of Baghdad. He had some 12,500 men

When the British army under General Sir Frederick Stanley Maude marched into Baghdad, crowds lined the streets, clapping and cheering. For generations they had been exploited by the corrupt Ottomans.

under his command, including around 2,300 survivors from the fall of Kut-al-Amara. Two divisions of 20,000 men under Ali Ishan Bey were on their way to Baghdad across the desert from western Persia (Iran), but it was unlikely that this force would arrive in time to help in the city's defence. Even if they did, the Turks would still only have 35,000 men at their disposal when they faced a British army of 120,000. The British would also be supported by cavalry, a flotilla of gunboats and planes for spotting and light bombing.

Khalil dismissed the option of avoiding this unequal fight by retreating from Baghdad. Simply handing the southern capital of the Ottoman Empire over to the British would be too much of a humiliation for the Turks. He also rejected the option of creating an aggressive 'forward' defence by abandoning work on the fortifications at Ctesiphon. For some reason, Khalil also discounted the flooding of the overland approaches to Baghdad. This would have caused Maude's men immense difficulties and the threat of flooding remained a worry for the British even after the capture of the city.

Instead Khalil chose to defend Baghdad itself. He built defences on either side of the Tigris to the south of the city and then he deployed the Turkish Sixth Army to defend the southeast approaches to the city along the Diyala River.

After waiting for a week at al-Aziziyeh, Maude resumed his advance on 5 March 1917. Travelling up the east bank of the Tigris he reached the Diyala three days later. Small-scale crossings under the cover of darkness on the following evening resulted

moved the bulk of his forces across the Tigris, so that he would be able to counter a British attack from the southwest. He left just one regiment on the Diyala which the British overrran on the morning of 10 March. Khalil was effectively outmanoeuvred.

Khalil's next priority was to guard his rear so he moved his forces to the west of their position in Tel Aswad. Their task was to protect the railway that started from Baghdad and ran all the way back to the heart of the Ottoman Empire and on to Berlin. The battle for Baghdad was then halted by a sandstorm. The Germans urged Khalil to stage a counterattack but by the time the weather had cleared he had decided to pull out of the city. At

in the successful establishment of a small bridgehead on the north bank. Taking the bulk of the forces across the well-defended river proved to be less easy. Instead, Maude built pontoon bridges several miles downstream and moved the main body of his forces to a position from where they could cross to the west bank of the Tigris. His aim was to outflank Khalil's defences along the Diyala and move directly on to Baghdad.

However, the German Army Air Service had just brought planes into the area. They spotted what the British were attempting to do and informed Khalil, who then

The re-captor of Kut and the victor of Baghdad: Major General Sir F. Stanley Maude, commanding in Mesopotamia.

eight p.m. on 10 March the retreat from Baghdad was under way.

On the following day Maude's troops entered the city without a struggle. Baghdad's 140,000 occupants lined the streets, cheering and clapping. For the last two years the Turkish Army had been requisitioning private merchandise and shipping it out of the city. General Maude issued a proclamation that read:

> *People of Baghdad, remember for twenty-six generations you have suffered strange tyrants who have ever endeavoured to set one Arab house against another in order that they might profit by your dissensions. This policy is abhorrent to Great Britain and her allies for there can be neither peace nor prosperity where there is enmity or misgovernment. Our armies do not come to your cities and lands as conquerors or enemies, but as liberators.*

However, Iraq did not gain its independence. The League of Nations gave Britain a mandate to run Iraq as well as Palestine, Trans-Jordan and Egypt. There was an uprising in 1920, so the British installed Lawrence of Arabia's friend Prince Faisal as king. He promised to safeguard British oil interests in Iraq, for which Britain paid him £800,000 a month.

Some 9,000 Turkish prisoners were taken at the fall of Baghdad. Britain had sustained 40,000 casualties over the entire campaign, many having died from disease. Maude himself contracted cholera after drinking contaminated milk. He died on 18 November 1917 and was buried just outside the city walls of Baghdad.

The capture of Baghdad was a decisive propaganda blow for the Western Allies and it ended Turkish activity in Persia. Meanwhile Maude's force moved on rapidly to capture the strategically vital railway at Samarrah.

Cambrai

The First Massed Tank Attack

1917

At Cambrai, the British finally showed that the tank could break the stalemate of trench warfare on the Western Front. Tanks went on to win the war, changing the face of war forever.

THE FIRST WORLD WAR broke out in August 1914. By October, the Western Front had solidified into a line of fortified trenches that ran from the Swiss Frontier to the North Sea. These were defended by artillery, barbed wire and machine guns, making them almost impossible to breach using infantry or cavalry. Something else had to be tried.

Lieutenant-Colonel Ernest Swinton, the official British war correspondent in France, put his mind to the problem. He realised that the answer was to build an armoured vehicle fitted with caterpillar tracks. The idea reached the ears of Winston Churchill, who was then at the Admiralty. The Landship Committee was set up to oversee what, for security reasons, were called 'tanks'.

Tanks went into action for the first time on 15 August 1916 during the first Battle of the Somme, but they did little to stem the 420,000 British casualties. In the following year, the three brigades of tanks had been built and they were then formed into a Tank Corps. It comprised nine battalions, each with three companies. These were divided into four platoons with four tanks in each. The corps com-

The tank was immune to machine-gun fire. It could crush barbed wire and cross trenches, and its tracks could even cope with the mud of the Western Front.

Despite the Allied victory, the town of Cambrai was utterly destroyed. This is how it looked on 1 September 1914, after a heavy German bombardment.

mander was Brigadier Hugh Elles. His chief of staff, and one of the most influential pioneers of tank warfare, was Lieutenant-Colonel J.F.C. Fuller.

Although the Corps had been formed, the tank had yet to prove itself. It was heavy, and made slow progress over muddy or heavily-shelled ground – as little as ten yards a minute or a third of a mile an hour. The driver's limited field of vision made it difficult to steer the tank in the right direction. Driving the tanks quickly was difficult and the crews were quickly exhausted by the heat inside them.

At Passchendaele, the disastrous British offensive that started in July 1917, tanks simply sank into the mud, leading to heavy losses. In all, the British lost 325,000 men during that campaign and the infantry began to see the tank as a failure. Even the crews began to lose their morale when they saw their tanks wasted in small-scale attacks.

Fuller met the situation head on. He searched his map of the Western Front for a place suitable for a large-scale attack by tanks. Between St Quentin and Cambrai there was rolling chalk downland, terrain that was especially suitable for the movement of tanks. The area had been quiet for some time, so it

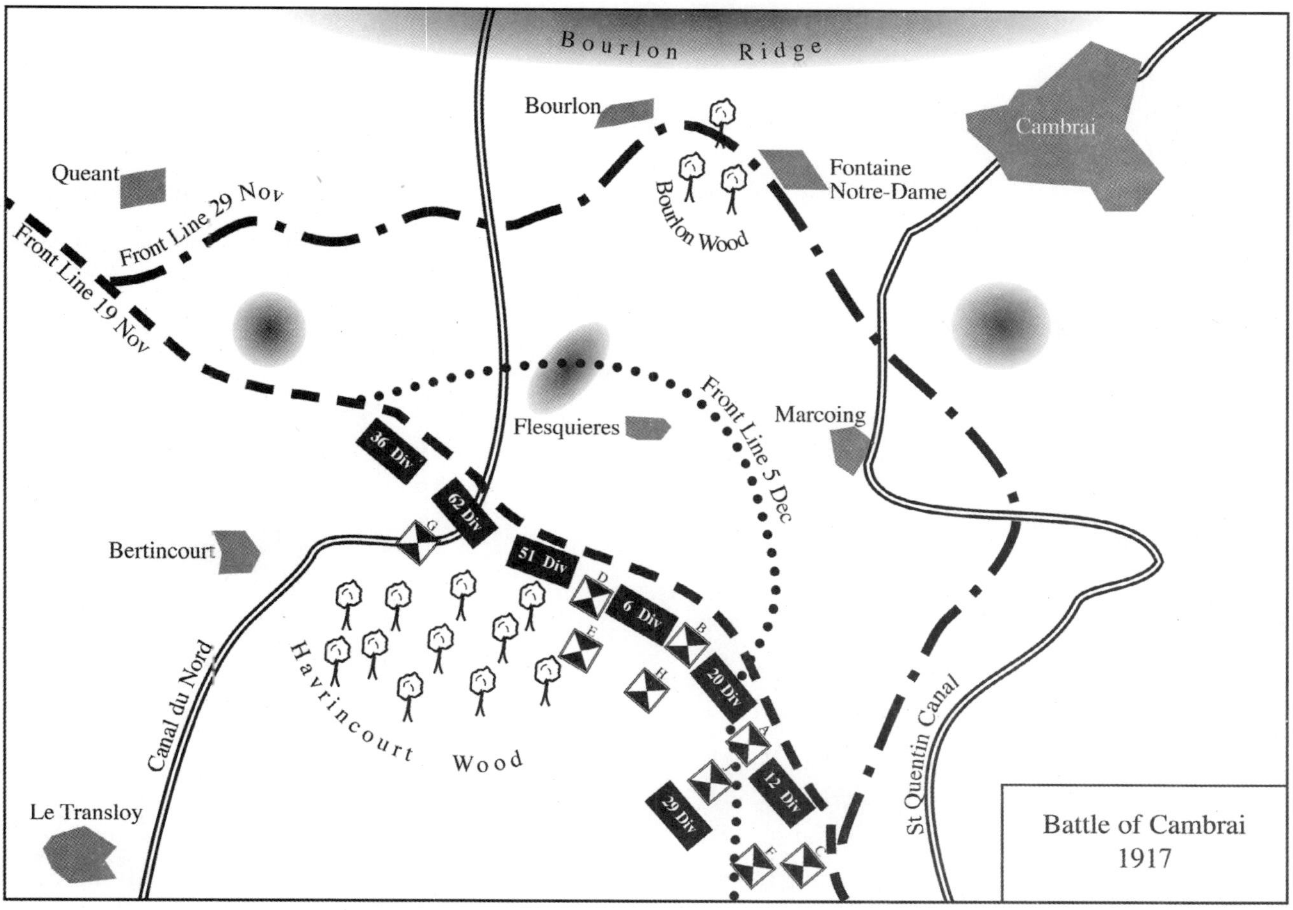

was relatively free of the shell craters that were the tank's greatest hazard.

He came up with a plan that would prove the worth of tanks once and for all – a lightning attack on St Quentin. Elles changed the objective to Cambrai and the plan was presented to General Sir Julian Byng, commanding officer of the Third Army that held the area. Byng liked what he saw and seized the opportunity to make an all-out offensive in his sector. While Fuller's plan called for six battalions of tanks, Byng called for all nine. In all, nineteen British divisions were assembled for the offensive, supported by five cavalry divisions with horses.

For the initial attack, eight British divisions were launched against three German divisions. Three lines of German trenches had to be breached. Even though the latest Mark IV tanks were twenty-six feet long, it would still be difficult for them to cross some of the wider sections, so Fuller attached fascines – bundles of sticks bound together with rope – to the front of his tanks. These were held in place by a quick-release mechanism and dropped into the trench to make a makeshift bridge.

Fuller formed his tanks into sections of three – one male 'advance' tank with a six-pounder gun and two female 'main body' tanks, carrying machine-guns, to protect the male from infantry attack. A male would first advance and flatten the wire for the infantry. Then it would turn to the left in front of the first trench, firing its gun to suppress the defenders. Next, its two females would advance. The first would drop its fascine into the trench, cross it, then turn left and work its way down the far side of the trench, machine-gunning the occupants as it went. The second would negotiate the first fascine, then drop its own fascine into the second trench, drive over it and machine-gun its way down the far side. The advance tank would then move across the two fascines and drop another fascine into the third trench before crossing it, with the infantry hopefully still close behind.

'Other things being equal, the most mobile side must win,' said Fuller.

Some 474 British tanks were secretly brought up to the front. Then at 6.20 a.m. on 20 November 1917, they appeared out of the early morning mist, taking the Germans by complete surprise. Elles himself led the attack with his head sticking up out of the hatch for better visibility. The ground was dry and they made good speed. The barbed wire, which shellfire routinely failed to destroy, was crossed without incident. The fascines were dropped. The tanks crossed the trenches and raked them with fire.

Previous assaults had used just a handful of tanks. Here the Germans were confronted with long lines of them. Armour-piercing bullets, which had been effective against early models, bounced off. Faced with this mechanized onslaught, the Germans threw down their weapons and surrendered or tried to flee. Some 7,500 prisoners were taken at the cost of only a few casualties. By 7.20 a.m. the British ripped a hole six miles wide and three miles deep through the Hindenburg Line. The infantry poured through it and by ten p.m. brigade headquarters had to move forward to keep up with the advance. After three years of stalemate no one was prepared for the speed of the breakthrough. Objective after objective fell and reports coming back from the front read, according to Fuller, 'more like a railway timetable than a series of battle reports'.

However, not everything went according to plan. General G.M. Harper ignored Fuller's carefully thought-out strategy. When attacking the village of Flesquières near the middle of the line he kept his infantry well back and sent the tanks in alone. They were drawn out in a line, abreast of each other. The German artillery on a ridge behind the village knocked out sixteen tanks. According to the despatch written by the Commander-in-Chief, Field Marshal Sir Douglas Haig, a single German officer was responsible for destroying all sixteen after his men had been killed or had fled.

However, the attack began to run out of steam on the following day. Battlefield intelligence could not keep up with the fast pace of this new type of warfare. There were gaps in the German defences that could have been penetrated, but recognizing and exploiting them was impossible. The Germans established a new defensive line around the salient. This spread the British tanks out along a longer line and they could launch only limited strikes involving forty or fifty at a time. Tanks began to break down and German artillery fire accounted for others. The initial success of the tanks had also taken the British commanders so much by surprise that they failed to take advantage of the situation by bringing up adequate infantry reinforcements.

Bad weather prevented the cavalry from exploiting the breakthrough. They stayed some six miles behind the front throughout the battle and took no part in it, marking what Fuller called 'the end of an epoch'.

By 27 November the offensive had been halted after an advance of some six miles. The tanks were withdrawn and the British began putting up barbed wire in front of their new positions.

On 30 November the Germans counterattacked with twenty divisions, using new *Stosstruppen* ('shock troop') tactics, which were yet to be seen on the Western Front. Only a month before they had been used to deadly effect when the Italian Army had been all but destroyed (Italy was on the Allied side throughout the First World War) at Caporetto in October 1917. The Germans abandoned the linear tactics that they had employed for the first three years of the war. They broke up their combat units into small independent squads each with a range of weapons – artillery, machine-guns and flame-throwers. These units were to advance individually, making no effort to stay in contact with the flank units. They were to advance as rapidly as possible, bypassing enemy strongpoints – who would be dealt with by troops following behind. Everything was done to maintain the momentum of the attack.

After a short and furious bombardment – compared with the lengthy barrages that had been used hitherto – the *Stosstruppen* attacked. High explosives, gas and smoke left the British bewildered. The Germans fell on them, concentrating their efforts on communications facilities and headquarters units in order to leave the enemy even more disorientated. They took advantage of gullies and dead spots in the terrain, coordinating artillery and machine-gun fire to deadly effect. Quickly overwhelming the new British trenches, they had advanced five miles by noon. By 5 December the British had been driven back, almost to their original positions. Casualties on both sides were about equal, with some 45,000 men lost on either side.

Even though no ground had been gained, it was recognized that tanks played their first decisive role at the Battle of Cambrai. Analyzing the Allies' failure to hold onto their gains Fuller said: 'The battle came to a halt because there was not a single tank or infantry unit in reserve. Though planned as a decisive attack, the battle was in reality no more than a raid – for without reserves, what else could it be?'

The Germans agreed.

'By neglecting to support a brilliant initial success,' wrote the German commander of all land forces, Field Marshal Paul von Hindenburg, 'they had let victory be snatched from them, and indeed by troops which were far inferior to their own, both in numbers and quality.'

Despite the British failure to exploit the initial success of their tanks, the Battle of Cambrai showed that armour was the key to victory on the Western Front. It was a lesson that was not wasted on the Germans, who used tanks to devastating effect during the first years of the Second World War.

Dunkirk

'The Miracle of the Little Ships'

1940

The collapse of the Allies in France in 1940 happened with frightening speed, trapping the British Expeditionary Force at the Channel port of Dunkirk. But Hitler, for reasons of his own, halted the advance allowing the British to escape.

IN 1939, AT THE OUTBREAK of the Second World War, a British Expeditionary Force was sent to France. Both countries had declared war on Germany over its invasion of Poland. Even so, the British and the French forces had no plan of attack. Instead they prepared for defensive action.

The British and the French had imagined that the main German attack would come through Liège and Namur in Belgium, as had happened in the First World War, across a plain that was perfect tank country. However, using a plan developed by General Erich von Manstein, the German main offensive began on a narrow front that took them through dense and hilly Ardennes Forest, which the French thought was impassable to tanks. On 10 May, Field Marshal Gerd von Rundstedt directed 1,500,000 men and over 1,500 tanks – two-thirds of Germany's forces in the west and nearly three-quarters of its tanks – against the weakest part of the front. It was defended by just twelve infantry divisions and four cavalry divisions, mounted on horses. The attack was brilliantly organized. A

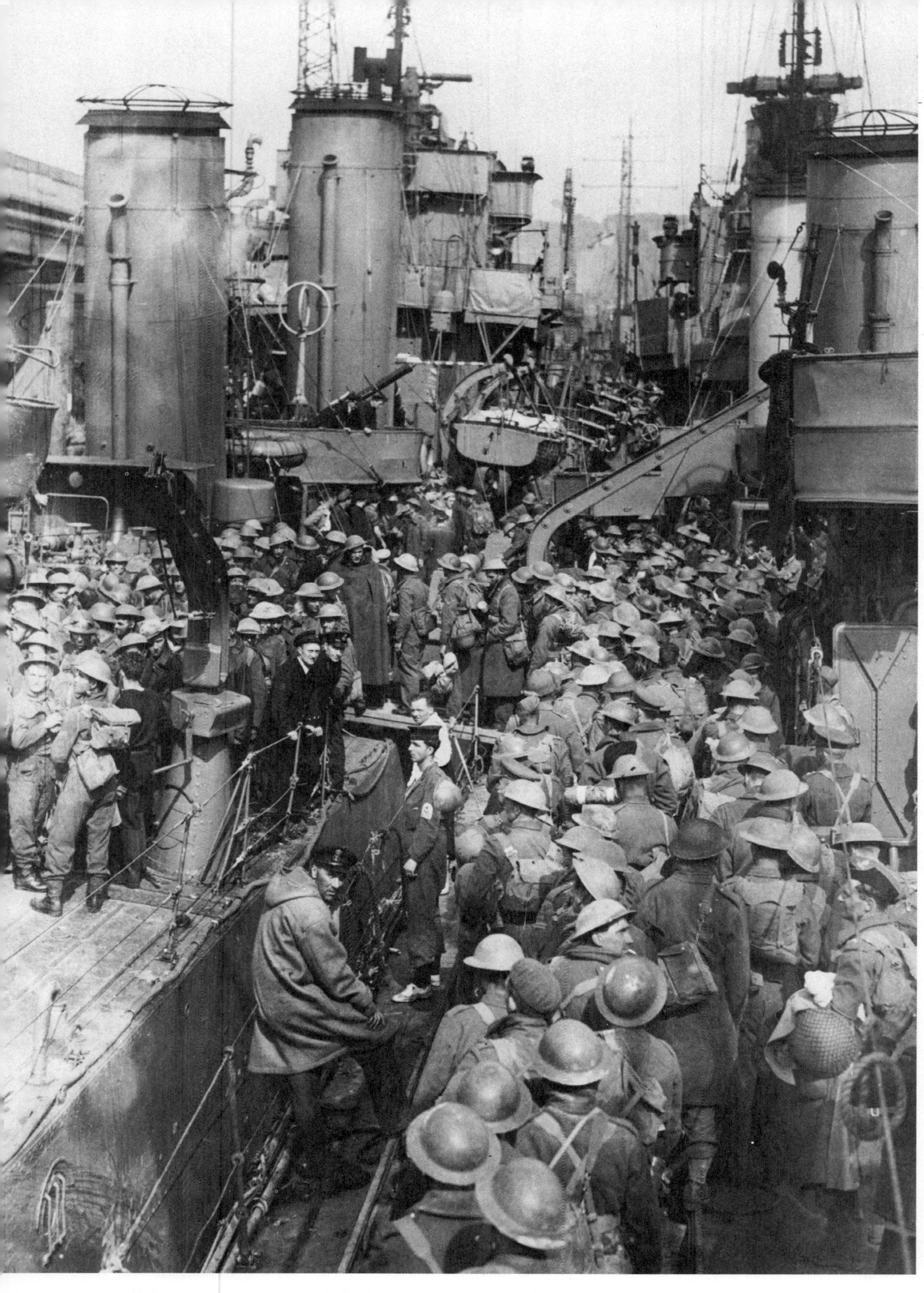

Not all the escaping troops were picked off the beaches by small boats. Others boarded larger ships in the docks. They were then whisked back to the crowded ports of southern England.

thrust through Luxembourg enabled the Germans to cover the thirty miles to the Belgian border in just three hours. Another thrust through the forest itself allowed the armoured divisions to speed down the narrow lanes. They reached France in less than three days, crossing the border on the evening of 12 May. The infantry followed, using pathways through the woods, travelling so fast that they reached the River Meuse just a day behind the armour. The French had not expected an advance in this area and the defences there were rudimentary. There were no fortifications in that sector and the French forces there had few anti-aircraft or anti-tank guns to take on the German dive bombers and armoured columns. The French cavalry divisions that rode in on horseback to reinforce the sector were forced to retreat to the Semois River on 11 May.

On 13 May, after the French defenders on the south bank had been devastated by waves of dive bombers, German infantry crossed the Meuse on rafts and in rubber dinghies at Sedan – the site of France's defeat in the Franco-Prussian War of 1870. The French had just a handful of aircraft in the air, while the German thrust was supported by 1,000 aeroplanes. German tanks crossed the river on the following day and on 15 May they broke through what remained of the French defences. It was estimated that the Germans could have been in Paris within two days. Instead, the Germans turned westwards towards the Channel. On the following day, the German spearhead covered almost fifty miles of open country. The advance was so fast that even the German high command were concerned that it was vulnerable. However, French resistance collapsed when the spearhead was joined by a diversionary German force that had come through Liège. Facing almost no opposition, the Germans reached Amiens on 19 May. German tanks entered Abbeville on 20 May and on 22 May they turned northwards towards Dunkirk and Calais. The French and the British suddenly found that they had been fighting the wrong war. They had calculated that the German advance would sweep across Belgium to the coast and then turn southwards, as it had done in the First World War. Instead it moved southwards into France, then swept around in an arc to the west and the north. This move was known as the *Sichelschnitt* ('sickle cut' or 'sickle stroke'). It broke all communication between the various Allied forces that were north and south of this 'Panzer corridor' and the French and British forces that had advanced into Belgium were now threatened by encirclement. As early as 19 May the British commander, Viscount Gort, had considered withdrawing the British Expeditionary Force by sea, but the British government wanted action for the sake of the alliance with France. Gort gave it to them. On 21 May, he launched an attack southwards from Arras against the Germans' right flank, in an attempt to break through to the French forces in the south. This kind of counterattack was just what the German high command had feared.

By that time, the head of the German column had swept through Boulogne and Calais. Dunkirk was now the only Channel port left in Allied hands. The Allies had set up their final defence line along the Canal d'Aire outside Dunkirk. On 24 May, the Germans were crossing the canal, ready to make their final push before taking the town when the German dictator Adolf Hitler stepped in and ordered them to halt their advance. News coming in about the counterattack at Arras was unclear and it seemed that the British were a genuine threat.

The German dive bombers virtually had the skies to themselves up to this point, but as they approached the coast they found themselves under attack from RAF fighters based in England. Nevertheless, Göring promised Hitler that he could neutralize the Dunkirk bridgehead with his Luftwaffe alone.

As it was, Gort did not have the armour to break through the Panzer corridor. He was running short

British troops fought a rearguard action, while the evacuees on the beaches and the shipping in the Channel were harassed by the fighters and bombers of the German Luftwaffe.

of supplies and ammunition and, on 25 May, he ordered the BEF to fall back on Dunkirk. As Gort no longer posed a threat, Hitler ordered that the advance on Dunkirk be resumed. But the hiatus had allowed the British to consolidate their defences. When the order came to advance again, the Germans met with considerable resistance. Almost immediately, Hitler ordered the German armour to stop. Hitler intervened personally on the morning of 24 May, ordering the Panzers to halt at the Canal d'Aire, just outside the port. Otherwise it seems certain that the Germans would have taken Dunkirk and Malo-les-Bains on the evening of the 25th. Hitler and von Rundstedt agreed that it would be best to reserve the Panzers for use against the remainder of the French army, which was deployed to the south under General Maxime Weygand.

The British government now decided that they had to save what could be saved. As early as 19 May, Churchill had ordered Admiral Bertram Ramsay to prepare for an evacuation. Already the call had gone out for small boats. The Admiralty quickly assembled 850 coasters, trawlers, ferries, motor launches and *schuyts* – flat-bottomed Dutch barges that had fled across the North Sea when the Germans invaded the Netherlands. Reluctantly, the Admiralty took thirty-nine destroyers off convoy duty to act as escorts, although these also embarked troops when they could get close enough to the shore. Now the race was on to evacuate the soldiers before the German advance resumed.

Operation *Dynamo*, as the evacuation was called, began at 18.57 on 26 May. That evening Hitler gave orders to resume the advance on Dunkirk. With the British in Belgium withdrawing towards Dunkirk, the Belgian Army was left to face the Germans alone. On 27 May it fell apart. King Leopold surrendered unconditionally on the following day and the French Pas-de-Calais flotilla joined the evacuation with some 300 vessels of every tonnage, including fifteen destroyers and torpedo-boats. However, on 27 and 28 May only 25,437 troops were taken off.

With resistance in Belgium over, the Luftwaffe began bombing the harbour at Dunkirk, putting it out of action. However, thanks to the air cover provided by the RAF Göring was unable to make good the boast that his planes could destroy what was left of the BEF. The harbour's bomb-damaged breakwater was still serviceable, which allowed many of the troops to be taken off by larger craft. The remainder were mustered on a ten-mile stretch of beach, where they were picked up by small craft that were largely manned by amateur sailors.

On 29 May 47,310 British soldiers were evacuated; on 30 May 120,000 men, including 6,000 French, were embarked. On 31 May, Gort relinquished command over the beaches to General Harold Alexander and 150,000 men, including 15,000 French, were shipped back to England. Britain handed over the defence of Dunkirk to the French XVI Corps under General Fagalde on 1 June and he managed to hold the Germans back until dawn on the 4th. Fagalde and some 40,000 men were taken prisoner – although 113,000 French soldiers had been taken to England.

In the eight days of Operation *Dynamo*, some 338,226 Allied troops, two-thirds of them British, were rescued. But almost all their equipment was abandoned. From the British Army alone the Germans acquired 1,200 field guns, 1,250 anti-aircraft and anti-tank guns, 11,000 machine guns and 75,000 vehicles. Of the forty-one destroyers that participated in the evacuation six were sunk and nineteen others damaged.

Another 220,000 Allied troops were rescued by British ships from Cherbourg, Saint-Malo, Brest, and Saint-Nazaire in northwestern France, bringing the total number of evacuated Allied troops to about

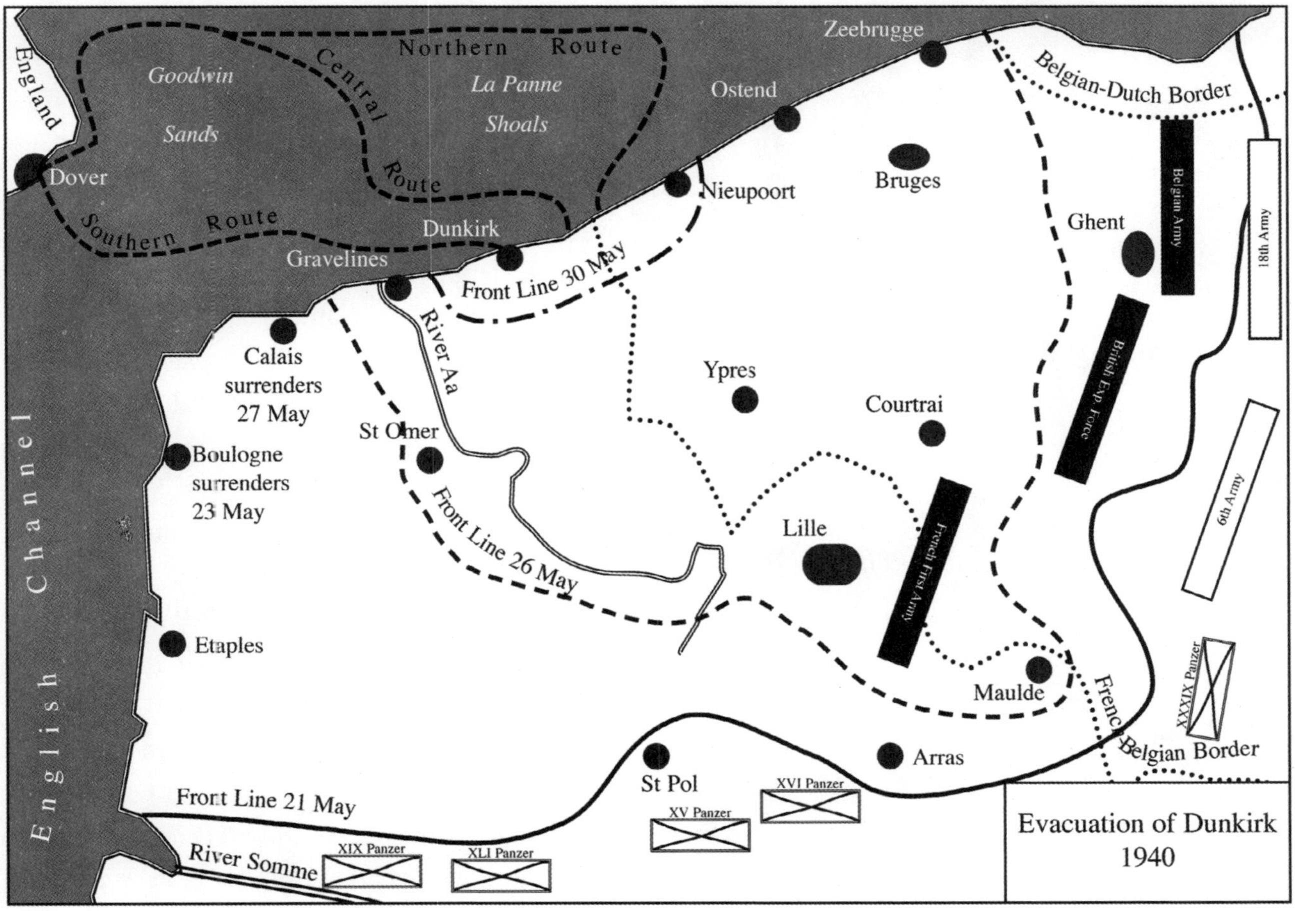

Evacuation of Dunkirk 1940

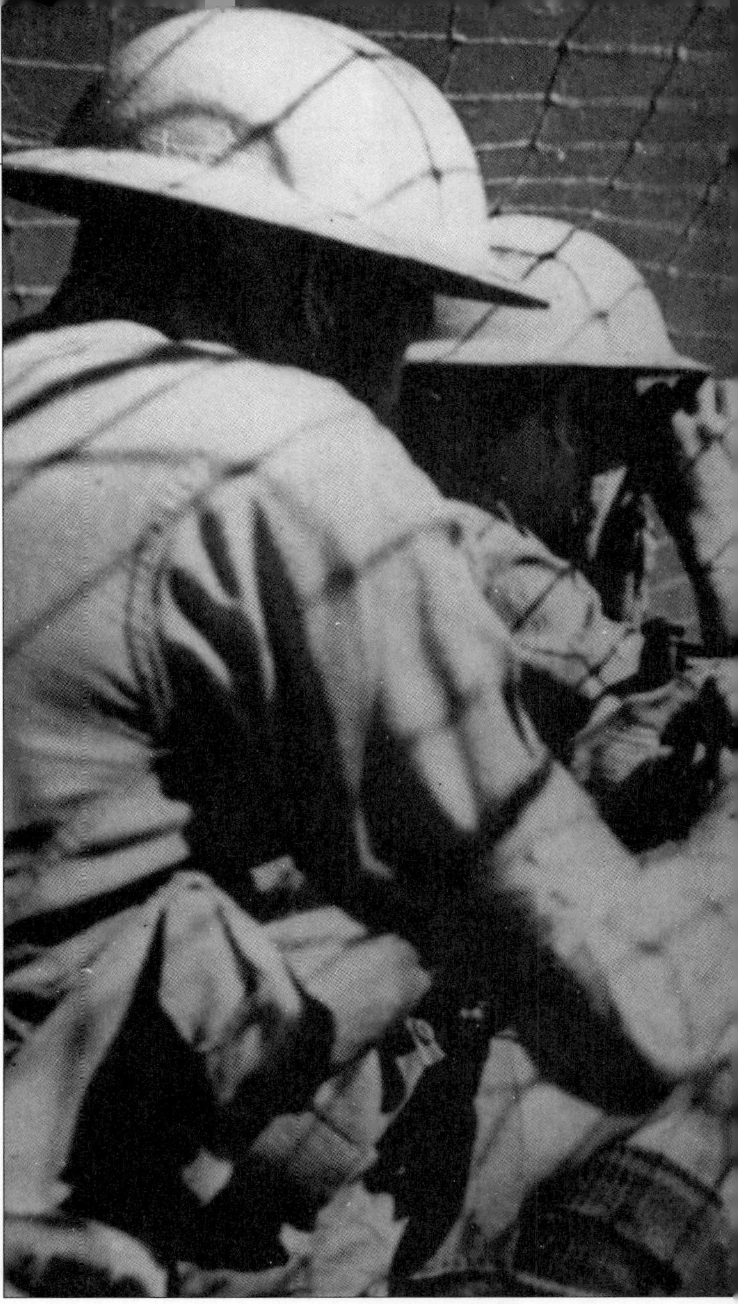

560,000. Within three weeks, however, the German army had taken more 1,212,000 Dutch, Belgian, French and British prisoners, with losses of 10,252 killed, 42,523 wounded and 8,467 missing.

Although the action at Dunkirk was actually a withdrawal, it was hailed as a victory by the British. In the long run it proved decisive because the bulk of Britain's most experienced troops had been saved. Controversy still rages about the reasons behind Hitler's decision to stay his hand and allow the British Army get away. It may have been one of the several key mistakes made by him during the Second World War, though some believe that Hitler still wanted to make peace with Britain and thought that this might be more easily achieved if the British Army was not forced into a humiliating surrender.

Tobruk

The Desert Rats Defy Rommel

1941

In the deserts of North Africa, General Erwin Rommel's Afrika Korps seemed invincible. But at Tobruk, a British force of largely Australians, New Zealanders and Indians showed that the German Panzers could be stopped.

ITALY'S INVASION OF LIBYA in 1911 meant that Mussolini already had one possession in North Africa. By the outbreak of the Second World War, some 150,000 Italian colonists lived there. So when the British rejected Hitler's peace overtures, Mussolini turned his attention to Egypt, which had been in British hands since 1882. He ordered Marshal Graziani to launch an offensive eastwards against the British troops in Egypt, who were under the command of General Sir Archibald Wavell. On 13 September 1940, the Italian 10th Army took the small border port of Sollum. They then advanced a further fifty miles into Egypt and occupied the British base at Sidi Barrani on 16 September. Six weeks later the British Western Desert Force under Lieutenant-General Richard O'Connor started a 'five day raid' which pushed the Italians back across the border on 10 December. Reinforced by the Australians, the Western Desert Force continued the advance and took the small port of Tobruk in northeast Libya on 21 January 1941. By

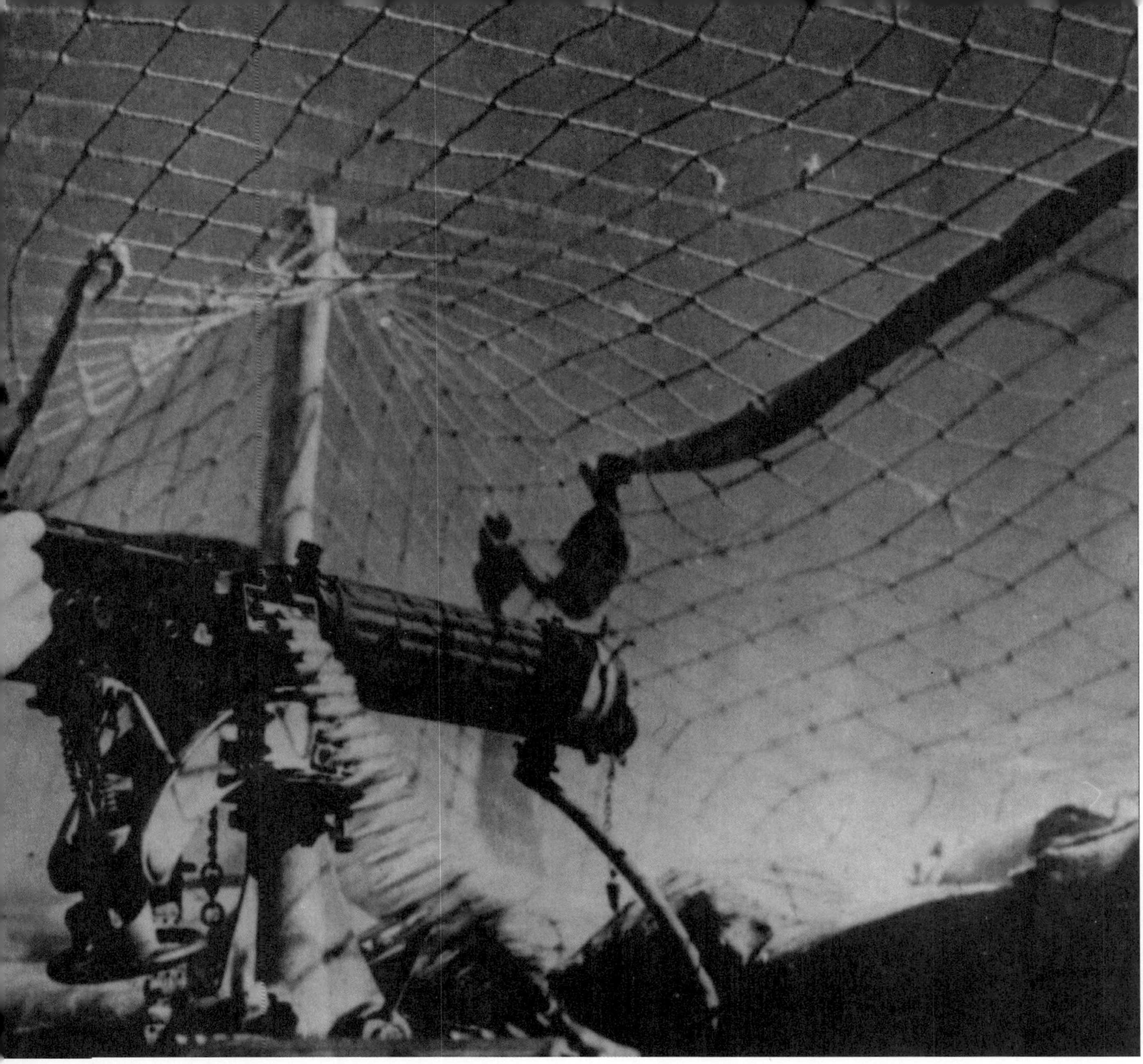

A soldier of the North County Regiment mans a machine-gun post. Tobruk was surrounded, but despite repeated German assaults, the British held the line.

the time the Italians had surrendered, on 7 February, they had been driven back for a distance of 500 miles by the British. Over 130,000 Italian prisoners had been taken, along with 400 tanks and 1,290 guns. Meeting no further resistance, the Western Desert Force could have gone on to take Tripoli, but their supply lines were already overstretched and British prime minister Winston Churchill wanted to divert men and resources to Greece.

Hitler came to Mussolini's aid. On 6 February, General Erwin Rommel, who had spearheaded the Panzer drive to the Channel, was sent with his Afrika Korps to Tripoli. He attacked El Agheila on 24 March, capturing O'Connor and throwing the British column back in the direction from which it had come. However, Wavell decided to hold Tobruk while the rest of the British force retreated into Egypt to regroup. As Tobruk had fallen so effortlessly on 21 January, its fortifications were largely intact. Its strongpoints, which were set out in alternating rows, were protected by concrete walls that were three feet thick. These offered protection against 15cm guns, the heaviest the Afrika Korps had at the time. It had an anti-tank ditch that was covered in camouflaged planks and sand and the perimeter defences described an arc that ran for twenty-eight miles around the port and reached a further nine miles inland. This was to be defended by the 9th Australian Division, reinforced by a brigade of the 7th, and the Sikhs of the 18th Cavalry Regiment. Major-General Leslie Morshead, commander of the 9th, told his men: 'There will be no Dunkirk here. If we have to get out, we will fight our way out. No surrender and no retreat.'

Artillery support was supplied by the Australian Royal Artillery and the Royal Horse Artillery. Although their twenty-five-pounder field guns were not designed as anti-tank weapons, they were very effective against Rommel's Panzers, bearing in mind that the standard anti-tank gun was the two-pounder. Tobruk was also defended by anti-aircraft batteries with seventy-five guns between them. Four Hurricanes were stationed there in the early days of the siege, but these were either shot down or withdrawn.

On 10 April, Rommel reached Tobruk and sent a motorised detachment to storm the town, but it was repulsed by heavy gunfire which killed its commander. On the night of 13 April, an infantry battalion of the Afrika Korps' 5th Light Division made its way through a minefield and across the anti-tank ditch. A counterattack destroyed the infantry battalion and Jack Edmondson, an Australian defender who went on fighting even though he was mortally wounded, was posthumously awarded the Victoria Cross. Meanwhile elements of the Afrika Korps had bypassed Tobruk and had reached the Egyptian border. From now on, the 22,000 men at Tobruk would have to be supplied by sea.

This was a dangerous business because the Luftwaffe had complete air superiority. However, the anti-aircraft gunners managed to keep the harbour open. The heavy batteries were armed with British 3.7-inch guns, which produced shrapnel, while light anti-aircraft batteries used Bofors 40mm guns backed up by captured Italian 20mm and 40mm Breda guns, which fired tracer shells that exploded on impact. Between them, they would throw up a barrage at a predetermined height. The German pilots got wise to this, however, and started hanging back to see what height the barrage had been fixed at before starting their bombing runs. The barrage was then spread more thinly, and over varying heights, to make it more difficult to penetrate. The Luftwaffe's response was to began dive-bombing the sites of the heavy guns, so the light anti-aircraft batteries with their rapid-fire tracers were moved in closer as protection.

Just before dawn on 14 April the Panzers attacked for the first time. They came on the left of the road that led south to El Adem. Thirty-eight tanks broke through the two lines of the zig-zagged perimeter defences and headed for the town. Three miles on they hit the second line of defence – the Blue Line. There they met point blank fire from British twenty-five-pounders. The Germans' artillery support and machine-gunners had been held up by the Australian infantry who stayed in position when the tanks broke through. In the face of the twenty-five-pounders, the Panzers had no choice but to retreat. As they did so, British tanks and Australian anti-tank guns pummelled their flanks. The routed Germans left seventeen tanks behind. Twelve aircraft had been shot down, 110 men killed and 254 were captured. It was the first time that Hitler's Panzers had tasted defeat.

Rommel realised that Tobruk could only be taken with an all-out attack, but he lacked the resources. Even the 15th Panzer Division, which was on its way, had suffered significant losses when the convoy carrying it was attacked on its way to Libya. By that time operations in the Balkans, and afterwards the Soviet Union, had starved Rommel of the tanks and men he needed for the capture of Tobruk. This small port later became the setting for the longest siege in British history.

Rommel bided his time for the next two weeks, bringing up more forces. By the end of the month he had some 400 German and Italian tanks at his disposal, against the defenders' thirty-one. On the evening of 30 April, he threw his men at Hill 209,

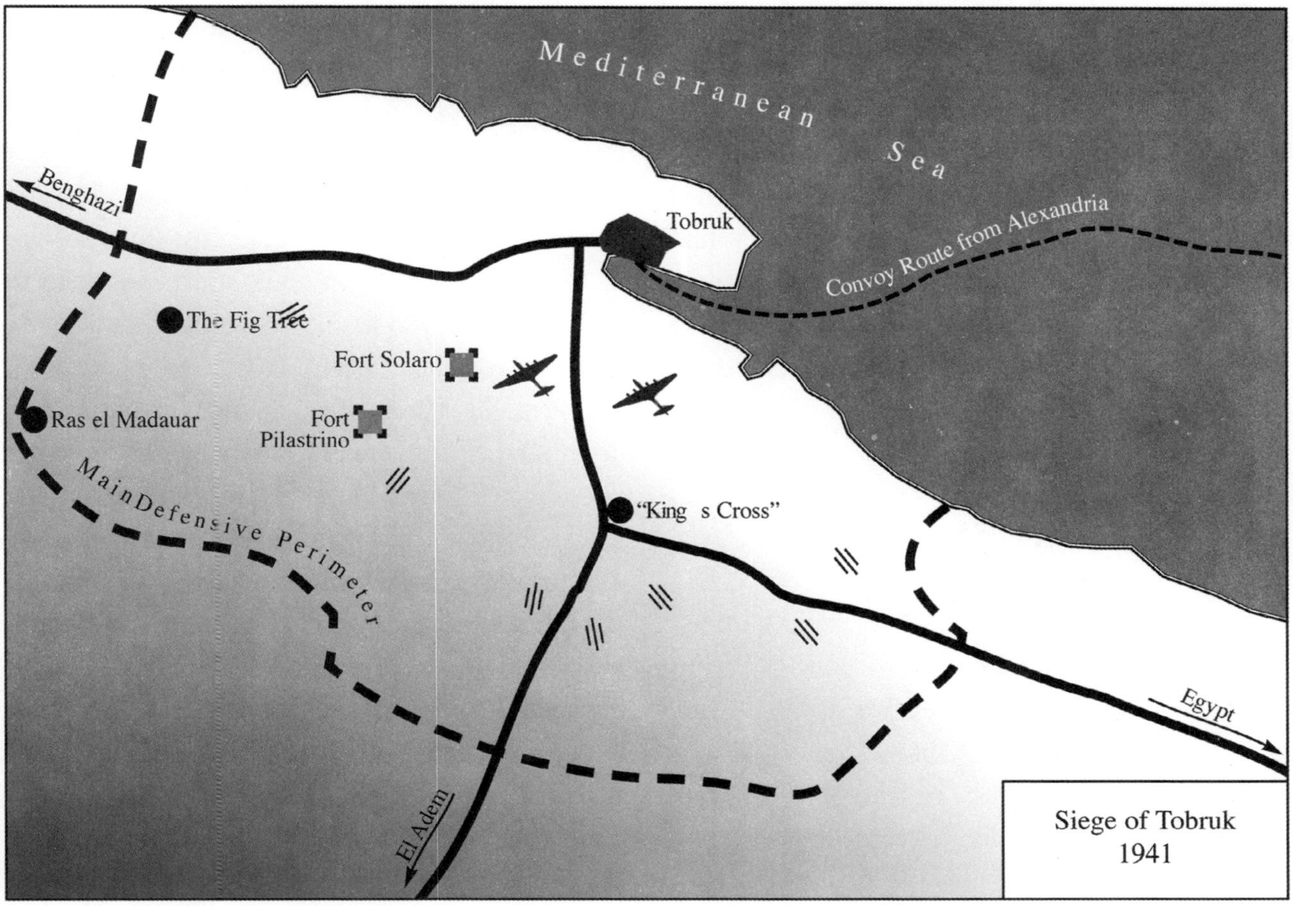

Siege of Tobruk 1941

known as Ras el Medauur, which was near the water tower on the southwest corner of the perimeter. Twenty-two Stukas began dive-bombing the Australian positions at 19.15 hours and an artillery barrage opened up at 20.00. This cut the telephone lines and neutralized the front-line defences.

Under the cover of the bombardment, the Germans blew gaps in the wire and cleared paths through the minefield. By 21.15 a German machine-gun battalion, positioned a mile inside the perimeter, opened fire on the reserve company. The Australians began a counterattack, but with poor communication, and they could not find the beleaguered perimeter posts in the darkness. By the following morning it was clear that the Germans had punched a hole through the outer defences that was a mile and a half wide. They captured seven perimeter posts and took more than a hundred prisoners. However, the Australians had put up such a determined resistance that they had taken the momentum out of the German attack.

Soon after 08.00 the Germans advanced again with forty tanks, but they were stopped by a minefield. Heavy shelling forced them to retreat, although a dust storm covered their withdrawal. Rommel tried to draw in the Allied armour by using a diversionary tactic with some twenty tanks, but Morshead was reluctant to commit his own tanks. He preferred to let mines and artillery shells do their work before risking his precious armoured reserve. Repeated air attacks failed to knock out the Allied artillery and by 09.00 the German attack had petered out.

As they could make no further progress in a forwards direction, Rommel's Panzers and their infantry support attacked the posts at either side of the mouth of the German bridgehead. One of them fell by noon, but the heavy shelling prevented the

Panzers from coordinating their efforts with their supporting infantry. Consequently, their attempts to take the other post failed. However, twenty-five light Panzers got beyond the perimeter posts and ran around the southern edge of the minefield. They were shelled all the way but by 09.15 they had reached Post R12, three miles east of Hill 209. There they were halted by fourteen cruiser tanks. Rommel then sent in another nine tanks. A sporadic tank battle broke out, but in spite of their superior numbers the Panzers were forced to withdraw after three of them had been lost.

The Germans tanks refuelled and began a new attack that afternoon. They were once more met by accurate British shelling. The Australians in the perimeter posts, armed only with Bren guns and rifles, put up fierce resistance. Two heavy Panzers tried to bombard one post into surrender from a range of seventy-five yards, but the Germans were repeatedly beaten back. By dusk half the defenders were wounded. The Germans attacked again in the twilight with tanks and flame-throwers and they took the post at 19.30. A second post fell on the following morning.

Having abandoned any attempt to drive forward directly onto the harbour, Rommel continued to push on inside the perimeter in the southeast until the bridgehead cleared the southern minefield. But he was stopped that evening by a counterattack against Hill 209. Impeded by the fading light and the dust kicked up by enemy shelling, the Australians advanced for more than a mile before they met resistance from anti-tank and machine-gun emplacements. By then they had lost the cover of their artillery barrage. Lacking the machine-guns they needed, the men withdrew. They had not retaken Hill 209, but they had had forced the enemy onto the defensive and had prevented the Germans from skirting around a vital minefield.

The German advance was halted by a sandstorm on 2 May, giving the defenders time to lay new minefields, bring up fresh infantry and strengthen their positions. The artillery continued to pummel the German positions and the Germans did not resume their offensive when the storm cleared next day. The garrison had lost just five tanks, while out of the eighty-one German tanks that Rommel had started with there were only thirty-five left in action. Of the forty-six that had been lost, however, only twelve had been completely destroyed. However, the Panzers had suffered their second defeat and their morale was shaken. On the other hand, the Germans had made a breach in the defences and had held a large salient.

Morshead planned to do something about that. He would send two battalions to attack the shoulders of the salient, retake the lost posts and cut off the enemy spearhead. At the same time, a third battalion would make deep raids into enemy territory. The problem was that the Germans held Hill 209 so they could watch as the Australians assembled. This gave them ample warning of the attack. After dark the Australians advanced under an artillery barrage and the Germans fought back with heavy machine-gun fire. Flares lit up the sky and German mortar and artillery fire brought the Australian advance on the northern flank to a standstill. On the southern flank, they retook one post but attacked another without success. The other attacks pushed the German outposts back by more than half a mile. The Germans had lost 1,700 men, compared to the garrisons' casualties of 797 – fifty-nine killed, 355 wounded and 383 missing. However, the German High Command grew alarmed at the losses and ordered Rommel not to attack again.

Morshead was jubilant. 'The actions before Tobruk in April and May are the first in which armoured formations of the German Army have been defied and defeated,' he said.

Churchill was also impressed. He sent a telegram which read: 'The whole Empire is watching your steadfast and spirited defence of this important

Nazi tanks manoeuvring on a hillside in Libya, unable to penetrate the defences of Tobruk, despite their superior numbers and weaponry. Even so they crowed that the defenders were caught like 'rats in a trap'. The British adopted the epithet.

outpost of Egypt with gratitude and admiration.'

Wavell's message to Morshead struck a more practical note. It read: 'Your magnificent defence is upsetting enemy's plans for attack on Egypt and giving us time to build up force for counter offensive. You could NOT repeat NOT be doing better service.'

The German radio propagandist William Joyce – known as in Britain as 'Lord Haw-Haw' because of his sneering voice – ignored the problems that Rommel was having. He crowed that the garrison were caught 'like rats in a trap'. A German newspaper then dubbed the British defenders the 'Rats of Tobruk', an insult they quickly embraced, calling themselves the 'Desert Rats'.

Tobruk was psychologically important from the Allied point of view, because it showed, for the first time, that the Germans could be stopped. The Panzers were not invincible. The German Blitzkrieg could defeated by minefields and artillery fire and infantry who stood their ground. Even the terror-bombers could be thwarted by dedicated anti-aircraft gunners. It also added a vital fillip to British prestige in the Arab world. Strategically, Rommel would have rolled on through Egypt if Tobruk had fallen. He would have taken the Suez Canal and the oilfields in the Persian Gulf and cut the British Empire in two. As it was, Britain was given time to recover from the disasters of Greece and Crete. The British forces could regroup in Egypt, while fresh American aid arrived via Britain.

The defence of Tobruk also kept Turkey – a

German ally in the First World War – out of the war. Accordingly, Hitler was prevented from using Turkey as a southern springboard for his attack on the Soviet Union, which delayed him by at least a month. Because winter is considered to be Russia's greatest general, this may have been crucial.

The greatest measure of the defenders of Tobruk's success was the fact that it took three battalions of Rommel's best troops and four Italian divisions to hold the salient around Hill 209. Morshead capitalised on this by maintaining a strategy of aggressive night patrolling in order to dominate no man's land and undermine the enemy's morale. In the meantime, the British maintained their harassing attacks on Rommel's forces on the Egyptian frontier, even though they were short of tanks. Their aim was to keep him from regrouping his whole force and turning it on Tobruk.

The actions before Tobruk were the first in which armoured formations of the German Army were defeated

After the evacuation of Greece, fifty tanks were diverted to Egypt. Wavell quickly organised Operation Brevity in order to relieve Tobruk. On 15 May 1941 the British captured the Halfaya Pass on the way to Sollum. But they were forced to withdraw on 17 May and the Germans retook the pass.

On the night of 15 May, the Germans launched an attack on three perimeter posts at Tobruk. It was thought that all three were lost, but when one was recaptured it was found that the other two had held out although they were desperately short of ammunition. Once they were resupplied, the Australians discovered that they were 'on a roll' and so they tried to recapture more of their outposts. Supporting fire came from thirty-nine British guns and a smoke screen was laid in order that machine-gunners from the Northumberland Fusiliers could sweep into the disputed area without being observed from Hill 209. The Germans laid their own smoke screen and barrage, however, and the British tanks lost their way in the dust and smoke. Even so, the Australian infantry carried on alone through intense fire in an attempt to take two posts. Unfortunately, the Germans were too well established and they not only held the concrete posts but also the intermediate positions that were able to provide flanking fire. At that point the Australians withdrew.

By June the two sides were consolidating their defensive positions. In the salient, the Germans had fallen back to a defensive line that was behind the positions they held on 3 May. By 26 June the Australians had been able to advance their line by 1,000 yards, reducing its length from over five miles to under four. This allowed the Australians to take one battalion out of the line and place it on reserve. On the other hand, the German line was more closely packed and the Germans had also mined no man's land, preventing any further Australian advances.

Wavell made a second attempt to relieve Tobruk, starting on 15 June. When this was beaten back by the 15th Panzer Division, General Sir Claude Auchinleck replaced Wavell as commander-in-chief in the Middle East on 1 July.

The Australians had held out in Tobruk for over three months. Factors such as heat, dust, flies, sand and poor food were affecting fighting ability and the Australian government asked that they be withdrawn. The bulk of the troops were evacuated in the late summer and replaced by the British 17th Division under Major-General Scobie. They were supported by the 1st Polish Carpathian Brigade and a Czechoslovakian battalion. However, some Australians stayed on with the original British forces.

While Rommel planned a new attack, General Auchinleck began organising Operation Crusader, a third attempt to relieve Tobruk, forming the 8th

Army under General Sir Alan Cunningham. Cunningham's plan was to send XXX Corps across the Libyan border to the south and deploy it at a place called Gabr Saleh. He hoped that Rommel and his Panzers would seize the opportunity for a tank battle because he believed that the better equipped and more numerous British and South African forces would win. Meanwhile, XIII Corps would overrun the frontier positions on the coast and push up the coast road towards Tobruk while Rommel was being crushed in the desert. The danger was that there would be a large gap between the two columns so the British would be vulnerable. Another column was drawn up between them, therefore, but it drew its strength from XXX Corps, thereby considerably weakening the force that was intended to take on Rommel.

Crusader got underway in torrential rain on 18 November. Unfortunately Rommel had plans of his own. Because he was making ready to take Tobruk, he kept his armour around Gambut on the coast road instead of moving to meet XXX Corps at Gabr Saleh. Worse yet was to befall Cunningham. The Eighth Army's operational plans fell into enemy hands after being brought to the front by a careless British officer. Because Rommel failed to meet XXX Corps at Gabr Saleh, the British pressed on. On 19 November, however, fifty of their new Crusader tanks were destroyed when they tried to take Bir el Gubi to the south of Tobruk. Another column pushed on towards Tobruk, but it was met by the Afrika Korps at Sidi Rezegh, who mounted a counterattack which destroyed much of their armour. Rommel could have wiped out the whole of XXX Corps if he had followed up on the following day. Instead, he took a gamble. With a hundred tanks he made a dash across the desert to the Egyptian border with the intention of cutting off the entire Eighth Army and attacking it from the rear.

The reverses took a terrible toll on Cunningham, who wanted to withdraw. Auchinleck urged him on in the belief that Rommel's bold move was an act of desperation. However, the strain was too much for Cunningham and on 26 November Auchinleck had to replace him with his own deputy chief of staff, Major-General Neil Methuen Ritchie. It was now Auchinleck who was really in command.

In a letter home, Rommel described his 'dash to the wire' as a great success. In fact, he had made little impression on the 4th Indian Division holding the rear, nor did he deprive Eighth Army of its supplies. Worse, his radio had broken down and he had left his Panzer group without orders for four days.

While XXX Corps had been decimated to the south, XIII Corps had been given an easier time of it while they were running along the coast road. The New Zealand Division broke through and on 25 November Scobie received a telegram telling him that the New Zealanders would make another attack on Sidi Rezegh on the following day. At the same time, the garrison was to attempt to break out. They did this in the midst of fierce fighting. At 13.00 hours they saw tanks on the horizon and then suddenly three red rockets burst in the sky. It was the 8th Army's recognition signal. Tobruk had been relieved at last. But not for long. In Rommel's absence, the 21st Panzer Division, which had been on the Egyptian border, was ordered to retreat. Rommel confirmed this order when he reappeared at his headquarters on the 27th. A confused battle followed in which the New Zealand Division was cut in two, with one half being sent back to Tobruk. In the mêlée, the commander of the 21st Panzer Division, General von Ravenstein, was captured.

Meanwhile, Auchinleck reinforced and reorganised XXX Corps and catapulted it back into battle. Rommel now only had a few tanks left so he withdrew his forces when he was told that he was not going to be resupplied until the latter part of December. He then attacked Tobruk from the east on 5 December. On the following day, a final counterattack failed and he ordered a general retreat, leaving behind an Italian division with orders to hold out as long as possible. Short of food and ammunition, it surrendered on 17 January.

The Siege of Tobruk lasted 242 days from 10 April to 7 December 1941, 55 days longer than the siege of Mafeking in the Boer War. It was the first defeat of German land forces in the Second World War.

Although the British managed to push Rommel 300 miles down the coast road he rallied at Gazala, in a counterattack that sent the British into full retreat. In June 1942, he finally captured Tobruk, which fell to the British again on 13 November 1942 after General Montgomery's victory at El Alamein.

Crete

German Airborne Victory

1941

During the invasion of Crete, the Germany deployed a massive force of airborne troops. Although the invasion was a success, the German casualties were so high Hitler never used his elite paratroopers again.

FOLLOWING GERMANY'S huge gains in the west in 1940, Italy found itself very much the junior partner in the 'Pact of Steel' that had been signed by Hitler and Mussolini in 1936. Mussolini wanted to make some territorial gains of his own, so without informing Hitler he sent 155,000 men across the border from Albania into Greece. Italy had invaded Albania in 1939. The Italian invasion of Greece was a disaster. Mussolini's seven divisions were halted by a handful of Greeks, who pushed the Italians back. By mid-December the Greeks occupied one third of Albania.

The British rallied to the defence of Greece, sending men and planes to airbases on the mainland near Athens. This put them within striking distance of the Romanian oilfields at Ploiesti, which were vital to Germany's attack on Russia, so Hitler had no option but to help Mussolini out once again. In March, there was a coup d'état against the pro-Axis regime in Belgrade, so the Germans and the Italians decided to invade Yugoslavia and sweep through into Greece. They made a lightning thrust through the Balkans, forcing the British to evacuate their forces from mainland Greece, although 20,000 remained as prisoners of war. By 11 May, the whole of Greece and the Aegean islands, with the exception of Crete, were in German hands.

However, the British wanted to hold on to Crete. It was just 500 miles from Alexandria and 200 miles from Tobruk. A symbol of British resistance in North Africa, Tobruk needed to be supplied by sea and would be in great danger if the Germans held the airfields at Heraklion, Réthimnon and Máleme on Crete.

The Germans needed Crete as well, but not just because they wanted to starve out Tobruk. The RAF were still within striking distance of the Romanian oilfields from the airbases there. Hitler was about to be deprived of Russian oil because of the attack on the Soviet Union – albeit temporarily, if all went well – so he could not afford to be without a supply from Romania, which had joined the Axis in early 1941. On 25 April 1940, in Führer Directive No. 28, Hitler ordered the invasion of Crete.

The use of airborne troops on Crete taught the British a valuable lesson. The Allies would use them to great effect later in the war.

A plan was drawn up to attack the island using an airborne division and three infantry regiments from the 5th and 6th Mountain Divisions. They would be landed by a hastily requisitioned flotilla comprising sixty-three motorized sailing ships and seven small steamers. This would be protected by two destroyers and twelve torpedo boats from the Italian Navy.

Defending the island were 41,500 men, 10,300 of whom were Greek. In addition to 17,000 British troops there was a large ANZAC force, comprising 7,700 New Zealanders and 6,500 Australians who had escaped from mainland Greece. On the way, they had abandoned much of their equipment and now they only had sixty-eight anti-aircraft guns, far too few to defend an island that measured 162 miles from end to end. They were also short of field guns, infantry weapons, ammunition, vehicles, entrenching tools, barbed wire, blankets and mess tins. They were led by General Bernard Freyberg, a hero of Gallipoli who had been wounded twenty-seven times during the First World War. However, he was the seventh British commander on the island in six months, and he had been given just three weeks to prepare the island's defences.

On 1 May, there were thirty-five operational RAF aircraft on Crete. By 19 May, incessant bombing by the Luftwaffe had reduced that number to only four Hurricanes and three Gladiators. These were sent to Egypt for safekeeping, but the air strips were only obstructed rather than being put out of action because it was intended that they would be used again as soon as possible.

The Battle of Crete began on 20 May. The Germans had an air fleet of 500 transport planes and seventy-two gliders, supported by 500 bombers and fighters. At 07.15 German gliders carrying elements of the 5th Mountain Division landed to the west and south of Máleme airfield. Soon afterwards there were more landings on Hill 107, which overlooked the airfield. However a third company, which aimed to take the nearby Tavronitis Bridge, landed among New Zealand troops. Although they sustained heavy casualties, they managed to take the bridge and hold it.

Then the parachute drop began. The 3rd Battalion of the 7th Parachute Division were supposed to drop around the airfield but again they landed among the New Zealanders. Within three-quarters of an hour 400 of the 600 paratroopers were dead. The 4th Battalion dropped west of Tavronitis and found themselves under attack from a band of civilians whom they quickly subdued, while the 2nd Battalion landed among Greek troops and armed civilians who butchered them. Only thirteen of the 2nd Battalion were still alive when they surrendered.

The 3rd Parachute Regiment dropped south of the nearby town of Canea, while the 2nd Company of the Luftlande Sturmregiment landed in fifteen gliders to the northwest. Their job was to subdue the anti-aircraft batteries there, but they soon discovered that the guns were dummies. The Northumberland Hussars in the area were real enough, though, and the 136 men who landed had soon sustained 108 casualties. But the 1st Company, landing to the southeast, managed to spike the anti-aircraft battery there before striking out to join up with other troops landing in the area.

The 3rd Parachute Regiment found itself widely dispersed. One company, carrying heavy mortars, dropped in a reservoir. Some men were drowned and all their equipment was lost. The survivors found themselves under fierce attack from the New Zealand and Greek troops in the area but they still

TOP: at a Greek mainland airport, some of the thousands of parachute troops are loaded onto transport planes.
CENTRE: invaders from the sky float down on Crete. LOWER: airborne troops armed with machine guns, rifles and grenades gained the foothold that enabled the Germans to win the most sensational victory in the history of modern warfare.

managed to take the village of Agia and set up their regimental HQ there. The divisional staff then flew in, but the glider carrying the divisional commander split its tow rope and crashed into the island of Aegina.

Things looked bleak for the Germans on the ground. Few of their objectives had been secured and the landing force was broken up into pockets, which were pinned down by the New Zealanders. Taking off from dirt strips in Greece also kicked up clouds of dust, so the planes carrying the troops had to be dispatched in discrete groups. This meant that the men were landed in small bands, often widely scattered, by which time preliminary attacks by bombers and fighters had alerted the defenders. One of the battalions landing around Réthimnon found itself among Australian troops. The paratroopers were pinned down in the drop zones and unable to reach their weapons containers. The two other groups that landed there had dug in. This meant that there were three discrete pockets of Germans around the airfield.

The troops that were dropped around Heraklion found themselves even more widely scattered and were under fire from the British troops who were holding the town. The second wave was even more unsuccessful than the first. Some 1,800 of the 3,000 men who had been dropped were dead and the survivors were in no shape to mount an offensive.

While the defenders had overwhelming superiority in men, armour and artillery, Freyberg took a generally pessimistic view of the situation. No counterattacks that night were capable of disrupting the enemy and concluding its fighting capability. In the morning, the commander of the 22nd New Zealand Battalion mistakenly thought that his forward positions had been overrun and ordered a withdrawal from Hill 107. In the confusion, the New Zealanders really were overrun and the Germans took the vital hill. Shortly after, another 550 paratroops were dropped and, with these reinforcements, the Germans captured the airfield. The Germans began to fly in ammunition even though incoming planes were subjected to withering machine-gun fire.

Reinforcements began landing at 16.00. Artillery fire wrecked some of the transports and others were damaged in collisions on the small airfield, but most of the troops got out safely. By 18.00 another 1,000 German troops were on the ground. The New Zealanders planned a quick counterattack, but by the time they had mustered their troops the Germans had landed in enough strength to hold on to the airfield.

The Germans also managed to strengthen their positions around Heraklion. They had begun house-to-house fighting in the outskirts when the Greek commander came forward to surrender the town. The British commander knew nothing of this and counterattacked, but was unable to dislodge the Germans.

The Royal Navy caught and sank the first flotilla of German sea-borne troops as they came in sight of Máleme. Over 500 officers and men of the 100th Mountain Regiment drowned and it was destroyed as a fighting force. Before the Royal Navy could sink the second flotilla in the Mediterranean, however, it came under an air attack. German Stukas sank two cruisers and four destroyers, while the battleship HMS Warspite and the aircraft carrier HMS Formidable were so badly damaged that they had to be sent to the United States for repairs. Even so, the second flotilla of German troops was taken back to Piraeus rather than risk further loss of life.

That night the New Zealanders tried to counterattack again at Máleme in order to prevent any more reinforcements being landed, but to the east of the airfield they ran into the remnants of the 3rd Battalion of the 7th Parachute Division who had been so badly mauled on the first day. Individual paratroopers scattered across the rough ground put up such a fight that they slowed the New Zealanders' advance. By dawn the ANZACs were far from their

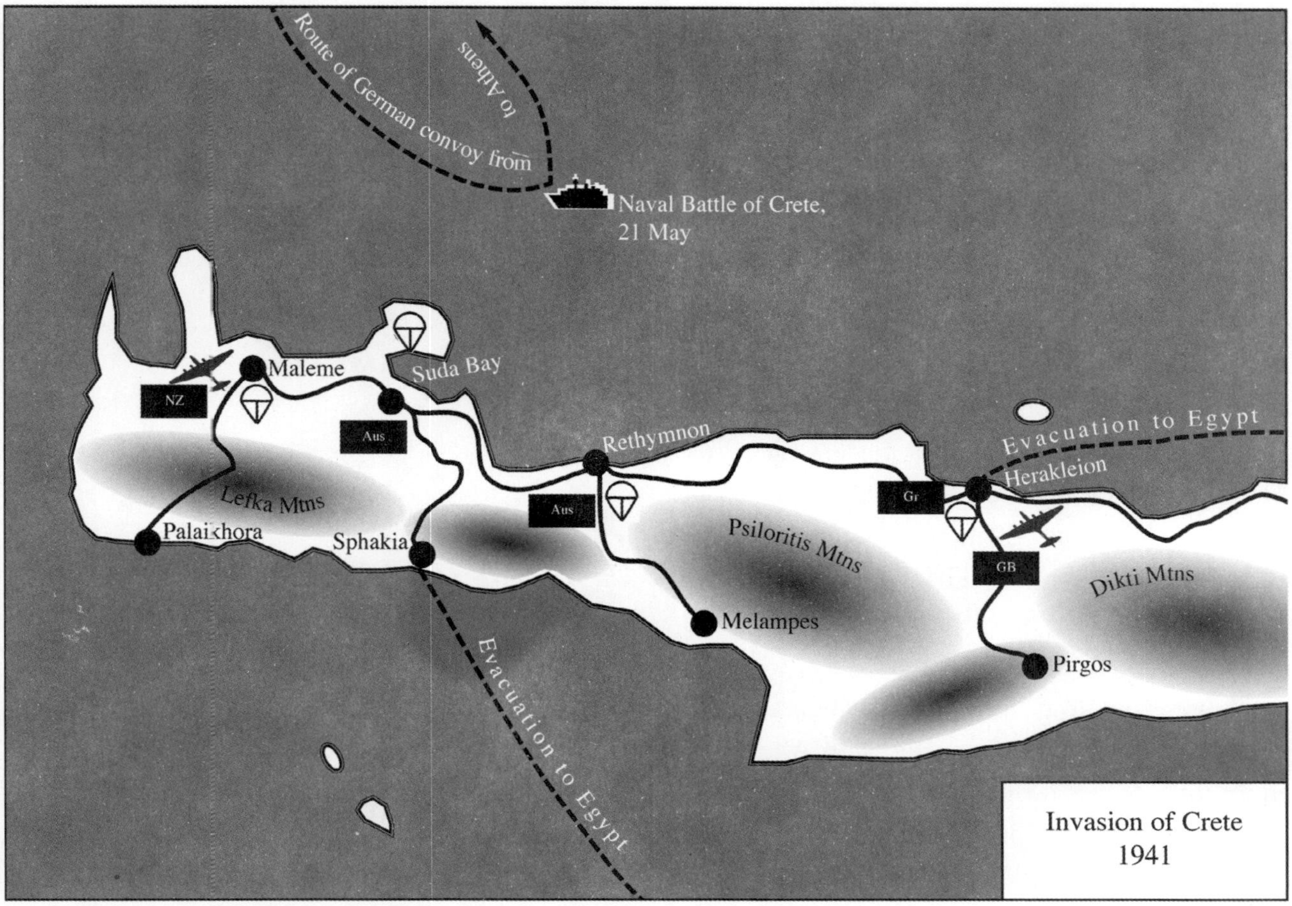

Invasion of Crete
1941

objective and German fighters and dive-bombers forced them to withdraw.

More Germans landed on the 22nd and Major-General Ringer flew in to take command. He divided his men into three Kampfgruppen, which were to push outwards at dawn on the following day. One group moved north towards the sea and found themselves up against armed civilians, including women and children. The Cretan Resistance was particularly savage. They tortured and mutilated any German who fell into their hands. A second Kampfgruppe moved into the mountains to the east, but was halted by the New Zealanders at the village of Modi. After fierce fighting, the New Zealanders were outflanked and they were forced to withdraw. This took their artillery out of range of the airstrip and the Germans could now land more reinforcements without coming under fire. Now the Germans brought in their artillery.

On 24 May, there were heavy German air attacks on the towns of Canea and Galatas and new battle groupings were drawn up. The Germans marched fifty miles in a flanking movement to cut off the main road from Canea and Réthimnon and join up with the paratroopers who had been stranded southeast of Canea since their drop on the 20th.

On 25 May, the Germans made a concerted attack on the key village of Galatas. The New Zealanders were ousted but retook the village in a bitter counterattack. By then their numbers were so depleted that they could not hold it, so withdrew that night. Now Canea lay within the Germans' grasp.

Under attack from the skies and with the Royal Navy unable to prevent further landings, Freyberg called for an evacuation on 27 May. Despite the danger, Admiral Andrew Cunningham, commander-in-chief in the Mediterranean, ordered the Royal Navy to go in and rescue Freyberg and his men.

When one of his aides pointed out that this put his ships in great danger, Cunningham replied: 'It takes the Navy three years to build a ship. It would take three hundred years to rebuild a tradition.'

The evacuation of Crete began on the night of 28 May. Altogether some 8,800 British, 4,704 New Zealanders and 3,164 Australians were brought out of the small port of Sphakia on the southern shore of the island and taken to Alexandria. Some 1,464 were wounded. Another 11,835 had been taken prisoner. On board the cruiser HMS Orion, Vice-Admiral Pridham-Wippell's flagship, a single German bomb killed 260 men and wounded 280. In all, the Royal Navy lost 2,011 officers and men.

The Germans lost 3,714 troops, who were either killed or missing, and they counted 2,494 wounded. Eight days of fighting on Crete had cost the Germans more than the entire Balkan campaign. After Crete, Hitler forbade any further large-scale deployments of paratroopers and plans to invade Cyprus and later Malta, were abandoned.

Alamein

The Tide Turns in North Africa

1942

Alamein marked the high-point of German expansion in the Second World War. Winston Churchill said, with some justification that before Alamein Britain did not have a victory; after Alamein "we never had a defeat".

AFTER ROMMEL'S VICTORY at Gazala, the Afrika Korps forced the British back down the coast road. The British tried to hold a line of fortification that ran south along the Egyptian border from Sollum to Sidi Omar. However, this shared a tactical weakness with other lines that the combatants had tried to hold in North Africa – the desert flank remained open. Rommel swept around it on 24 June, advancing over a hundred miles in one day. However, realising that the line could not be held, the British Eighth Army had already fallen back to Mersa Matruh, 120 miles east of the frontier. The situation was now des-

Two British infantrymen force the crew of a German tank to surrender as a sandstorm clouds the battlefield at El Alamein on 25 October 1941. At last, the British had learnt how to challenge the might of the German Panzers.

perate. The Luftwaffe was already in range of Alexandria. If the Eighth Army failed to hold Rommel back there was nothing to stop him taking Egypt, the Suez Canal and the oilfields of the Persian Gulf. He could then go on to attack the beleaguered Russians' southern flank.

The commander of the Eighth Army, Major-General Neil Methuen Ritchie intended to make one final stand at Mersa Matruh, but the British commander in Egypt General Sir Claude Auchinleck realised that a defensive line there would suffer exactly the same weaknesses as the one at Sollum. On 25 June, therefore, he sacked Ritchie and took personal command of the Eighth Army. On the following day he issued new orders. There would be no new line at Mersa Matruh but instead he intended to keep his all troop formations fluid. Mobile columns would strike at the enemy from all sides. To that end he reorganized into brigade battle-groups made up of artillery – always the British strength in North Africa – supported by armour and infantry.

On 27 June, Rommel caught up with the Allies

again. There were a series of punishing skirmishes with units of the British forces being bypassed, cut off and having to break out eastwards. Eventually, they fell back on a line at El Alamein, just sixty miles from Alexandria. There Auchinleck was determined to block any further advance.

Auchinleck's line at El Alamein differed from the one at Sollum because it did not have an open flank to the south. It ended at the Qattara Depression, which comprised 7,000 square miles of salt lakes and marshes that were impassable to tanks and other heavy military vehicles. The German spearhead reached the El Alamein line on 30 June. It was manned by Australians, the original 'desert rats' who had survived the siege of Tobruk, along with British, South African, New Zealand and Indian troops who had fallen back across the desert. And critically, they would be supported by the RAF at El Alamein.

Having come so far, so fast, the Afrika Korps was now exhausted. And it was at the end of a very long supply line. Its first assaults failed to break through, so it began to lay extensive minefields when it halted to build up its forces. Throughout July 1942 assault was met by counter-strike, with neither side giving way.

On 13 July, Rommel launched his newly re-equipped Afrika Korps into what became known as the First Battle of El Alamein. Again the Panzers were halted and that night Auchinleck counterattacked. Indians and New Zealanders overwhelmed two Italian divisions and contained a counter-strike by the Panzers.

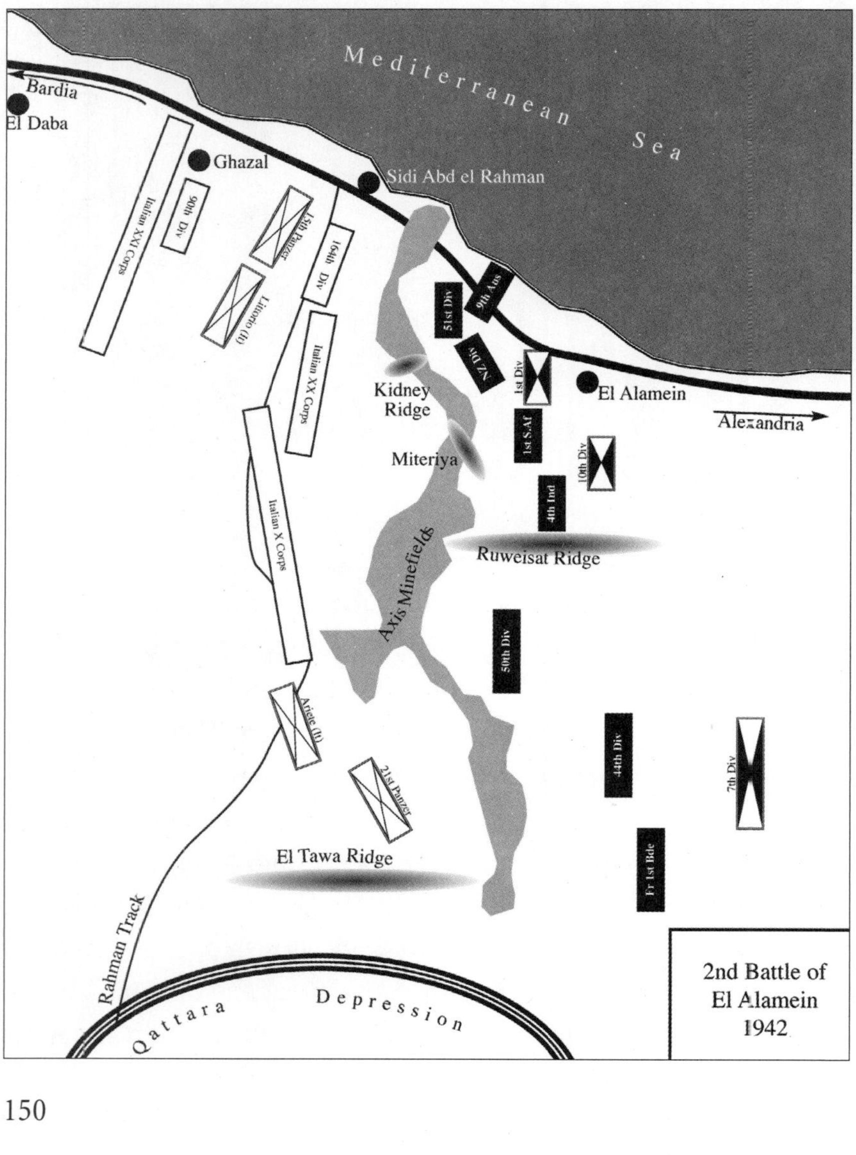

2nd Battle of El Alamein 1942

The battle became a war of attrition, leaving some 10,000 dead. Rommel quickly used up all the supplies that he had taken at Tobruk. He had been reinforced with 260 tanks but after the fall of Tobruk Roosevelt had sent the British a hundred self-propelled guns and 300 Sherman tanks. The Shermans were armed with 75mm guns that at last gave the British a tank to rival Rommel's Mark III and Mark IV Panzers.

Although Auchinleck had stopped Rommel's advance he had not pushed him back and, on 4 August, Churchill arrived in Cairo to see what could be done. Auchinleck told him that he intended to delay any offensive until September in order to give the new reinforcements that he had just received time to acclimatize. Churchill would countenance no delay, sacked him on the spot and appointed Sir Harold Alexander as commander-in-chief in the Middle East. Command of the Eighth Army was given to General Bernard Montgomery, who took over on 13 August. Montgomery quickly reorganized the Eighth Army so that it fought in divisions, with units giving each other mutual support.

The Eighth Army was expecting Rommel to go on the offensive at some time around the full moon on 26 August. It was anticipated that he would attack, as usual, to the south of the line. He was then expected to break through, surround the Eighth Army within a matter of hours and then rush on to take Cairo. The spot he would choose for his attack was defended only by a minefield. But Montgomery had also spotted the weakness in his defences. He prepared positions behind the minefield so that any attacking force would have to run the gauntlet of six-pounder anti-tank guns and dug-in tanks.

Rommel's long supply lines meant that he had problems obtaining fuel. This delayed the attack until 31 August, giving the Allies more time to prepare. He had been hoping that his attack would take the British by surprise. However, the attacking force was bombarded by the RAF two hours before it set off. It comprised 200 Panzers, 243 Italian medium tanks and thirty-eight light tanks. Troops advancing in front of the tanks to lift the British mines came under heavy fire from well dug-in soldiers. More air strikes were called in. The commander of the Africa Korps was badly wounded and the commander of the 21st Panzer Division was killed.

Rommel narrowed the front and his column made its way through two minefields but was eventually stopped by a third. The Panzer divisions also found that they could make only slow progress on the soft sand. Casualties were heavy as the stalled column came under heavy artillery fire but then a sandstorm blew up, grounding the RAF and blinding the artillery.

On 1 September the storm lifted and the Panzers continued their advance but British armour drove them back. The Germans tried another offensive in the afternoon, but they were beaten back again. Montgomery tightened a ring of steel around the Afrika Korps. They tried to break out and failed, sustaining heavy casualties. Meanwhile they were being bombed by day and by night. By the afternoon of 3 September, Rommel's men were in retreat. Montgomery now aimed to go on the offensive, but he did not feel that his reinforcements were sufficiently welded together to give chase. As it was he let the Germans hold on to a strong point between the two minefields at the end of the El Alamein line.

On 7 September, he broke off the battle and began making new preparations. He had worked out a plan of deception to keep the enemy's strength at the south end of the line. He deployed a dummy pipeline, dummy supply dumps and dummy vehicles in that sector. Radio traffic was stepped up in the southern part of the line to suggest that an attack would be launched from there early in November.

The real attack would be launched further north. The guns and tanks massed there were moved in at night and carefully camouflaged. Slit trenches were dug out into the desert for the infantry to attack from. These too were camouflaged to prevent German aerial reconnaissance from being aware of the British intentions. As the six-week period of preparation grew to a close, the RAF stepped up its attacks on enemy airfields, effectively grounding the Luftwaffe by 23 October – the night of the attack.

Montgomery had abandoned the conventional wisdom of desert warfare. He would not attack to the south and try to turn the flank, nor would he take on the enemy's armour then deal with the infantry later. He would begin by sending a diversionary force against the armour in the south in order to make Rommel think that the main thrust would come there. Meanwhile there would be a

massive bombardment, first of all of the artillery positions in the north and then the infantry positions. Montgomery's infantry would then infiltrate down their slit trenches to take on German troops still dazed from the bombardment. There would inevitably be vicious hand-to-hand fighting, but Montgomery calculated that his men would get the best of it. After that, the armour would pour through the hole made by the infantry, systematically annihilate the German troops and then get into position at the rear to take on any remaining armour on ground of their own choosing. Even if they could not destroy the Panzers completely, the Germans would not be able to hold ground without infantry and would have to retreat.

There was a full moon on the night of 23 October. This was vital because thousands of mines would have to be lifted in order to make a hole in the enemy's defences. The minefields were 5,000 to 9,000 yards in depth and strengthened with booby-trap bombs and barbed wire. At 21.40 the Second Battle of El Alamein began when more than 1,000 guns along the whole line opened fire simultaneously on the German artillery. Twenty minutes later they switched their aim to the enemy's forward positions. As a huge curtain of dust and smoke rose over the enemy, the British infantry moved in with fixed bayonets, to the skirl of the pipers.

The Germans resisted valiantly, but by 05.30 the next morning two corridors had been opened and the armour began moving down them. Then things began to go wrong. The infantry still had not made it all the way through the minefields when they were met with fierce resistance. This left the armour dangerously exposed. By dusk the following day, one column of armour had made it through but the 10th Armoured Division was still in the middle of the minefields and was taking shelter behind the Miteiriya Ridge. Its commander, General Lumsden, had always been critical of Montgomery's plan. He thought it was suicidal to send tanks through narrow corridors in minefields where there was well-dug-in heavy anti-tank artillery. If one tank was hit, those behind it could not move and would be sitting ducks.

Lumsden was summoned to Montgomery's HQ and there he explained his position. Montgomery then called Brigadier Alec Gatehouse who was commanding the spearhead and ordered him to send the 10th Armoured Division over the Ridge. Gatehouse refused to waste his division in such a reckless fashion. After a robust exchange of views, Montgomery ordered him to send one regiment over the ridge, instead of the entire division. Of the forty-nine tanks of the Staffordshire Yeomanry that went over, only fifteen limped back. Gatehouse had been right.

Nevertheless, the advance continued and by the morning of 25 October two armoured columns had reached the enemy's positions. The situation on the battlefield had grown confused and the Germans

British General Bernard Montgomery made his reputation at El Alamein. He then forced Rommel out of North Africa, headed British forces in the invasion of Italy and commanded all Allied land forces on D-Day.

made a number of bloody counterattacks. One of them, on the vital salient known as Kidney Ridge, was led by Rommel himself. All were repulsed and things gradually turned in the British favour. On 27 October the 1st Armoured Division alone knocked out fifty German tanks while repeated sorties by the RAF broke up the Panzer formations.

With the two armies locked in fierce fighting, it became apparent to Rommel that everything depended on which side would be exhausted first. However, Montgomery had been skilfully transferring units to the line in order to build up a force that could deliver a knockout punch. Those that remained were told to adopt a defensive posture, but to employ aggressive patrolling and artillery fire in order to give the impression that the advance was continuing.

On the night of 28 August, the 9th Australian Division drove a wedge down the coastal road. This was what Rommel was hoping for. If the British attempted to move around him to the north, he would be able cut their forces in two. So he moved his Panzers to the north. However, Montgomery did not follow up with a major attack down the coast. Instead he sent the 2nd New Zealand Division in against a weak point in the German line that was defended by the Italians.

The battle was reaching its climax. Rommel told his commanders that they must fight to the death, although shortage of fuel meant that he was already considering withdrawal. Then, on the night of 30 October, he began to think that his luck was in. The Australians rose from their trenches and moved forward against fierce resistance. This would inevitably exhaust the tenacious Australians. However, a force of Panzer Grenadiers found themselves surrounded in a fortified position known as Thompson's Post. The other Panzers attacked repeatedly in an attempt to relieve them and they managed to get through to the survivors after three days of fighting.

Meanwhile, the full weight of Montgomery's remaining forces were thrown against a 4,000-yard stretch of the front. At 01.00 on 2 November, two British infantry brigades moved through the New Zealanders' lines and attacked. They were followed by 123 tanks of the 9th Armoured Brigade. Their objective was to destroy the anti-tank screen, especially the lethal 88mm guns. Montgomery told its commander, Brigadier John Currie: 'I am prepared to accept one hundred per cent casualties.' Currie led the attack personally.

The tanks, which were followed by infantry with bayonets fixed, ran over mines. As the sun came up, they were hit by dug-in German anti-tank guns. All but nineteen of the 9th's tanks were knocked out and 230 of Currie's 400 men were killed. However, the attack achieved its objective. The 1st Armoured Division plunged through the new corridor that had been created. When Rommel realised that he had been tricked, he sent formations of Panzers south. On the following day anti-tank guns were moved into position, but by that time the British had expanded their salient to the south and were pushing relentlessly westwards. A tank battle ensued, but the German and Italian tanks were held in check by the RAF and by artillery fire. After two hours, the German counterattack petered out. That afternoon, Rommel tried again, throwing an Italian armoured division into the fray. But more and more British reinforcements were pouring through the gap and fanning out behind it.

The Afrika Korps was down to just thirty-five tanks when Rommel decided to withdraw. But then he got an order from Hitler, telling him to hold the position to the last man.

'There will be no retreat, not so much as a millimetre,' read the Führer's message. 'Victory or death.'

Rommel knew that to hold his current position would be suicidal. But then, it would also be suicidal to disobey Hitler. When General von Thoma, head of the Afrika Korps, asked for permission to retreat, Rommel refused to give it, but he turned a blind eye when von Thoma pulled back anyway. Von Thoma was captured soon after and did not have to face Hitler's wrath. After twelve days of fighting, the Axis forces were now in full retreat. Fuel was low and there were only enough vehicles to cover the Germans' retreat. The hapless Italians were abandoned and they surrendered by the thousand.

Brigadier Gatehouse asked permission for the 10th Armoured Division to give pursuit. He was sure that he could outrun them and destroy them in forty-eight hours. But Montgomery refused because Rommel had already shown that he could suddenly mount a counterattack that could turn a rout into a new offensive. The retreating column was bombed and strafed by the RAF and the 8th Armoured Brigade managed to head off a German column and also take a large number of prisoners, tanks and lorries. Other units also gave pursuit, but a downpour on 7 November turned the road into a quagmire and the Afrika Korps got away. It left 10,000 men behind it. Another 20,000 Italians had been captured and 20,000 more had been killed or wounded. There were 450 knocked-out tanks on the battlefield, along with seventy-five that had been abandoned by the Italians due to lack of fuel. Over 1,000 enemy guns had been destroyed or left behind.

The British Eighth Army sustained 13,500 casualties during the Battle of Alamein. Some 500 British tanks had been knocked out, although 350 of those could be repaired, and a hundred guns had been lost also. In Britain, the church bells had been silent for years because they were to act as an invasion alarm. Churchill ordered that they be rung out in celebration. Speaking of the victory at El Alamein at the Mansion House in the City of London on 10 November 1942, he said memorably: 'Now is not the end. It is not even the beginning of the end. But it is, perhaps, the end of the beginning.'

For Britain, the Battle of Alamein was a turning point. For three years the British had been battered in Europe, on the Atlantic and in the Far East. 'After Alamein,' wrote Churchill with some justification, 'we never had a defeat.'

Eventually, the Eighth Army pushed the Afrika Korps out of Libya. Then, following a series of American landings in Morocco and Algeria, the Germans were forced out of North Africa all together. This led the way to the Anglo-American landings on Sicily and the mainland of Italy itself.

Stalingrad

Hell on the Eastern Front

1942–43

In his political manifesto Mein Kampf *Hitler envisaged a German homeland that expanded to the Volga. At Stalingrad, the Nazis came within yards of his ambition. But, at a terrible cost, the Russians pushed the Germans back.*

IN THE SUMMER OF 1941, Hitler attacked the Soviet Union. His armoured units penetrated deep into Soviet territory. The onset of winter halted the offensive on the outskirts of Moscow. Still dressed in their summer uniforms, his men suffered terrible privations on the Eastern Front that winter. But Hitler was not downhearted because most of the Soviet Union's European territory was now in his hands and, by February 1942, the Soviets' winter counterattack had petered out. Now Hitler began to make plans to crush the Red Army once and for all. The renewed campaign would include an attack on Stalingrad (now Volgograd), a city that stretched some thirty miles along the Volga and was some 600 miles southeast of Moscow. It was a huge new industrial city and was paraded as one of the great achievements of the Soviet system. It also bore the name of the Soviet Union's leader, who had organized its defences against the White Russians in the civil war that followed the founding of the Soviet state. Stalin realized that the city must be held at all costs. If it fell, so would he.

Stalingrad was also crucial for Hitler. It was a symbol of Communism and it had to be crushed. It was also an important centre for the mass production of armaments. Once it had been taken, his victorious army would head up the Volga to encircle Moscow, while a second army would move southeast to take the oilfields of the Caucasus and threaten Turkey and Persia (Iran).

The German army in southern Russia was then split into two groups, under the overall control of Field Marshal von Bock. Army Group B, under General Freiherr von Weichs, was much the stronger of the two. It comprised the Fourth Panzer Army under General Hoth, the Second Army and the powerful Sixth Army, under Field Marshal Friedrich Paulus, all supported by other crack infantry and Panzer divisions. By comparison Army Group A was practically a reserve force. It included the crack First Panzer Army under Field Marshal Ewald von Kleist, which was going to take the oilfields of the Caucasus, and the Seventeenth Infantry Army. But the numbers were made up with Italian, Romanian and Hungarian troops. Altogether there were now

A key German objective was the Soviet tractor factory in Stalingrad. There the workers continued building munitions between assaults: when an attack started they grabbed their guns.

twenty-five Panzer divisions compared with nineteen the year before. Hitler was also fielding as many men as before, although the Romanians and Hungarians were not highly regarded as soldiers. However, the war was very different now. The Wehrmacht no longer seemed invincible and Hitler was no longer infallible. German soldiers now feared being posted to the Eastern Front, where the brutal treatment of the civilians – including mass shootings, burnings, summary execution and the deliberation starvation of men women and children – was sure to invite retribution.

In the spring of 1942, Stalin made a counterattack on the Kerch Peninsula in the Crimea. This was crushed and the Germans took 100,000 prisoners. Two fresh Siberian divisions sent to relieve Leningrad were encircled. Then 600 Russian tanks, two-thirds of their force, punched through the Romanian Sixth Army to take Kharkov. But then the trap closed. Von Kleist crushed the southern flank of the Soviet advance on 18 May, while Paulus swept down from the north. The Soviets lost nearly 250,000 men, along with all their tanks. The stage was now set for Hitler's summer offensive.

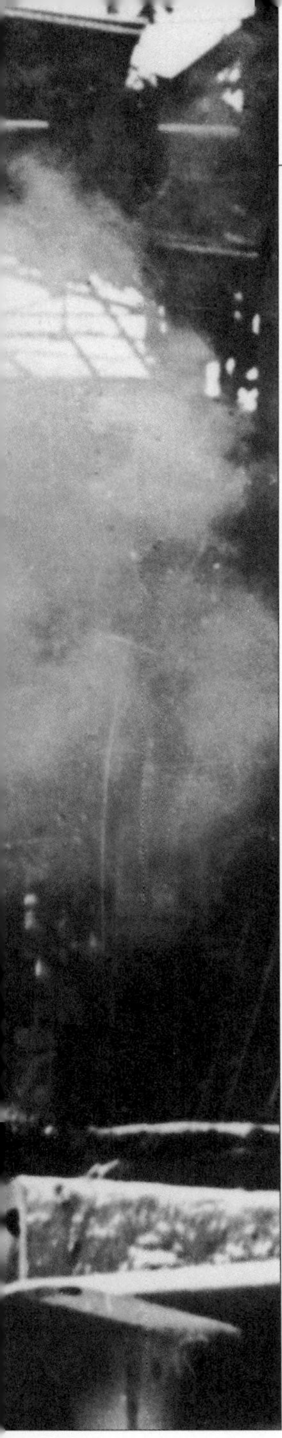

On 28 June, on a wide front stretching from Kursk to Rostov, the Panzers roared across the open steppes. The dust pall they kicked up could be seen for forty miles around and it was soon joined by smoke from burning villages. There were no significant forces to oppose them because the reserves were still being held back for the defence of Moscow. The Red Army put up a fight at the industrial town of Voronezh and when von Bock attempted to crush them, rather than bypass them and continue the offensive, Hitler sacked him. Army Group A, led by von Kleist's Panzers, then crossed the River Don and headed southwards towards the oilfields, while Army Group B headed for Stalingrad.

Army Group A progressed quickly, and they were almost in sight of the oil derricks of the Caucasian field by 9 August. However, the Fourth and Sixth Armies – with 330,000 of Germany's finest soldiers – advanced more slowly over the 200 miles to Stalingrad and became strung out. As they massed to mount an assault, Stalin made the decision to commit the Moscow reserve to the defence of Stalingrad and the desperate race to get them there began. Between 25 and 29 August, Paulus's Sixth Army made a ferocious attempt to storm the city before the reinforcements could arrive. Meeting stiff opposition, Paulus asked Hoth's Fourth Panzer Army for help. It attacked from the south, forcing the Soviet Sixty-Fourth Army, which was defending the southern part of city, to extend its flank to meet the threat. The Soviet front was now eighty miles wide, but only fifty miles deep. Paulus threw his entire Sixth Army, now supported by the Fourth Army Corps, against it. On 22 August, German troops penetrated the northern suburbs and on the 23rd they reached the Volga, within mortar range of a vital railway bridge. The Soviet Sixty-Second Army in the northern sector was now outflanked and the Luftwaffe were then called in to deliver an all-out night bombardment. The idea was to demoralize the defenders and cause panic among the citizens. Most of the civilian population fled to the other side of the Volga and the authorities began evacuating the largest factories. When Stalin heard of this, he stopped the evacuations. The result was that the factories themselves became centres of resistance. Workers in the tractor factory continued producing new tanks and armoured cars until the Germans were on their doorstep. After that, they would sling ammunition belts over their overalls, pick up grenades, rifles and anti-tank weapons and take up their positions in the firing-points or bunkers with their comrades from the Red Army. The remaining women, children and the elderly hid in cellars, sewers and caves in the cliffs above the Volga.

Despite the fierce fighting that followed the terror bombing, the German advance in the north of the city was halted. In the south, Hoth's Panzers pushed the Sixty-Fourth Army back, but they failed to penetrate the line and once they entered the heart of the ruined city their advance ground to a halt also.

For Hitler, Stalingrad was going to be where the war was won or lost. He summoned his commanders to his new forward headquarters at Vinnitsa, over 500 miles away in the Ukraine. The drive up the Volga was vital to the success of his Russian campaign, he told them. New Hungarian and Romanian armies were brought in to protect the left flank along the Don and three new infantry divisions were sent to reinforce the Sixth Army. Stalin, too, believed that the war would be won or lost at Stalingrad. He moved in a new team of

German and Soviet troops took to fighting building by building, with one side occupying one floor of a building while the other side occupied another.

commanders headed by General Georgy Konstantinovich Zhukov, who had masterminded the defence of Leningrad and Moscow.

The Germans were the masters of the Blitzkrieg. They were not accustomed to slow, grinding, man-to-man fighting through the rubble of a ruined city. The Russians, by contrast, quickly learned to adapt their tactics to the new situation and every move the Germans made cost them dearly. After weeks of ceaseless fighting against crack German troops, the Red Army still held a nine-mile strip along the banks of the Volga. A series of gentle curves in the Volga and a number of small islands prevented the German ground troops from bombarding all the river crossings with artillery and mortar fire. The Luftwaffe did not bomb them either, nor did the Soviet artillery on the other bank shell them. Instead, they continued to throw everything they had against the Soviet enclave on the west bank.

Hitler authorized a new offensive on 12 September. On the following day Paulus sent in three Panzer divisions backed by eight divisions of infantry. Against them, the Soviets had forty tanks, all but nineteen immobile. The Sixty-Secondnd Army had been reduced to just three infantry divisions, the remnants of four others and two battle damaged tank brigades. And there were no reserves, because every man had already been thrown into the battle. However, the Soviet headquarters was on the spot. General Vasili Chuikov had made the dangerous crossing of the Volga and had set up his command post in a dugout by the river, near Pushkin Street bridge. With their backs to the river, Chuikov inspired his men with the words: 'There is no land across the Volga.' For those who did not get the message, there were firing squads to deal with the deserters. Hundreds were shot.

The Germans flung themselves at the middle of the Russian line and they broke through and seized Mamaye Hill on the afternoon of the 14th. From the high ground there they could concentrate artillery fire on the vital ferry link from Krasnaya Sloboda. The 76th Infantry Division overwhelmed the defenders at a ruined hospital in the middle of the Soviet line. Victory now seemed certain and many Germans got drunk on looted vodka. The only resistance now seemed to be snipers.

Chuikov then threw his nineteen tanks in and the battle resumed. That night the fighting came within 200 yards of Chuikov's headquarters and staff officers joined in. But the Germans still pushed forward and the vital central landing stage came under machine-gun fire from close range. On the night of 14 September, Russian Guardsmen were forced to scramble ashore under fire. There was no possibility of them counterattacking as a coherent division because they were soon dispersed in isolated pockets among the ruins, with no intercommunication.

The street fighting had also broken up the German formations. They now fought through the devastated streets in small battle groups each comprising three or four Panzers and a company of German infantrymen that had to laboriously clear each pocket individually. Russian riflemen and machine gunners hid in ruined buildings and craters and behind mountains of rubble. They hid until the Panzers had gone by and then attacked the infantry. The Panzers then either found themselves attacked by roving T34s or they ran into anti-tank guns or dug-in tanks. In the narrow streets, the Panzers were vulnerable both to grenades dropped from directly above and to anti-tank guns, of which the Russians had a plentiful supply. Their armour-piercing shells were only able to make comparatively small holes in the buildings, most of which had been destroyed anyway. The battle hinged on house-to-house combat fought with bullet, grenade, bayonet and flame thrower.

The Germans found that it took a whole day and numerous casualties to advance 200 yards. Even then the Russians returned at night, knocking holes in attic walls so that they could reoccupy buildings over the heads of the Germans. Victory still seemed near, however. A German salient ran down the Tsarita tributary to the Volga itself. They had almost complete control of much of the city and the landing stages and most of the river crossings were within range of their guns. The Russians' only lifeline lay to the north where the ferries were out of range.

It did not seem to matter how much of the city the Germans occupied – the Russians would still not give up. The remains of the 92nd Infantry Brigade formed isolated pockets of resistance across the south of the city. The grain elevators there, although bombed and blasted, still stood defiant. At all levels, from top to bottom, they were occupied by pockets of Guardsmen and Russian Marines who repelled wave after wave of attackers. Their stout resistance brought the German assault inexorably to a halt.

For the Germans, two months of fighting for a narrow strip of the ruined city of Stalingrad was a propaganda disaster. The German people were told that the Russians were throwing wave after wave of men into the battle and were exhausting their reserves. In fact, the opposite was true. During September and October, the Germans threw no fewer than nineteen newly-formed armoured brigades and twenty-seven infantry divisions into the battle. In that same period, only five Soviet divisions crossed the Volga. Zhukov sent only the bare minimum needed to hold off the Germans, so that he could build up strength for a counterattack.

At around this time a crucial change was made in the Red Army. Since the Red Army was formed in the wake of the 1917 Revolution, its officers, many of whom came from the former Imperial Army, were stripped of their badges of rank and their every move was watched over by political commissars attached to each unit. Now old-fashioned gold-braided epaulettes were distributed. Old regimental traditions were revived. Political interference ceased and soldiers were told that they were fighting, not for the Communist party, but for Mother Russia.

While Russian spirits received a boost, German morale sagged. The Russian artillery fire grew steadily heavier. Meanwhile the nights began to draw in. The skies became grey and the weather chilly and the Germans began to fear that they would be spending another winter in Russia. Quickly Paulus planned a fourth all-out offensive. This time he was determined to score a great victory because he had heard that Hitler was considering promoting him to Chief of the High Command. Hitler had promised publicly that Stalingrad would fall 'very shortly'.

Forty thousand Russians now held a strip of the city that was barely ten miles long. At its widest it reached a mile and a quarter inland from the west bank of the Volga and at its narrowest it measured 500 yards. But the Russians defending it were hardened troops who knew every cellar, sewer, crater and ruin of this wasteland. They watched the German advances through periscopes and then cut them down with machine-gun fire. Snipers stalked the cratered streets or lay camouflaged and silent for hours on end awaiting their prey. Against them were pitched veteran German troops, who were demoralized by the losses they had taken, or raw recruits who could in no way be prepared for the horrors they were about to face.

On 4 October, the Germans were just about to launch their offensive when the Russians counterattacked in the area around the tractor factory. This threw the Germans off balance. Although little ground was lost, it cost them many casualties. The Luftwaffe sent in 800 dive bombers and the German artillery pounded the city mercilessly. Occasionally a pet dog would escape from a bombed building, race through the inferno, leap into the river and swim to freedom on the other side. After a five-hour bombardment, which shattered glass deep below ground and killed sixty-one men in Chuikov's headquarters, the German attack eventually went ahead.

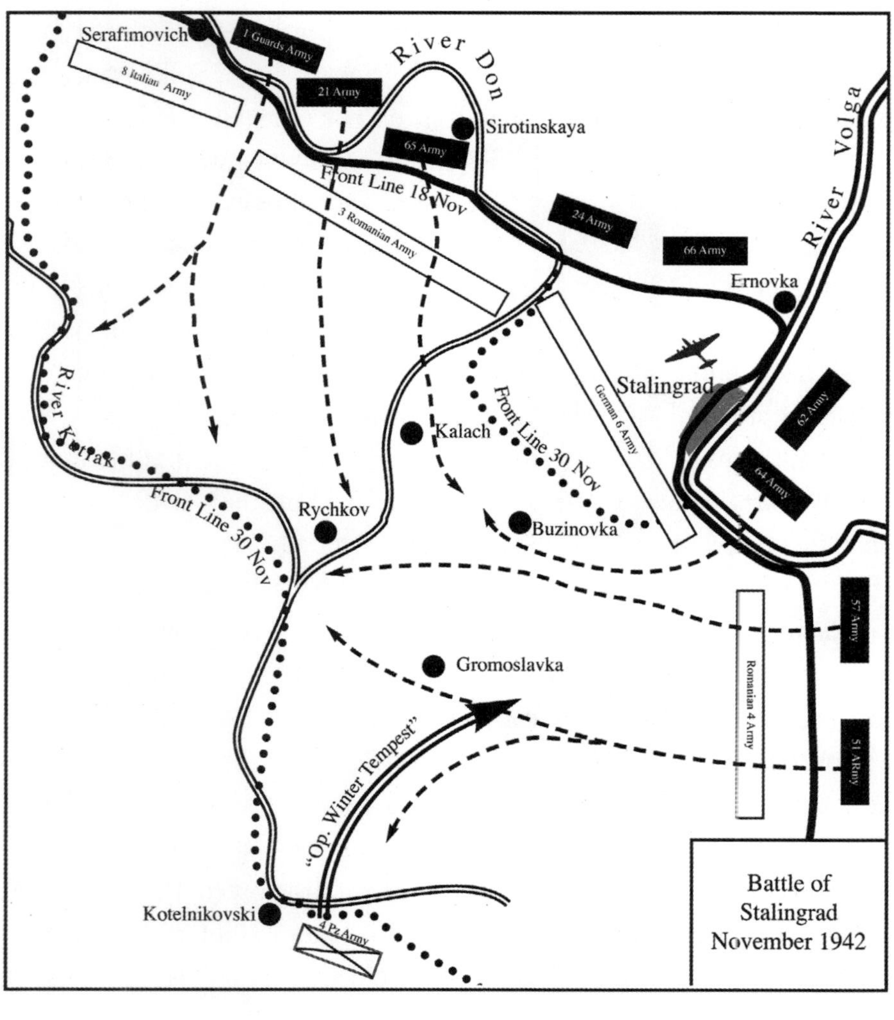

On 14 October two new armoured divisions and five infantry divisions pushed forward on a front that was just three miles wide. They found themselves lured into special killing grounds that the Russians had prepared, where houses and sometimes whole blocks or

squares had been heavily mined. Combat became so close that the Germans would occupy one half of a shattered building while the Russians occupied the other. When the Russians prepared a building as a stronghold they would destroy the stairs so that the Germans would have to fight for each floor independently. When it came down to hand-to-hand fighting it was usually the Russians who came off best. If they lost a building, the survivors would be sent back with the first counterattack to retake it. That day, 14 October, according to Chuikov, was 'the bloodiest and most ferocious day of the whole battle'.

The Germans pushed forward towards the tractor factory by the sheer weight of numbers but the Soviets reinforced it with 2,300 men. After an entire day, the Germans had taken just one block. Although it took enormous casualties, however, the tractor factory eventually ended up in German hands and the Soviet forces were pushed back so close to the Volga that boats bringing supplies across the river came under heavy machine-gun fire.

Next door to the tractor factory, the ruined Red October factory looked as though it might fall too but at the last moment a Siberian division was put in. Its men were told to fight to the death. They dug in amongst the shattered concrete, twisted girders, heaps of coal and wrecked railroad trucks. Behind them were the icy waters of the Volga – there was nowhere to retreat to.

Unable to dislodge the fanatical Siberians, the Germans bombarded them with mortars, artillery and dive-bombers. But the Siberians had dug a series of interconnecting trenches, dugouts and strong points in the frozen ground around the factory. When the barrage was lifted and the German armour and infantry went in they found themselves under blistering attack. After forty-eight hours of continuous fighting hardly a man was left of the leading Siberian regiment, but the German offensive had been halted.

The onslaught on the Red October factory continued for the next two weeks. The Germans made 117 separate attacks – twenty-three on one single day. The Siberian division held out, backed by artillery from across the river that was directed by observation posts hidden in the ruins.

'Imagine Stalingrad,' wrote a German veteran, 'eighty days and nights of hand-to-hand fighting. The streets are no longer measured in metres, but in corpses. Stalingrad is no longer a town. By day it is an enormous cloud of burning, blinding smoke. It is a vast furnace lit by the reflection of the flames.'

Paulus's offensive was at a standstill. The defenders of the city were unyielding and he had no more men to throw against them. For the moment there was a stalemate, but winter was on its way. Then the sixth Army received reinforcements in the form of a number of battalions of Pioneers. These would be used in the vanguard of a new offensive along a front just 400 yards wide. Instead of fighting from house to house, they would move through the sewers, cellars and tunnels under the city.

The offensive began on 11 November with a bombardment that turned what remained of the city into rubble. The first rush of fresh troops took the Germans through the last 300 yards under the city to the bank of the Volga. When they reached it, however, the Russians emerged from their hiding places behind them, cutting them off. The German advance troops were trapped but surrender was not an option. They were far past the point at which prisoners were taken. The attack collapsed into sporadic pockets of desperate, hand-to-hand combat in hidden caverns under the rubble and on both sides men fought with unmitigated savagery. The troops were filthy, smelly, unshaven and red-eyed. They were high on vodka and benzedrine. No sane, sober man could fight in such conditions. After four days, only Russians were left. Then a terrible silence fell over Stalingrad – the silence of death.

At first light on 19 November the air was full of

sound again when 200 Russian guns opened fire to the north of the city. On the next day hundreds more opened up to the south. While the Germans had been exhausting their forces by fighting inside the city, Zhukov had been busy building up a new army, massing 900 brand-new T34 tanks, 115 regiments of the dreaded Katyusha multi-rocket launchers, 230 artillery regiments and 500,000 infantrymen.

Two spearheads attacked the northern and southern tips of the German forces. The German flanks were turned fifty miles north and fifty miles south of Stalingrad and the Red Army rushed forward to encircle the German forces inside the city. This took the Germans completely by surprise. Paulus had imagined that the Russian reserves were drained and that the German High Command was bracing itself for a new Russian winter offensive against Army Group Centre at Rzhev. The flanks of Paulus's Army were held by Rumanian troops who were ill-equipped and had little stomach for fighting. As far as they were concerned, this was Germany's war.

The Germans never knew what had hit them. They found it impossible to judge the scale or the direction of the offensive. Paulus sent some Panzers to the north but they could not stem the tide there. Twenty miles to the rear of the main German forces besieging Stalingrad was the town of Kalach and the bridge across the Don that was a vital part of Paulus's supply line. Demolition charges had been placed so that the bridge could be blown up if the Russians threatened to take it, but on 23 November the Russians took them by surprise by turning up in a captured Panzer. They machine-gunned the guards and removed the demolition charges.

Meanwhile, the Russians' southern pincer had smashed through the Germans' lines and had turned northwards so that the two spearheads met at Kalach that evening. They had encircled 250,000 Germans and made the most decisive breakthrough on the Eastern Front. One Italian, one Rumanian and one Hungarian army had been defeated and 65,000 prisoners taken. Three days later the Russians had deployed thirty-four divisions across the Don and were breaking out to the north. Some armoured columns stayed behind to trouble Paulus's rear, while Russian infantry moved around the Germans and dug in. More than 1,000 anti-tank guns were deployed to prevent a German break-out and the Germans menacing Stalingrad were hit by heavy artillery from the other side of the Volga.

Hitler told Paulus to hold his ground until

Some 91,000 Germans were taken prisoner at Stalingrad. Few would return from Soviet captivity. In all 300,000 Germans were lost in the battle. From Stalingrad, the Germans would suffer one long, almost uninterrupted, retreat.

'Fortress Stalingrad' was relieved. Göring told Hitler that his Luftwaffe could fly in 500 tons of stores a day. Paulus was not wholly convinced and aware that the winter was imminent he prepared a force of 130 tanks and 57,000 men for a break-out. Hitler countermanded this. He had still not given up on his hope of capturing Stalingrad and so he ordered General Erich von Manstein, author of the tank attack through the Ardennes, to collect up the remaining Axis forces in the region and relieve Paulus.

Reinforcements were rushed to Manstein from Army Group Centre at Rzhev and Army Group A in the Caucasus. The attack began on 11 December and was led by Hoth and his Fourth Panzer Army. Following them was a convoy of trucks carrying 3,000 tons of supplies. They would make their attack from the southwest and punch their way into the city where Paulus was still holding his position. The ground was frozen, which made it good going for the Panzers and the heavy snow made them difficult to spot. The Russians in Stalingrad were also having a hard time and ice floes coming down the Volga menaced their ferries.

However, the Russians also knew how to turn the snow to their advantage. The winter sky had deprived the Germans of air reconnaissance. As Hoth made progress towards Stalingrad, he did not notice the Russians who were hidden behind the snow in the gullies that criss-crossed the landscape. At dusk and dawn, T34s would emerge and attack the infantry's trucks and the supply convoy that followed the Panzers. The German armour would then have to halt, turn around and deal with them, thereby slowing the advance. However, on 17 December Hoth reached the Aksay River, thirty-five miles from Stalingrad, where Zhukov had sent 130 tanks and two infantry divisions to meet him.

The powerful XXXXVIII Panzer Corps was planning an attack to relieve Stalingrad from the northeast but 450 Russian T34s suddenly came rumbling across the ice of the Don. They smashed the Italian, Romanian and Hungarian armies in that sector and pushed on towards Voronezh. The XXXXVIII was so busy containing this thrust that a counter-thrust towards Stalingrad was out of the question.

To the south, Hoth was in trouble as his northeastern flank crumbled along its entire 200-mile length. Manstein now realised that the only hope for the 250,000 Germans in Fortress Stalingrad was for Paulus and Hoth to attack either side of the Russian line simultaneously. Paulus refused to try to break out and declared that Hitler had ordered him to stay where he was. There was to be no retreat from Stalingrad. Besides his ill-fed troops were not physically strong enough to make the attack and they only had enough fuel to travel for twenty miles, which would barely take them to the Russian lines. Göring was still promising that he would supply them and Hitler wanted Paulus's army in position for a new offensive in the following spring.

On 19 December Hoth crossed the Aksay and on the 21st Manstein told Hitler that it was vital for the Sixth Army to attempt to break out and meet him. However, Hitler backed Paulus so Manstein had no choice but to recall Hoth. He had lost 300 tanks and 16,000 men in the failed attempt to relieve Paulus. With Hoth pulling back, Army Group A also had to withdraw as it risked being cut off in the Caucasus.

The Sixth Army was now left to its fate. It was fanciful to believe that it could hold its position all winter. The infantry were running short of ammunition and the maximum allocation was thirty bullets a day. The Russians now had the 250,000 beleaguered Germans surrounded by 500,000 men and 2,000 guns. Meanwhile the retreating German forces were being chased out of southern Russia by a new Soviet offensive.

In an effort to free up more manpower, on 8 January the Soviets offered Paulus the chance to surrender on the best possible terms. There would be food for the hungry, medical care for the wounded, guaranteed repatriation for everyone at the end of the war and the officers would even be allowed to keep their weapons. But Hitler had taken personal charge of Fortress Stalingrad from his bunker in Poland and he refused these terms. Instead he promoted Paulus to the rank of Field Marshal and told him to fight on.

It had been estimated that the remains of the Sixth Army could be sustained on 550 tons of supplies a day – fifty tons more than Göring, at his most optimistic, had promised. The Luftwaffe had 225 Junkers Ju 52s available for the task. The nearest airfields were then an hour and a half away by air and it was assumed that each plane could make one flight a day. In fact only rarely were more than eight of the Junkers serviceable on any one day. Two squadrons of converted Heinkel 111 bombers were brought in, but they could only carry one and a half tons of supplies each. Then as Russians advanced the Sixth Army had to be supplied from airfields even further away. As the weather closed in, air supplies grew erratic. The Soviets massed anti-aircraft guns along the flight paths so the Sixth Army could then only be resupplied at night. In all, 536 German transport planes were shot down and the average supply drop fell to sixty tons a night. The bread ration was cut to one slice a day and one kilogram of potatoes had to feed fifteen men. The horses of the Rumanian cavalry were eaten. Dogs, cats, crows, rats, anything the soldiers could find in the ruins was consumed. The only drinking water came from melted snow.

As the tightening Russian noose forced them to retreat, the Germans found that they were too weak to dig new defences. They slept with their heads on pillows of snow. Frostbite was endemic and any wound meant that death was almost inevitable. Even if the wounded man's comrades were strong enough to carry him to the first aid post there were few medical supplies left and there was little that the doctors could do. Suicide was so common that Paulus had to issue a special order declaring it dishonourable. Even so, when the rumour circulated that the Russians were taking no prisoners, everyone kept one last bullet for themselves.

On 10 January the Russians began their final attack. The perimeter shrank by the hour. By 24 January, the Germans were forced back behind the line the Russians had held on 13 September. The command structure collapsed. Medical posts and make-shift hospitals were full of wounded men begging their comrades to kill them. The airstrips – their only lines of supply – were taken and the remnants of the Sixth Army were forced back into the ruined factories, the cellars and the sewers of the city. But still Hitler would not surrender.

Finally, on 30 January, Paulus's command post was overrun and he was captured. Two days later resistance was at an end. In all, 91,000 frozen and hungry men, including twenty-four generals, were captured. As they were marched away a Soviet colonel pointed at the rubble that was Stalingrad and shouted angrily at a group of German prisoners: 'That's how Berlin is going to look.' Two entire German armies were wiped out including their reserves. Some 300,000 trained men had been lost. They were irreplaceable. The battle had been a blood bath. In the last stages alone, 147,200 Germans and 46,700 Russians had been killed.

Stalingrad was the decisive battle on the Eastern Front. It humiliated what was once thought to be an invincible German army. On 5 February 1943 the Red Army newspaper *Red Star* wrote:

> *What was destroyed at Stalingrad was the flower of the German Wehrmacht. Hitler was particularly proud of the 6th Army and its great striking power. Under von Reichmann it was the first to invade Belgium. It entered Paris. It took part in the invasion of Yugoslavia and Greece. Before the war it had taken part in the occupation of Czechoslovakia. In 1942 it broke through from Kharkov to Stalingrad.*

Now it was no more. This was a terrible blow to German morale. With the destruction of the Sixth Army at Stalingrad, the German offensive in Russia was over. The tide had turned and the Red Army would eventually push the Wehrmacht all the way back to Berlin and beyond.

In captivity, the tide turned for Paulus too. Once one of Hitler's favourite generals, as a German prisoner of war he agitated against the Führer. If they did not make peace, he warned, the whole of Germany would be turned into one 'gigantic Stalingrad'. He joined the Soviet-backed 'Free Germany Movement', broadcasting appeals to the Wehrmacht to give up the fight. After the war, he testified at the International Military Tribunal at Nuremberg. After his release in 1953, he settled in East Germany and died in Dresden in 1957.

Kursk

The Greatest Tank Battle

1943

Kursk was the largest tank battle in history. It demonstrated that the Red Army could defeat the Germans in mechanized warfare – the very thing that had given the Nazis their astonishing victories earlier in the war.

AFTER THEIR DEFEAT at Stalingrad in the winter of 1943 the Germans were on the retreat in Russia. However, in the summer of 1943, they tried to seize the initiative once more. A huge salient 150 miles wide had developed around Kursk with the Soviet lines protruding a hundred miles westwards into the German lines. On 15 April 1943 Hitler ordered Operation *Zitadelle* ('Citadel') to 'encircle the enemy forces situated in the region of Kursk and annihilate them by concentric attacks'. The German tank strategist General Heinz Guderian opposed this. He feared that they would suffer heavy tank casualties, tanks that they would not be able to replace in 1943. The new Panther tanks that the plan depended on were suffering teething troubles and he thought that they should be 'devoting our new tank production to the Western Front to have mobile reserves available for use against the Allied landings which could be expected with certainty to take place in 1944'.

General Walther Model, commander of the German Ninth Army on the Eastern Front, was also against the operation. It might have been successful in March, he said, but in May it had no chance. He produced air reconnaissance photographs that showed that the Russians had prepared strong defences at Kursk in anticipation of a German pincer movement and had withdrawn most of their mobile force from the salient. But Hitler ordered the assault to go ahead 'for political reasons'.

As it was, the Panther tanks were not ready until the end of May and the operation was put back until 15 June. By that time the Germans had assembled an assault force of fifty divisions – 900,000 men. These would be led by seventeen armoured divisions with 2,700 tanks and mobile assault guns.

The problem was that the Soviets knew what the

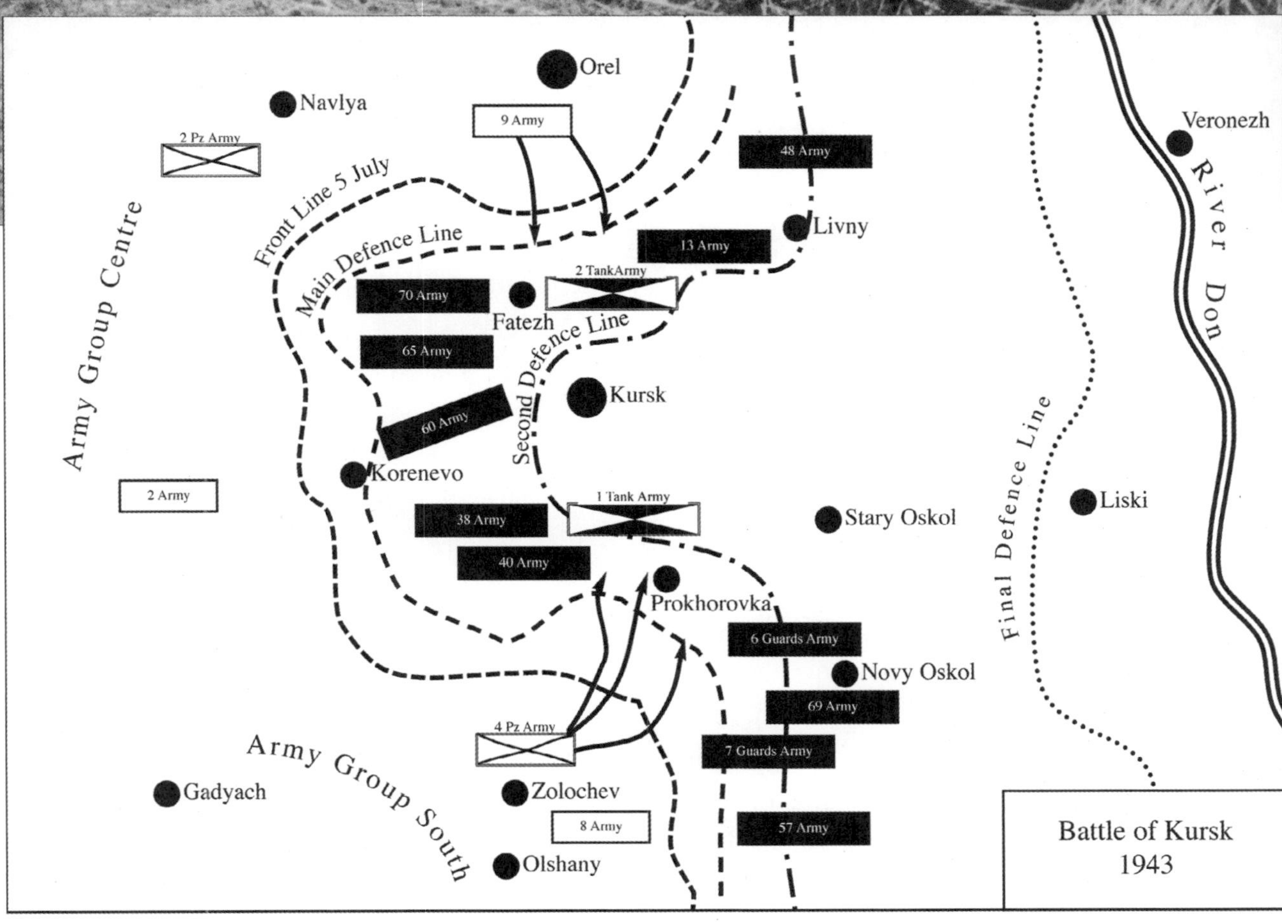
Orel
Navlya
9 Army
2 Pz Army
48 Army
Veronezh
River Don
Front Line 5 July
Main Defence Line
Livny
13 Army
2 TankArmy
70 Army
Fatezh
Army Group Centre
65 Army
Second Defence Line
Kursk
60 Army
Final Defence Line
Korenevo
2 Army
1 Tank Army
Stary Oskol
Liski
38 Army
40 Army
Prokhorovka
6 Guards Army
Novy Oskol
69 Army
4 Pz Army
7 Guards Army
Army Group South
Gadyach
Zolochev
8 Army
57 Army
Olshany
Battle of Kursk
1943

Not only were the Germans defeated in tank battles on the ground, the Red air force easily took control of the skies from the Luftwaffe. The Soviets were now on their way to Berlin.

Germans were planning. Soviet spies had infiltrated the German High Command and Stalin heard of Operation *Zitadelle* 48 hours after Hitler had issued his orders. The Red Army had plenty of time to organize defences between sixteen and twenty-five miles deep into the salient. Their plan was to let the Germans exhaust themselves in their offensive and then smash them in a counter-offensive. Soviet intelligence was so comprehensive that Stalin knew how many divisions he faced and how they were equipped. He also had details of the chain of command, the position of the reinforcements and the supply columns and the exact timing of D-Day and zero hour. This allowed the Russians to lay 400,000 mines that would channel the German armoured units into nests of anti-tank guns.

The Soviet defences were formidable. They had 6,000 anti-tank guns, 20,000 other artillery pieces, howitzers and mortars and 920 rocket launchers. They outnumbered the Gemans in the field with seventy-five divisions and 3,600 tanks. In all, there were two million men , supported by 4,000 aircraft.

The German offensive was put off until 5 July, giving the Soviets more time to prepare their defences – which easily outstripped the German offensive capability. Some twenty minutes before zero hour the Soviets bombarded the German assembly points. German Panzers were used to making lightning attacks but by the evening of the first day they had advanced only six miles through the Soviet

defences. One reason was that the new tanks had been built with a cannon but no machine guns, making them useless against infantry.

The northern thrust of the pincer was halted on the second day just twelve miles from the start line. The southern arm manage to penetrate twenty miles and when they were eight days into the battle they had taken 24,000 prisoners and destroyed or captured a hundred tanks and 108 anti-tank guns. Even so the gap between the two jaws of the pincers was still seventy-five miles. On 12 July, the Soviets announced that the first phase of the battle was over. They launched an offensive of their own against the Germans' Orel salient immediately to the north.

Hitler now faced a dilemma. He had already lost 20,000 men. His offensive had stalled and he now had to withdraw some of his forces to defend Orel. Meanwhile British and American forces had landed in Sicily on 10 July, opening a second front. Troops would have to be sent to defend southern Italy. As a result Hitler called a halt to *Zitadelle*.

The Soviets now had the initiative. They boasted an artillery barrage that was 'ten times heavier than at Verdun'. The aim was to bombard the German minefields, blowing up as many mines as possible in order to reduce Russian casualties in their advance. Overhead there were huge air battles with heavy losses on both sides, but the Red Army broke through after three days.

Behind the German lines partisans began blowing up the railways to prevent supplies and reinforcements reaching the front. On the night of 20–21 July alone 5,800 pieces of track were blown up. In all, between 21 July and 27 September there were 17,000 attacks by partisans on the railways. The Germans were forced to abandon the Orel salient, burning the crops behind them.

To the south things were no better. The Germans were outnumbered by seven to one. And the Soviets kept bringing up reinforcements. Hitler refused to allow the troops there to withdraw to new defensive positions and on 30 July a Panzer group had a limited success, forcing the Red Army back over the River Mius. They left behind them 18,000 prisoners, 7,000 tanks and 200 guns. However, on 3 August the Soviets pounded the gap between the German armies to the north and the south of Kursk and sent a huge mechanised force through the breach. Within four days, they had advanced seventy miles.

German Panzer groups roamed the battlefield fighting sporadic actions, but nothing could halt the Soviet onslaught. While the Germans lost men as they pulled back, the Red Army gained conscripts with every mile they took. The German army fought on for almost two years but after Kursk there was nothing they could do to prevent the Red Army from driving forward all the way to Berlin.

British positions at Kohima, Burma, where the Royal West Kents, with support from 1st Punjabis, held out against overwhelming Japanese attacks for fourteen long days in April 1944.

Kohima & Imphal

Fourteenth Army Holds the Line

1944

The Japanese had taken over south-east Asia with astonishing speed. They seemed invincible. But when they tried to take India, the British and Indian armies used new tactics to turn them back.

KOHIMA IS A TOWN in the Naga Hills in northeast India. It lay on the only road from the British railhead at Dimapur, thirty miles to the northeast, to the supply depot in Imphal, sixty miles to the south. From April to June 1944, it was the site of one of the most bitterly-fought battles of the Second World War.

India had always been a target of Japan's expansion during the Second World War. However, the Japanese High Command had long considered that moving troops across the terrain of Upper Burma made the task almost impossible, particularly since General Charles Orde Wingate's irregular forces, the Chindits, successfully operated behind Japanese lines.

By 1944 the Japanese had suffered repeated defeats at the hands of the Americans in the Pacific and needed a victory to boost their morale. The High Command decided on a 'March on Delhi'. In addition to dealing a crippling blow to the British Empire by installing an Indian nationalist government under Subhas Chandra Bhose, head of the 7,000-man Japanese-backed Indian National Army, they would knock out the America air bases that were supporting the anti-Japanese nationalist forces in China.

However, at the same time, General William Slim – whose Fourteenth Army had already halted the

Japanese advance at Chittagong (now in Bangladesh) and Impal in India – was planning the reconquest of Burma. For eighteen months he had been building up logistical bases at Imphal and Dimapur.

In early 1944 the Japanese Fifteenth Army – under the command of General Renya Mutagachi, 'the victor of Singapore' – received orders to put a stop to the British preparations in Assam and march on northern India. The Japanese offensive was known as 'U-Go'. Within it three Japanese divisions, the 15th, the 31st and the 33rd, were assigned to the destruction of the Anglo-Indian forces at Kohima and Imphal. Another offensive known as 'Ha-Go' to the south on the coast at Arakan was aimed at drawing off reserves. However, the Japanese were unaware that the British and Indian troops based in Assam in 1944 were properly trained for the coming battles, unlike their predecessors in 1942. Slim had also developed new tactics. Instead of the wholesale retreat in front of the invading Japanese that had characterized the British campaigns in the early part of the war, British units would now stay put and allow themselves to be surrounded in strongly-defended positions where they could be supplied by air. This would effectively halt the Japanese offensive because they could not risk leaving the enemy in the rear. It also gave them the problem of supplying the besieging forces while their supply lines were being harassed by the Chindits.

The Japanese plan was for the 31st Division to split into three columns that would cut off the Kohima-Imphal Road and surround the hill station from three different angles. Meanwhile the 15th and 33rd divisions would surround Imphal to the south. By 22 March elements of the British IV Corps – the 17th, the 20th and the 23rd Indian Divisions – that were based in and around Imphal were engaging the

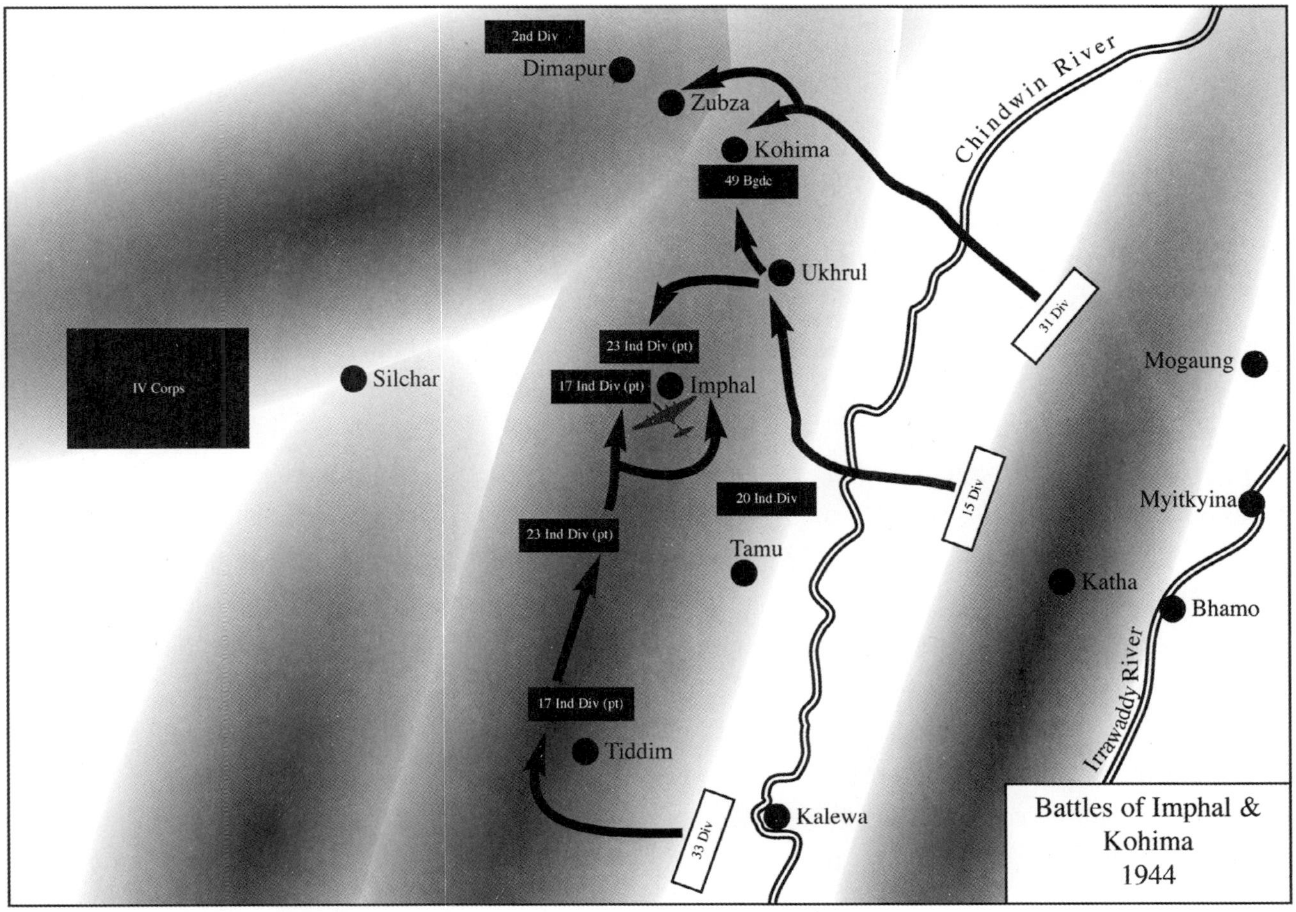

first of the Japanese troops. Then on the 24th came the bad news that Wingate had been killed in a plane crash while visiting his troops in northern Assam.

General Slim knew that a major Japanese offensive was underway, but British intelligence had assumed that no more than a few battalions would be able to cross the system of parallel ridges, some as high as 7,000 feet, between the Chindwin River and Kohima. However, with the Kohima-Imphal road cut off, and the town surrounded, it became clear that an entire Japanese division was bearing down on Kohima.

The only troops stationed in the Kohima area were a few units of Assam Rifles and the 1st Assam Regiment, who had been stationed east of Kohima and had pulled back after heavy fighting. Slim sent the 5th and the 7th Indian Divisions – who had seen action in Arakan – by air to reinforce both Imphal and Kohima.

The battle-hardened 161st Indian Brigade of the 5th Indian Division was flown to Dimapur in late March. From there it moved down the road towards Kohima. By early April, it was setting up defensive positions in and around the hill station. They dug in with a series of trenches along Kohima Ridge. The bitterest fighting would take place on Garrison Hill and a long wooded spur on a high ridge to the west. The position was so small that only one battalion of the 4th Royal West Kent Regiment could be deployed there. The remainder of the 161st Indian Brigade and its artillery were placed in Jotsoma, two miles west of Kohima. Units from Jotsoma were sent forward to reinforce the 4th Royal West Kents during the fighting.

By the evening of 5 April the defenders had just assumed their position when more than 12,000 men of the Japanese 31st Division attacked. Realising that they were vastly outnumbered the 4th Royal West Kents were forced to shorten their defences. After the first assault, they withdrew from the more isolated positions, thereby giving the Japanese significant inroads into the ridge and handing over positions they were preparing for their own defence. However, on 7 April morale was boosted when reinforcements in the form of the 4/4 Rajput Regiment arrived from Jotsoma.

On 8 April, the Japanese launched a series of attacks on the northeast defences.. By the 9th the British had been forced back. There was hand-to-hand combat in the garden of the district commissioner's bungalow and around the tennis court. By then, the Japanese had cut the road between Jotsoma and Dimapur and the tracks between Jotsoma and Kohima. The defenders of Kohima could expect no more reinforcements and on 10 and 11 April they were again forced to shorten their lines.

The defenders of Kohima halted the Japanese advance and forced the 31st Division into a battle of attrition. This was very much to the advantage of the British, who were supplied daily by air. The Japanese had not carried supplies with them, thinking that they would take what they needed from the British. They were soon reduced to eating bamboo shoots, grubs and whatever they could find in the jungle. The siege lasted thirteen days and Earl Mountbatten, the supreme allied commander in Southeast Asia, described it as 'probably one of the greatest battles in history.. the British–Indian Thermopylae', and praised the 'naked heroism' of the defenders.

On 13 April, the Japanese launched another assault against the British positions on the ridge. The troops who were mounting a defence around the district commissioner's bungalow came under increasingly heavy artillery and mortar fire. They also had to repel frequent infantry assaults and bayonet charges, with grenades being tossed across the tennis court. These attacks were eventually beaten off by the artillery on Jotsoma ridge, which found itself under attack. Again, however, the British

Lieutenant-General Sir William Slim, commander of the Fourteenth Army in Burma. 'Uncle Bill', as his troops affectionately knew him, was one of the greatest military strategists of the Second World War.

and Indian troops there were able to fight off the Japanese.

The turning point of the siege came on 14 April. While the Japanese kept up their artillery bombardment of Kohima and Jotsoma, there were no infantry attacks. The Japanese now realized that their position was impossible. Observing that his men were starving, the commander of the 31st Division, General Sato, asked to be allowed to withdraw. However, General Mutaguchi, who was commanding the action from a pleasant hill station some 300 miles behind the lines, told him that the throne of the Emperor depended on his staying in place. Sato remained even though other commanders were replaced and he was warned that he would be court-martialled if he retreated.

Meanwhile the 2nd British Division had arrived at Dimapur and were coming to down the road to Kohima, destroying Japanese roadblocks on their way. Morale soared when news of this reached Kohima on the 15th.

The Japanese launched one last desperate attack on the evening of 16 April. Positions changed hands more than once in heavy fighting, but mounting casualties forced the British to withdraw to the Garrison Hill. This tiny enclave was assaulted from the north, the south and the east. The position seemed hopeless but on the morning of 18 April the British artillery opened up from the west against the Japanese positions. The 2nd British Division had arrived with tanks from XXXIII Corps. But it was only when a tank was manhandled onto the tennis court that the Japanese were forced from their positions and the siege was lifted. The defenders had suffered over 600 casualties. The last Japanese were only driven out of the Kohima area on 13 May. None were captured and the surrounding jungle reeked of unburied corpses.

While Kohima was being attacked, Imphal valley was completely surrounded by the Japanese army, who had installed heavy artillery on the hilltops. However, they had no air support because all the Japanese aircraft were needed in Arakan, where British forces were then counterattacking. The attack on Imphal was headed by Netaji ('Respected Leader') Subhas Chandra Bose and the India National Army, but they did not receive the help they expected from the local people. However, two Japanese soldiers disguised themselves as local workers, stole an aircraft from the airstrip at Palel and dropped leaflets which claimed that Bose had come to liberate India from the British. The leaflets also allied him with the pacifist independence leader Mahatma Gandhi. That episode made little difference but on 14 April 1944 the Indian tricolour was hoisted for the first time at Moirang, thirty miles south of Imphal on the Tiddim road.

Imphal itself was besieged by the Japanese 15th Division, which had surrounded the town, dug-in on the peaks to the north and cut the Kohima road. The difference was that, unlike Kohima, Imphal had an airstrip. Captain P.A. Toole of 305 Field Park Company in the Indian Army landed there in a Dakota in early April 1944. He recorded that when he arrived there was a blazing plane at the end of the runway and gunfire in the distance. 'I had been through the blitz but this was real war and not like the movies,' he said.

He was lucky. Many planes were lost. Although there were no Japanese aircraft in the skies, landing at Imphal was tricky under continuous ground firing from the tops of the hills. By then the Japanese had caught on to the trick of having a Royal Air Force fighter circle the valley several times in order to confuse the Japanese artillery, while the cargo planes put down on the airstrip below. Even so, the air campaign was successful. Dakotas flew in food and other supplies, including forty-three million cigarettes to maintain morale and 12,000 sacks of mail. The RAF also evacuated 13,000 casualties. Out in the jungle, the Japanese received nothing from the outside. Behind the Japanese lines the Chindits had destroyed the railways in Burma and prevented 300 trucks from getting through.

On 22 June 1944 the Fourteenth Army joined the column advancing down the road from Kohima and made contact with the IV Corps who were holding Imphal. Ukhrul, a Japanese stronghold to the east, between Imphal and Chindwin, was cleared by mid-July with heavy Japanese casualties. At Bishenpur to the south the Japanese 33rd Division held out against the 17th (Black Cat) Division, but they were eventually routed when the British artillery bombarded their positions so heavily that not a single leaf was left on the trees.

By early August 1944, Myitkyina, 200 miles to the east in Burma, was captured. This left the Japanese around Imphal stranded. The monsoon was at its peak and the Japanese soldiers suffered from the heat, the plague, mosquitoes, malaria, hunger, shortage of ammunition and homesickness. Subhas Chandra Bose's dream of liberating India failed. He flew back to Singapore and was never heard of again. Meanwhile the sick and malnourished Japanese soldiers retreated through the hills and plains of Manipur. Despite the monsoon, the British started an advance that would be the beginning of the reconquest of Burma. The Japanese Fifteenth Army was finished. Some 50,000 bodies were counted on the battlefield but how many more were left unburied in the jungle is not known.

Slim was knighted at Imphal by the viceroy on 15 December. His Fourteenth Army went on to retake Burma, destroying the Japanese and INA forces there. However, the war was ended by the atomic bombs that were dropped on Japan in August 1945. Any further action against the Japanese in South-east Asia was unnecessary and the men who had fought so gallantly at Kohima and Imphal began to see themselves as part of the 'forgotten army'.

D-Day
The Liberation of Europe
1944

The Red Army were advancing from the east. The Western Allies were moving up the Italian peninsula. But it was not until the Allies made an amphibious assault in Normandy that the cage slammed shut on Hitler.

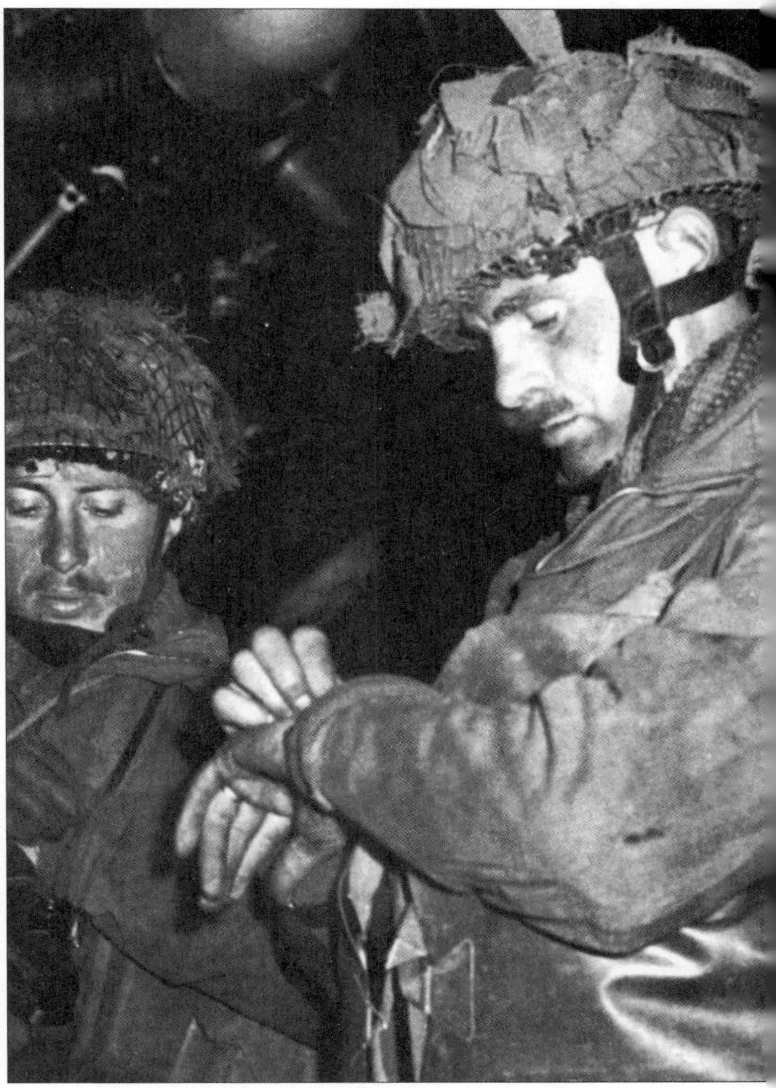

British airborne troops synchronize watches before spear-heading the attack on Normandy before dawn on 6 June, 1944. Their task was to seize key bridges behind the beaches.

SINCE THE SOVIET UNION had come into the Second World War in 1941, it had been urging Britain to begin a second front in western Europe. When the US entered the war, they wanted to make an attack on the Germans in France as soon as possible but the British were more circumspect. Having been in the war longer that their new allies, the British felt that it would be foolish to risk everything in a single reckless operation. Many of the British commanders had experience of the carnage of the First World War and were afraid of throwing men against enemy lines in a frontal attack – which is inevitable if you make an amphibious assault against a fortified coastline. As First Lord of the Admiralty in the First World War, Churchill himself had been responsible for the disastrous amphibious assault at Gallipoli in the Dardanelles where 250,000 men, largely Australians and New Zealanders, were lost before the 83,000 survivors could be evacuated. Britain's worst fears were realised when 5,000 Canadians, 1,000 British and fifty US Rangers staged a disastrous raid on the Channel port of Dieppe in August 1942, for 2,600 men were lost. The American Army was still untested, so President Roosevelt was persuaded to join the war in North Africa.

When this was brought to a successful conclusion, Churchill proposed an attack on the 'soft underbelly of Europe'. On 10 July 1943 an Anglo-American force landed in Sicily. Italian resistance collapsed and on 25 July Mussolini fell from power and was arrested. The German forces, under Field Marshal Kesselring, were then evacuated from Sicily and prepared themselves to defend the Italian mainland.

On 2 September, a small Allied force landed on the 'heel' of Italy and quickly captured the ports of Taranto and Brindisi. On the following day Montgomery's Eigth Army crossed the Strait of Messina and landed on the 'toe' of Italy, meeting with little resistance. That same day the new Italian government agreed to change sides and its capitulation was announced on 8 September. On 9 September the combined US–British Fifth Army under General Mark Clark landed on the 'shin' at Salerno. This was where Kesselring had expected the attack to come. The situation was precarious for six days, but the Fifth Army eventually broke out, taking Naples on 1 October.

Italy declared war on Germany on 13 October 1943. This was not unexpected, and Kesselring had already consolidated his hold on central and Northern Italy. He also held the Allies at the Gustav Line, a defensive line that ran right across the narrow peninsula of Italy some sixty miles south of Rome. To circumvent this, the Allies landed 50,000 men north of the Gustav Line at Anzio. They met with little resistance, but instead of driving directly on to Rome the landing force stopped to consolidate the beachhead. Kesselring quickly counterattacked, almost pushing the Allies back into the sea.

The main Allied force was held up by the German defenders at Monte Cassino, a mountain-top monastery that occupied a pivotal position on the Gustav line. The Eighth Army was then switched from the Adriatic side of the peninsula to the western flank. The Allies managed to breach the Gustav Line to the west of Monte Cassino on the night of 11 May 1944. It was then outflanked and it fell to the Polish Corps of the Eigth Army on 18 May. On 26 May, the main Allied force joined up with the beachhead at Anzio and on 5 June 1944 the Allies drove into Rome.

However, progress on such a narrow front as the Italian peninsula was bound to be slow and it did little to divert German strength from the Russian front. By this time the Red Army was making good progress against the Wehrmacht. By sheer weight of numbers it would eventually overwhelm the German army and overrun Germany. Even if the Allies pushed Kesselring all the way to the Alps it would have been impossible to cross them before the Red Army had swept right across Germany, perhaps also taking the rest of western Europe as many people feared. By the spring of 1944 a landing in France was politically vital.

The delay in staging an amphibious assault across the English Channel gave the Germans time to fortify the coastline. They built what they called the

Rommel inspects an artillery battery in the Atlantic wall. Although the Germans knew a cross-Channel invasion was imminent, a brilliant British deception operation led them to believe that it would come at the Pas de Calais, not in Normandy.

'Atlantic Wall', which ran down the west coast of Europe from the Arctic Circle to the Pyrenees. By the time of the invasion 12,247 of the planned 15,000 fortifications had been completed, along with 943 along the Mediterranean coast. Also 500,000 beach obstacles had been deployed and 6.5 million mines had been laid.

The huge extent of the wall was partly the result of a campaign of misinformation called Operation *Fortitude*. The British had used this ploy to feed the Germans with the idea that a landing might come anywhere at any time. Hitler would have to spread his forces thinly in order to defend his empire against attack from the west.

At the beginning of the war, the British had arrested every German spy in Britain. They had turned many of them into double agents so that they could be used to feed false information back to their spymasters in Hamburg and Berlin. Disinformation was also conveyed by means of the radio traffic that the Germans intercepted. The British had also broken the German Enigma code, so they were

British troops of the 13th/18th Hussars suffer a temporary hold-up on the beaches. Their casualties are relatively light compared with those of the Americans on Omaha beach.

able to know if their deception was working or not. On occasion the British even fed the Germans the information that the invasion would come in the South of France or Norway, or perhaps through the Balkans or the Black Sea. This meant Hitler had to disperse his troops to the four corners of his empire.

However, the major thrust of Fortitude was to convince Hitler that the western Allies would take the most direct route. They would take the shortest Channel crossing at the Straits of Dover to the Pas-de-Calais. It would be easy for them to support the landings with air and artillery cover from England at that point. Also, it would give them the shortest route to Paris and even Germany itself. This deception was reinforced by the fictional First US Army Group, a non-existent army apparently mustered in Kent, ready for embarkation at Dover. Radio traffic poured out of Kent and set builders from theatres and film studios were employed to make mock tanks and landing craft that would look like the real thing in German aerial reconnaissance photographs. One badly-wounded prisoner of war, a Panzer officer who was being returned to Germany, actually saw the First US Army Group with his own eyes – although the tanks and trucks he saw were not in Kent at all but in Hampshire, ready for embarkation at the southern ports. He was also introduced to General Patton, who had been represented to German intelligence as the commanding officer of FUSAG. Hitler became convinced that FUSAG existed and that this was where the attack would come from. So much so that he kept his mighty 15th Army in the Pas-de-Calais and his Panzers east of the Seine for seven weeks after the Allies had landed on the beaches in Normandy.

The Calvados coast in Normandy was chosen as

the site of the landings because it had a number of wide flat beaches. The forces that landed on them would then be able to join up quickly and form a single bridgehead. It was poorly defended, however. The fortifications there and in other places had been built by slave labourers who had weakened them by deliberate sabotage. Many of the defenders were Russians, Poles or other Eastern Europeans who had little motivation to fight against the Americans or the British. Any Germans who were there were either too old to fight on the Russian front or else too young. Others had been wounded in action.

The other advantage enjoyed by the Calvados coast was its lack of a major port. The conventional wisdom was that for an invasion to succeed the landing force would have to seize a port in order to get men and materiel ashore quickly enough to defend themselves against a counterattack that would aim to push them back into the sea. This was another reason why Hitler and his High Command were so convinced that the attack would come in the Pas-de-Calais, where there were three ports – Calais, Boulogne and Dunkirk. However, the raid on Dieppe had taught the British that an attack on a heavily-defended port was not a good idea. Even if a landing force managed to take it, the Germans had placed demolition charges within the harbour facilities of all the ports they had occupied. Once these had been set off they would render the port useless and the invasion would inevitably fail. Instead, British planners came up with an ingenious solution – the Allies would bring their own harbour. Two prefabricated 'Mulberry' harbours would be built in sections which would then be towed across the Channel and assembled at the landing beaches. The Americans laughed when they first heard the idea, but began to take it very seriously when they realised that landing in an area that had no existing port would give the invasion force the element of surprise.

The Allies' plans were well advanced when, in November 1943, Hitler sent his most trusted commander, now Field Marshal Erwin Rommel, to take charge of the Atlantic Wall. He found it wanting, especially in Normandy and he began to strengthen it. Then, just a week before the Allied landings, the battle-hardened 352nd Infantry Division, direct from the Russian Front, was posted to man the defences along what was to become Omaha Beach.

Southern England had become a huge parking lot for tanks, trucks and aeroplanes during the late spring of 1944. There were weapons and ammunition dumps in country lanes and village pubs were full of soldiers from every part of the English-speaking world, along with Poles, Czechs, Hungarians, Free French and Jews from Germany, Austria and all parts of Nazi-occupied Europe. In all, more than six million people were involved in the D-Day landings. Twenty US divisions, fourteen British, three Canadian, one French and one Polish division were billeted in southern England, along with hundreds of thousands of other men who be-

Assault troops of a Royal Navy demolition unit went ashore from landing craft to blow up beach obstacles which would have made the amphibious landings impossible.

longed to special forces and headquarters units. There were also communications staff and corps personnel. Then suddenly, as this huge force made its way to the embarkation ports, silently at night, these men simply disappeared.

In the ports, waiting out to sea, were the 138 battleships, cruisers and destroyers that would bombard the French coast. They were accompanied by 279 escorts, 287 minesweepers, four line-layers, two submarines, 495 motor boats, 310 landing ships and 3,817 landing craft and barges for the initial assault. Another 410 landing craft would join them as part of the ferry service that would get more personnel and equipment ashore after the beachhead had been secured. A further 423 ships, including tugs, would be involved in the construction of the Mulberry harbours; the building of the 'Pluto' pipeline that would pump petrol under the Channel; and the laying of the telephone cables that would connect the commanders on the ground to SHAEF (Supreme Headquarters, Allied Expeditionary Force) in London. Another 1,260 merchant ships would also be involved in supplying the landing force, making a total of over 7,000 vessels.

Some 10,000 aircraft were also deployed in Operation Overlord. They would bomb key fortifications, drop paratroopers, tow gliders carrying airborne troops, attack enemy formations and protect the airspace above the beaches.

For political reasons the head of the invasion needed to be an American and Churchill got on well with General Eisenhower – who had demonstrated his competence as a commander in Operation Torch and the landings in Sicily and Italy. However, four British officers under Eisenhower were actually running the landings – Air Marshal Sir Arthur Tedder, Eisenhower's deputy; Admiral Sir Bertram Ramsay, in charge of the operation at sea; Air Chief Marshal Sir Trafford Leigh-Mallory, responsible for air operations; and General (later Field Marshal) Bernard Montgomery, the leader on the ground. This caused some resentment among American officers, who felt that they should have been represented at the high levels of command. However, one reason for the choice of Eisenhower as supreme commander was his skill in handling the rivalries between British and Americans.

When Montgomery was appointed on New Year's Day 1944, he first threw away the invasion plans that the American planners had been working on since 1942. He considered that the front in the American plan was too narrow and that the assault force was not big enough to do the job. He raised the number of divisions landing on the beaches from three to five and the number of airborne divisions from one to three. Montgomery presented his plan to the military commanders and senior politicians at St Paul's School in West Kensington on 15 May 1944. It was accepted. A key part of the plan was that equal numbers of British and American troops would be landed on D-Day itself. But as losses mounted the battle-ravaged British would be unable to sustain this commitment, while the US had an almost bottomless well of recruits. Eventually, the war in western Europe would become a predominantly American affair. In order to reflect this, Eisenhower himself would take over command of the land forces once the beachhead was well established.

D-Day was to be 5 June 1944. By then the Allies had complete air superiority over France and the bombing campaign had softened up the enemy. Much of it was directed against the railways in order to prevent men, weapons and ammunition being brought to the front. Bombing and sabotage by the French Resistance had knocked out 1,500 of the 2,000 locomotives that had been available. Eighteen of the twenty-four bridges over the Seine between Paris and the sea had been destroyed, along with most of those over the Loire. Marshalling yards, crossings and other vital parts of the railway system had been attacked and bombs and rockets had knocked out nearly all the radar stations along the northern coast of France.

As 5 June approached, the fine, sunny days that had lasted throughout May came to an end. The defenders along the Atlantic Wall, who had been kept on constant alert by false alarms for months, began to believe that the Allies had missed their chance. Rommel himself took the opportunity to go back to Germany to see his wife on her birthday. On the following day, 6 June, he was to have a meeting with Hitler.

The first-wave Allied troops had already embarked on 4 June when the weather worsened and a storm blew up. Eisenhower had no option but to postpone the invasion. However that night the meteorologists calculated that there might be a break in the weather on the following day and Eisenhower gave the order for the invasion fleet to sail. Broad lanes across the channel had been swept by navy minesweepers and as the invasion fleet headed out to sea huge waves of RAF heavy bombers flew overhead to bombard the coastal defences with 5,200 tons of bombs. As dawn broke on 6 June, the USAAF's medium bombers and fighters took over and continued the pounding of the emplacements behind the invasion beaches.

Under Montgomery's plan the US had two landing beaches – Utah at the base of the Contentin peninsula and Omaha further to the east, along the Calvados coast. The three British beaches – Gold, Juno and Sword – lay further still to the east. The two fronts were each about twenty miles long. During the night, between midnight and 03.00, one British and two American airborne divisions landed on what Hitler called Festung Europa (Fortress Europe) behind the Atlantic Wall. The British 6th Airborne Division landed east of Caen to seize vital bridges across the River Orne in order to prevent the Panzers that were stationed to the east from attacking the landing force's left flank. In addition, the American 82nd and 101st Airborne dropped at the base of the Contentin peninsula in order to prevent troops stationed in Cherbourg from counterattacking. They were also charged with securing the causeways across the flooded areas behind the invasion beaches.

The paratroopers had been carried across the Channel on 1,100 planes from twenty different airfields. The British paratroopers were dropped too far east, but they caught the enemy by surprise all the same. They took the village of Ranville and secured the landing zones for the gliders that would bring in more men and anti-tank guns about two hours later. These aircraft dropped close to the bridges and seized all but one of their objectives – the bridge at Troarn that carried the main road from Caen to Le Havre and Rouen. A team under Major Rosveare then grabbed some explosives, commandeered a jeep, drove hell-for-leather for the bridge and blew it up. Meanwhile 150 British paratroopers attacked the coastal battery at Merville that covered Sword beach. After fierce hand-to-hand fighting that cost half their number the paras captured the battery and destroyed its guns.

The American airborne landings fared rather worse. Heavy flak and clouds caused the transports to disperse. The pilots flew too high and too fast scattering the paratroopers of the 101st Airborne over an area of 375 square miles. Of the 6,100 men that had been dropped, only 1,000 made it to their rendezvous point. The 82nd had better luck and managed to capture St Mère Église on the road from Cherbourg. It was the first town in France to be liberated and, by dawn, the Stars and Stripes fluttered outside the town hall in the place where the Nazi swastika had hung for four years. The American gliders also had a bad time. Only twenty-two of the fifty-two gliders landed in the drop zones and most were badly damaged on impact. This left the airborne troops short of transport, signals equipment and anti-tank guns, which made it impossible for them to capture the bridges across the River Merderet. The paratroops that were dropped west of the Merderet found themselves in a region bristling with German strongpoints. They were so widely dispersed that all their efforts went into survival rather than securing their objectives. But although they did not take the bridges, they fully engaged the German 91st Division where it stood and it made no move against the beaches.

Throughout the night, German headquarters received sporadic reports of paratroopers landing. Because the troops and the French resistance had set about cutting the telephone wires, however, it was impossible for anyone in command to get a clear picture of what was going on. At 02.45 General von Rundstedt's headquarters received a report saying: 'Engine noise audible from the sea on east coast of Cotentin.' This was dismissed and the Germans only became aware of the impending invasion when the landing craft were twelve miles off shore. Even then, it was thought to be a diversionary attack to draw the German defenders away from the Pas-de-Calais where the real invasion would come.

At first light, a combined Allied fleet of 200 warships began bombarding the Normandy coast. Then the landing craft started their run-in. The seas were heavy and most of the men, who had been fed a hearty breakfast, were seasick. To add to their misery they were soon soaked to the skin from the spray as waves broke over the front of the landing craft. A piper played a highland reel in the front of one of the British landing craft. In another Major C.K. 'Banger' King of the East Yorkshire Regiment read stirring extracts from Shakespeare's Henry V over the Tannoy. In front of the landing craft that carried the troops was a line of amphibious tanks. Behind those were craft carrying artillery and multiple rocket launchers which began to bombard the Germans. The German fortifications had been built to stand bombing and naval gunfire. Although the occupants were dazed from the bombardment, most of the emplacements were still intact and they were ready to mow down the infantry as they came rushing from their landing craft. However, they did not expect to be fired on by artillery mounted on the landing craft, nor were they ready for the sight of amphibious tanks trundling up the beaches ahead of the troops.

There were more surprises. Tanks fitted with huge revolving drums of flailing chains were landed in order to clear the minefields. Other tanks carried bridges, or bundles of logs that could breach walls or fill in ditches. Some tanks were even fitted with flame-throwers for clearing out machine-gun nests. The whole idea of the Atlantic Wall was to destroy the invaders before they had a chance to get off the beaches. This would prove to be impossible.

Montgomery's plan was for the British to engage the German Panzers in the vicinity of Caen. They would then hold them there before finally destroying them. Meanwhile the Americans were to clear the Cotentin peninsula. Once they had taken Cherbourg, the Allies could build up their strength and break out of the beachhead to the south. The key to this was for the British 1st Corps, which landed on Sword and Juno beaches, to join up with the 6th Airborne on the Orne. The British 3rd Division landed on Sword beach, near the mouth of the Orne, and took less than an hour to secure the beach and push inland. They had travelled nearly two miles from the shore when they were stopped by the German infantry and the 88mm self-propelled guns of the 21st Panzers. This took the British troops by surprise. They had been extensively trained for fighting on the beaches, where many of them expected to die. Once they had survived that, they were not quite sure what to do and it took eight hours before they linked up with the 6th Airborne.

To the west of the British sector, the 50th Division – which had seen action in North Africa – and the 8th Armoured Brigade fought their way through the enemy defences within an hour. By 12.00 the beach-

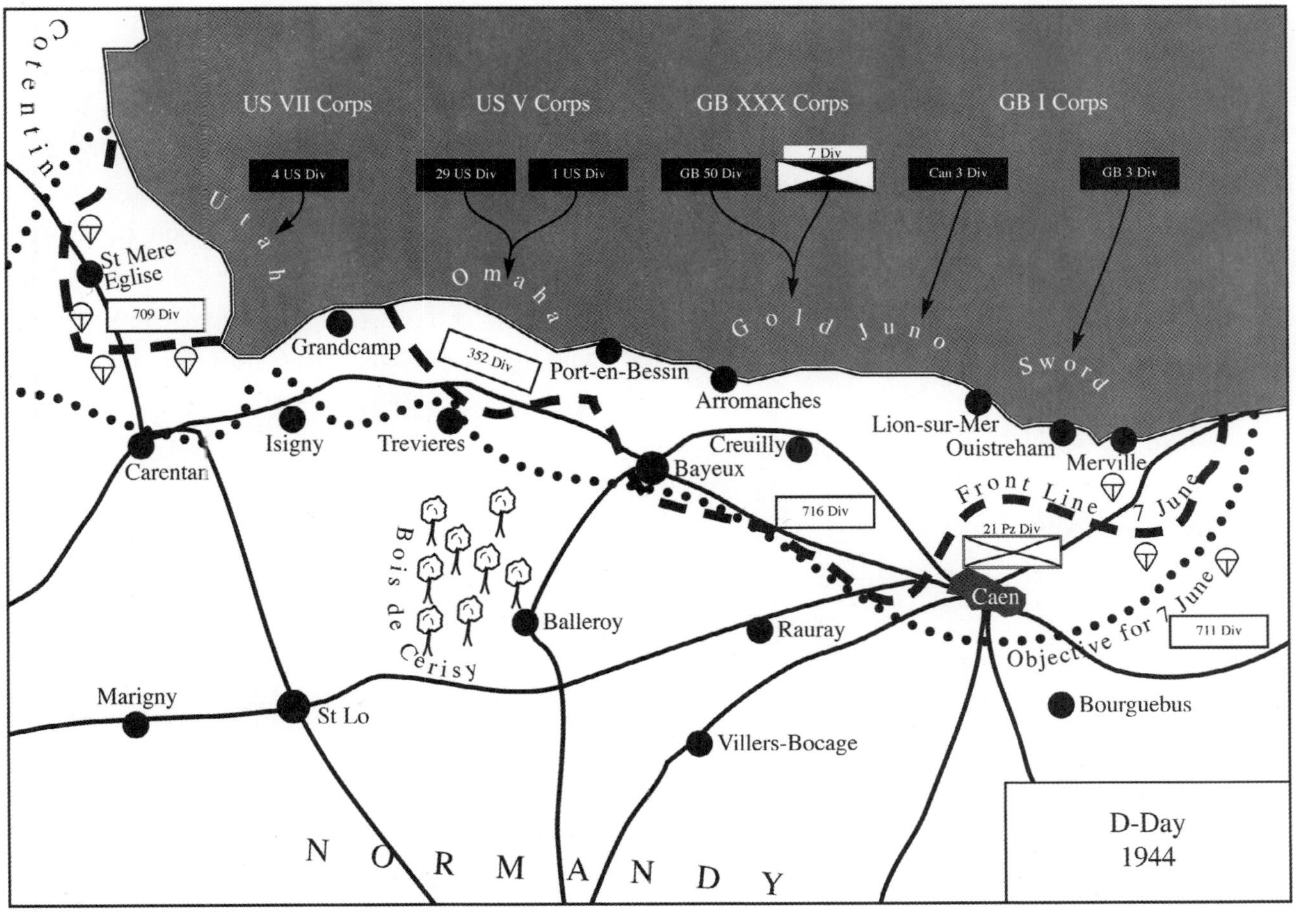

head was three miles wide and two and a half miles deep. The British infantry and armour, supported by further naval barrages, had cleared the beaches around Arromanches, the site of one of the Mulberry harbours, by sunset. At that, word was sent for the harbour's huge cassons to begin their journey back across the Channel. By the time it was dark, British patrols had reached the outskirts of the historic town of Bayeaux and the 50th Division's beachhead was six miles wide and six miles deep.

The Canadians who landed on Juno beach, between Sword and Gold, had a harder time because their landing zone was obstructed by a reef which delayed their landing by half an hour. The amphibious tanks and the obstacle-clearing tanks that should have gone ashore ahead of the infantry were held back. When the tanks finally came ashore, it still took the Canadians several hours to overcome the enemy strongpoints at the mouth of the Seulles. At that point they found that they did not have the specialized armour they needed to clear the beach exits and men and vehicles backed up onto the sands.

For the men of the US 3rd Infantry Division, Omaha Beach would become their Calvary

To the east of Juno the lack of tanks meant that the Canadians took heavy casualties in the hundred-yard dash to the shelter of the sea wall. However, a ship almost beached herself to bombard the German defences and the Canadians began to stream off the beach. By nightfall, they had taken the town of Bernières and had travelled seven miles inland – the furthest any of the Allied forces had reached on the first day. When they were probing the main Bayeaux-Caens road within three miles of Caen they joined up with the British 50th Division. The result was a combined Anglo-Canadian beachhead that was twelve miles long and almost seven miles deep.

On Utah beach, to the west of the American section, thirty-two amphibious tanks went in under a huge bombardment that was provided by two battleships, two cruisers and twelve destroyers. Twenty-eight of the tanks managed to cover the two miles to shore. When the first wave of infantry hit the beaches and traversed the 500 yards to the foreshore, they found that they were met by only occasional gunfire. This sector had been lightly defended because the area behind it was flooded and no attack had been expected there. The 4th Infantry Division had actually landed on the wrong beach. However, within three hours they had clear avenues through the beach obstacles and minefields and their tanks rushed forward to seize the causeways over the flooded areas.

By contrast the landings on Omaha beach were little short of a disaster. The beach itself was far from ideal. The 300 yards of sandy foreshore was backed by a steep bank of shingle. Behind that was a sea wall or sand dunes, beyond which was a plateau some 150 feet deep, with defensive positions along the top. Four ravines cut the face of the plateau. These were the only beach exits and they were well defended. At either end of the plateau the cliffs rose to a hundred feet in height.

Although the beach was unsuitable for an amphibious assault it was chosen because the Allies needed to take a beach between Gold and Utah if a single beachhead were to be established. But worse, this was where the battle-hardened 352nd Infantry Division had been stationed. The Allies knew this, but the American troops, who were new to combat, were not told in case it sapped their morale.

Omaha beach was more exposed that Utah and only four of the amphibious tanks managed to cover the four miles to shore without being swamped. Poor visibility meant that the initial bombardment had failed to neutralize the enemy's defences. The rockets from the multiple rocket launchers that followed the infantry had landed harmlessly in the shallows.

When the landing craft hit the beaches and their ramps were dropped the troops rushing out were met with a withering fire. Soon the sea was choked with blood and dead bodies. Those who survived did so by hiding behind the beach obstacles that the engineers should have blown up. The second wave of troops met a similar fate, apart from a small section who had managed to land on a part of the beach that was now wreathed in smoke. Almost a whole infantry company managed to reach the sea wall and pick their way through the minefield behind, but that was only because they had been blown to the east of their designated landing zone. Strengthened by a formation of Rangers who had come in behind, they made their way up to the plateau in time to prevent a counterattack on the beach. Even further to the east, two battalions had managed to get ashore under the cover of heavy smoke from burning undergrowth and a building set on fire by the naval bombardment. They made their way off the beach before the German artillery got the range of those who followed them.

The main force found themselves pinned down behind the shingle bank, where they were subjected to murderous machine-gun and artillery fire. Colonel G.A. Tayler rallied his regiment. 'Two kinds of people stay on this beach,' he told them, 'the dead and those who are going to die.' Some brave men then picked themselves up and attacked the German defences. Others scaled the cliffs to the left and moved off to join up with the British.

Even so, General Huebner, commanding officer of the 1st Infantry Division, realised that something drastic had to be done. He organized a further naval bombardment of the German fortifications, despite the risk of hitting his own men. The destroyers sailed so close to the shore that they were hit by rifle fire, but they did their job so effectively that the Germans came out with their hands up. It was not until 19.00, however, that the paths through the minefields had been cleared and the obstacles blown up or bulldozed aside so that the armour could leave the beaches. They then advanced on the fortified villages behind.

By dusk, the Omaha beachhead was only 1,200 yards deep. Beyond it the enemy was massing for a counterattack. Instead of pushing the Americans back into the sea at Omaha, though, the Germans rushed all their armour towards what they considered to be a greater threat – the British and the Canadians advancing on Caen. One battalion of the 352nd Infantry Division was sent to deal with the American paratroops in Cotentin and another was sent against the British, leaving only one battalion to check the Americans pouring off Omaha. On the following morning, the British from Gold turned eastwards to join up with the Canadians from Juno. Towards evening, they had cleared the remaining strongpoints between them and the British beaches now formed one continuous beachhead. However, the move on Caen had stalled. The landscape of northern Normandy is known as bocage country. This is characterized by small fields separated by thick hedges on high banks and sunken roads. It is easy terrain to defend. Hundreds of German tanks and 88mm guns were dug in and camouflaged and the Allied forces had to fight their way hedgerow by hedgerow through this country. However, the Allies' bombers, fighters and accurate naval gunnery support – which could lob shells inshore over a distance of sixteen miles – made it difficult for the Germans to gather themselves into the formations necessary to stage a concerted counterattack. The best the defenders could do was to slow the Allied advance rather than halt it entirely or turn it back.

Tank warfare expert Colonel-General 'Fast Heinz' Guderian had boasted that the Panzer Lehr would 'throw the Anglo-Americans into the sea', but their 260 tanks were beaten back by air assaults. On D+1

Although resistance along most of the beaches was surprisingly weak, there were still strongpoints inland. These had to be painstakingly eliminated.

an SS Division was sent to the front but it simply disintegrated under air attacks that employed bombs and rockets – its men ended up hiding in the woods until dark. The Allied planes did not even have to wait until the enemy reached the battlefield before engaging them. They would attack the trains that were bringing them to the front, sometimes at a distance of up to thirty miles.

Also on D+1 the American airborne troops had begun to form themselves into a coherent fighting force. The ten-mile stretch between the Utah and the Omaha beaches was still held by the enemy. However, with the help of RAF Typhoons and naval bombardment the Royal Marines from Gold beach had taken the small fishing port of Pont-en-Bessin, halfway between Gold and Omaha's left flank. On the following day, forces from the British and the American beaches linked up.

Montgomery kept up the pressure on Caen, often engaging in bloody battles that were designed to keep the enemy off balance. They were costly in terms of British casualties but they forced the Germans to use their tanks as dug-in artillery and they also took the pressure off the Americans. The

160 British troops who took the key village of Bréville suffered 141 casualties. Once it was taken, though, the eastern end of the beachhead was secure. After fierce fighting, US troops took Carentan on 12 June and the Omaha and Utah beachheads were finally joined, giving the Allies one huge enclave along the Normandy coast sixty miles long and fifteen miles deep. The German front in the west began to crumble. An American thrust across the Cotentin peninsula to Barneville on the Atlantic coast successfully cut off Cherbourg. Another push created a twenty-mile salient to the south.

By D+12, there were 500,000 men ashore. With twenty divisions now in Normandy, the Allies had managed to build up their forces faster than the Germans. The destruction of railways and bridges and the constant air attacks – the aeroplanes were now flying from airstrips inside the beachhead – made it impossible for Rommel to bring battle-ready formations into the area. Divisions had to be broken up and it was necessary to travel at night, with the infantry often on foot or on bicycles. Tanks could not be massed for a large assault on the beachhead so they were just used piecemeal to plug the line. Two SS Panzer Divisions brought in from the Eastern Front were devastated long before they reached the battlefield.

On 19 June, disaster almost overtook the Allies when the worst storm for nearly fifty years blew up in the Channel. It raged for over three days and three nights, during which time a dozen ships were sunk out at sea and 800 vessels were driven ashore. The Mulberry harbour at Arromanches was badly damaged but it was still useable. However, the one that lay off Omaha beach was smashed to pieces. Suddenly the Allies were not only short of supplies and ammunition but they were also robbed of their air cover. It was the perfect opportunity for Rommel to counterattack. But his forces were deployed for defence and were in no position to seize their last chance to push the Allies back into the sea.

Once the storm broke, the amphibious trucks used during the beach assaults were employed to ferry supplies ashore. By the end of the month the daily tonnage that was being landed was back to pre-storm levels. Bits of the Mulberry harbour at Omaha were salvaged and were used to patch up the one at Arromanches. Within two weeks 700 out of the 800 ships that had been beached were repaired and re-floated. By 27 June, the port of Cherbourg was in American hands but it had been so badly damaged and booby-trapped that it could not be used for several weeks.

The British had planned to attack Caen on the 19th. The attack had been delayed, however, and it was finally launched on 26 June. The British, with massive artillery support, managed to take the key highpoint, Hill 112, to the south of Caen. On the following day there was a massive armoured counterattack which employed the remnants of the SS divisions that had been brought in from Russia and a Panzer division brought up from the south of France. These formations came under withering air attack from the RAF's rocket-firing Typhoons. As the German tanks advanced through the bocage country, they were vulnerable to the British Piat anti-tank weapon that could be fired at close range from behind the hedgerows. Both sides still threw everything they had into the fray. A five-day battle raged over Hill 112 and the fighting became so intense that the little River Odon was dammed with human bodies. The result was a stalemate and the British did not completely overrun Hill 112 until 10 July.

It rained heavily throughout July. The fighting became literally bogged down and both sides feared that the battle for Normandy might turn into the kind of trench warfare and endless carnage that had been seen in World War I. Public opinion in Britain and America became restive. Meanwhile, Hitler replaced his commander in the west, Field Marshal Gerd von Rundstedt, with Field Marshal Gunther von Kluge, a hardened veteran of the Russian Front.

At the cost of 11,000 casualties, US troops had crossed the fields and marshes of western Normandy to take the smouldering ruins of St-Lô, which stood at the head of a good road that ran south to the Loire Valley. A plan with the codename of Operation Cobra was hatched to make a break-out here using a fast-moving tank column under General Patton. To pull this off, Montgomery would need to keep the German tanks pinned down to the east. The Canadians made an attack on the airfield at Carpiquet, suffering grievous casualties. The British then launched a renewed onslaught on Caen, after the RAF had dropped 2,500 tons of bombs on it. After two days of fierce fighting, the British captured the northwestern part the city, above the River Orne. A renewed attack from Hill 112 resulted in 3,500 British casualties.

'The battleground at Falaise was unquestionably one of the greatest killing-grounds of any war'

Montgomery planned to maintain the pressure with Operation Goodwood, a massive attack against prepared positions to the east and the south of Caen. On the eve of the battle, Rommel was shot in his staff car by the machine-guns of an RAF fighter, after which he took no further part in the fighting. He committed suicide while he was convalescing, after being implicated in a plot to kill Hitler.

The British lost 1,500 men and 200 tanks on the first day of Goodwood but still failed to make a break-through. However, they kept up the pressure for seventy-two hours before the offensive was halted by a thunderstorm. Goodwood had one unexpected effect, though. It finally convinced Hitler that there was not going to be an attack on the Pas-de-Calais – the Normandy landings were the real thing and so he ordered the 250,000 men of his Fifteenth Army into the battle. Because of the devastation caused by the Allies' air attacks it took them a month to reach Normandy. By that time the Allies had a million men ashore and the Fifteenth Army proved to be too little too late.

Montgomery took a great deal of criticism for the failure of Operation Goodwood. However, the Chief of the Imperial General Staff, Field Marshal Alan Brooke, pointed out that not only had it drawn in most of the German armour as planned but it had destroyed it faster than it could be replaced. General Omar Bradley, now commanding the US forces in Normandy, also appreciated the strategy. It had allowed him to get his men into position for a break-out.

Patton landed on Utah beach on 6 July without even getting his feet wet and he began to assemble his Third Army from a well-camouflaged bivouac on the Cotentin peninsula. With the Fifteenth Army on its way to the east of the front, Hitler felt that it was safe to move seven of his divisions, including two Panzer divisions, to the west, bringing the number there up to sixty-five. This strengthened the German line against any US break-outs but it also lured them into a death trap. On 25 July, 3,000 USAAF bombers dropped 4,000 tons of high-explosive fragmentation and napalm bombs onto a five-mile stretch of the German front to the west of St-Lô. The German commander General Bayerlein claimed that this raid turned the area into a *Mondlandschaft* – a moonscape. He estimated that seventy per cent of the German troops in that section were put out of action – they were either dead, wounded or demented. Patton's troops slowly moved forward through the bocage country – what the GIs called the 'Gethsemane of the hedgerows'. By 27 July, Coutances was taken and by 30 July, Avranches and the German retreat had turned into a rout. Within twenty-four hours, Patton pushed three divisions through the five-mile gap that had opened at

Avranches. His men were now out of the bocage country and onto the open roads of Brittany.

Montgomery was still making slow progress in the east and he turned his troops to the south with the Canadians advancing on Falaise. Bradley sent Patton and his Third Army on a long sweep south, then east, to encircle the Germans. Hitler saw the danger too late. He had ordered von Kluge to remove four armoured divisions from the British front and deploy them against the Americans, but von Kluge could not disengage them until 7 August. Hitler planned a counterattack against the bottleneck at Avranches. His aim was to close the gap and cut off Patton's supply lines. But he was 800 miles away in his headquarters, the Wolf's Lair, in East Prussia. His commanders on the ground in Normandy were against the attack. They knew that the battle of Normandy was lost and that they should make an orderly retreat across the Seine.

Hitler threw in the four divisions of the Fifteenth Army that he had been holding back at the Pas-de-Calais. Allied bombers cut off the German retreat by bombing the remaining bridges along the Seine. Meanwhile Patton was making quick time across the open roads of northwest France, taking Le Mans on 8 August. To the north, on their way to Avranches, five Panzer and two infantry divisions ran into a single American division at Mortain. The Americans held them until other Allied units came to their help. Powerful US formations struck back through Vire, while the British pushed down from the north against Condé and Patton turned up towards the north to close the trap. The Germans were now caught in a small pocket between Mortain and Falaise, where the Allied air forces relentlessly bombed and strafed them. By 14 August, the only way out was through an eighteen-mile gap between the Canadians at Falaise and Patton's 3rd Army. Patton wanted to drive on to Falaise and close the gap but by then his speeding army had lost its coherence and Bradley ordered him to stop. By this time German units were being cut down by the French Resistance or surrendering wholesale to the Allied forces. Von Kluge got lost in the confusion. Soon after he reappeared he was relieved of his command and afterwards committed suicide. By 17 August the Falaise gap was down to eleven miles and the German forces were streaming eastwards though it. By 18 September, it had been squeezed into six miles and air attacks on it were so relentless that any attempt to get through it resulted in almost certain death. It was sealed on 20 August.

General Eisenhower said of the battle:

> *The battlefield at Falaise was unquestionably one of the greatest killing grounds of any of the war areas. Roads, highways and fields were so choked with destroyed equipment and with dead men and animals that passage through the area was extremely difficult. Forty-eight hours after the closing of the gap, I was conducted through on foot, to encounter a scene that could be described only by Dante. It was quite literally possible to walk for hundreds of yards at a time, stepping on nothing but dead and decaying flesh.*

Some 10,000 Germans were killed in six days in the Falaise Pocket and 50,000 prisoners were taken. Of the 20,000 to 50,000 who escaped, many more would be killed before they reached the Seine. Thousands more who were cut off elsewhere gave themselves up to the Allies. Two Panzer divisions and eight divisions of infantry were captured almost complete. In all, German casualties in Normandy amounted to 400,000 men, half of whom were captured. The Allies' casualties totalled 209,672 men, of whom 36,976 were killed. The Germans also lost 1,300 tanks, 1,500 guns and 20,000 vehicles. What remained of the German army in western Europe ran headlong for the German border. On 25 August 1944, after four years of occupation, Paris was liberated.

Iwo Jima

A Japanese Island Fortress

1945

Island-hopping across the Pacific, US troops met fanatical resistance from the Japanese who would rather die than surrender. But the battle for Iwo Jima would be more gruelling than anything they had met before.

WHILE THE WAR raged in Europe, US forces were island-hopping across the Pacific. They were still fighting in the Philippines and in Borneo when plans were created for the invasion of Japan. The planners decided that this would begin with landings on Kyushu, the most southerly of the major Japanese islands.

In the closing months of 1944, the B-29 Super-Fortresses that were stationed on the Mariana Islands, under General Curtis E. LeMay, began a campaign of bombing. But it was a round trip of 3,000 miles from Saipan to mainland Japan, a long flight even for the SuperFortresses. However if the US forces took the little volcanic island of Iwo Jima in the Bonin Islands, which lay some 760 miles to the southeast of Japan, they would halve the distance to Tokyo and, with fighters stationed there, the USAAF would be able to defend its bombers over their targets. Iwo Jima was a doubly important target because Japan considered the island to be its 'unsinkable aircraft carrier'. It was a radar and fighter base whose aircraft intercepted the Super-Fortresses on their bombing missions over Japan.

Irregularly shaped, Iwo Jima is about five miles long and anything from 800 yards to two and a half miles wide. The Japanese were determined to hold on to it. They garrisoned the island with 21,000 troops under Lieutenant-General Kuribayashi Tadamichi and it had the strongest defences of all the Japanese possessions in the Pacific. It had been under constant bombardment since the fall of the Marianas in July 1944, but the prolonged fighting in the Philippines had delayed the attack, giving the Japanese a few months to build up the island's already formidable fortifications. As on other Pacific

US Marines on Iwo Jima blow up a cave connected to the extensive Japanese network of underground defences, February 1945. The Japanese had built over 3 miles of tunnels on an island covering only 8 square miles.

islands, they had created underground defences, making the best possible use of natural caves and the rocky terrain.

For days before the landings, Iwo Jima was subjected to massive bombardment by naval guns, rockets, and air strikes using bombs carrying the recently developed napalm. But the Japanese were so well dug in that no amount of shelling or bombing could knock them out.

On 19 February, the Fifth Amphibious Corps under General Harry Schmidt went ashore on the south of the island. Schmidt confidently predicted that he would take the island in four days. But it was not going to be that easy. In fact, it was going to be the most costly battle in US Marine Corps history.

As the first wave of Marines crossed the beach, which was just 200 yards wide, they were caught in a savage crossfire and were pounded with mortars fired from pits just a few feet wide. Flame-throwers, explosives and tanks were needed to clear them. Of the 30,000 men who landed on the beaches on the first day, 2,400 were hit by the Japanese. The

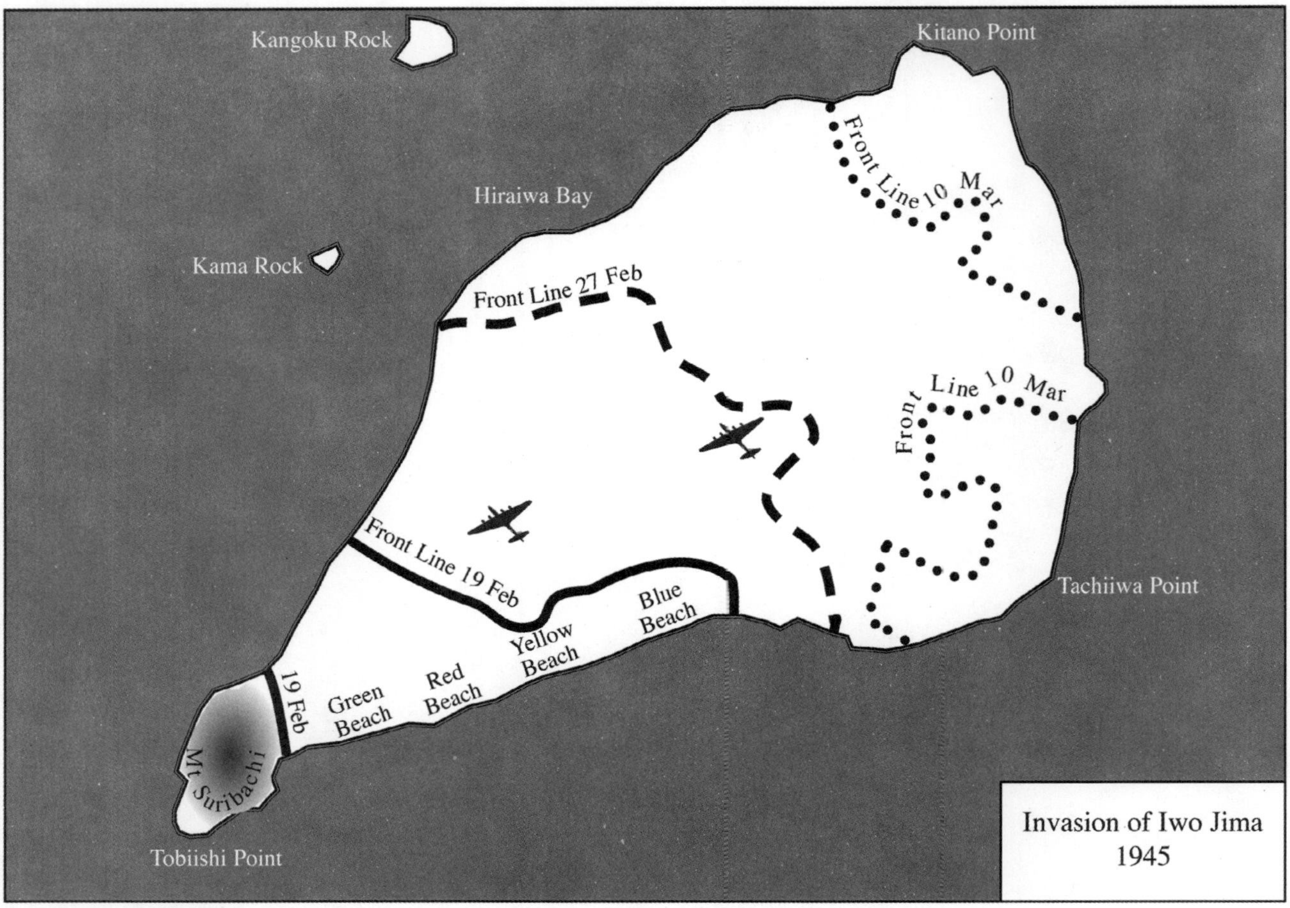

Marines soon had a 4,000-yard-long beachhead, but they could only move slowly inland because of the island's ashy volcanic soil.

The 5th Marines then divided their forces. Half struck inland and took the first of the two Japanese airfields – a third airfield was under construction. The other half turned south to take Mount Suribachi. Such was the strength of the Japanese positions that it was not until D+3 that Mount Suribachi was surrounded. On the next morning the 28th Marines occupied 200 yards of the lower slopes. Planes then pounded the Japanese positions.

On 23 February, the F Company of the 2nd Battalion came back from patrol and reported that the Japanese had gone to ground. A larger patrol under Lieutenant Harold G. Shrier eventually reached the crater and took the summit after a brisk firefight. The raising of the American flag by six Marines on Mount Suribachi was photographed by Joe Rosenthal of the Associated Press. It became one of the best-known images of the Pacific war and statues, paintings and American postage stamp designs have been based on it. The photograph actually depicts a second flag being raised over Mount Suribachi. The first flag was raised by Lieutenant Shrier some hours earlier, but it was too small to be seen by the other troops on the island and a bigger one, borrowed from a ship, was substituted for propaganda purposes.

While the 5th Marines moved up the west coast, the 4th Marines fought their way up the east coast. Despite a naval bombardment, air strikes and fire from Marine artillery, the 4th were stopped by mines and anti-tank guns. The 5th managed to take some Japanese emplacements under heavy fire and had advanced by 500 yards at the end of the first day.

The fighting was so intense that the 3rd Marines, a floating reserve, needed to be landed. They were to

The raising of the Stars and Stripes on Mount Surbachi was one of the most enduring images of the war. However, it was actually a recreation; a smaller flag had been erected on the summit earlier.

take the northern plateau, a strange lunar landscape that had been eroded into weird shapes by wind and rain. It was perfect defensive terrain for the determined Japanese force and flame-throwing tanks had to be brought up to incinerate them in the shell-proof bunkers. Eventually the Marines achieved the capture of all the hills overlooking the third airstrip and, by 28 February, all three airfields were in American hands.

The Marines had achieved their objective, but the fighting was far from over. They went on to attack Hill 382 and Hill 362A. Both hills were warrens of bunkers and tunnels. The crest of Hill 382 had been hollowed out to make a huge bunker that housed anti-tank guns and tanks were hidden in the gullies. To the south there was a natural bowl that had been named the 'Amphitheatre' by the Marines and a huge rock that was known as the 'Turkey Knob'. Marine casualties were so high in that area that these features were jointly known as the 'Meatgrinder'.

The Marines abandoned their normal practice and attacked at night when they attempted to capture the complex on Hill 362A. Even though they took the enemy by surprise, it took six days – from 2 to 8 March – to take the position.

Then, on 8 March, the Japanese counterattacked at a point between the 23rd and the 24th Marines. But the attack was over open ground, with no artillery support. They pulled back, leaving 650 dead.

The Marines continued up the centre of the island and by 9 March they had reached the northeast coast. On 15 March, the Japanese made a number of attempts to infiltrate the American lines, but were pushed back. The last pocket of resistance, at Kitano Point on the northern tip of the island, was reported secure on 25 March. However, on the following day some 350 Japanese emerged from the blackened rocks. It is said that they were led by Kuribayashi himself. They charged into the bivouac area where the men of the 5th Pioneer Battalion were sleeping. The Marines' 8th Field Depot and the US Army's VII Fighter Command set up a defensive line and by sunrise some 223 Japanese lay dead.

After that all resistance collapsed. Over 20,000 Japanese, including Kuribayashi himself, had been killed and only 261 were taken prisoner. The Marines and the Army lost 6,812 of their number and a further 19,189 were wounded. However, the lives of 24,761 American pilots and aircrew were saved by using Iwo Jima as a forward air base.

The Battle of Iwo Jima produced a costly but decisive victory. Now the all-out assault on the Japanese mainland could begin and, in the next five months, over 2,000 SuperFortresses flew bombing missions from the airfields of Iwo Jima. However, the scale of the recent fighting had left the Americans with a worrying question. If the Japanese had fought so ferociously for an island of just eight square miles, which they had only gained in 1891, what sort of resistance would the Americans face when they landed on the main islands of Japan itself?

Berlin

The Downfall of the Third Reich

1945

The war in Europe came to a terrible climax in Berlin. The city had already been damaged by RAF bombing. Red Army artillery would demolish it. Then the death of Hitler eventually brought Germany's capitulation.

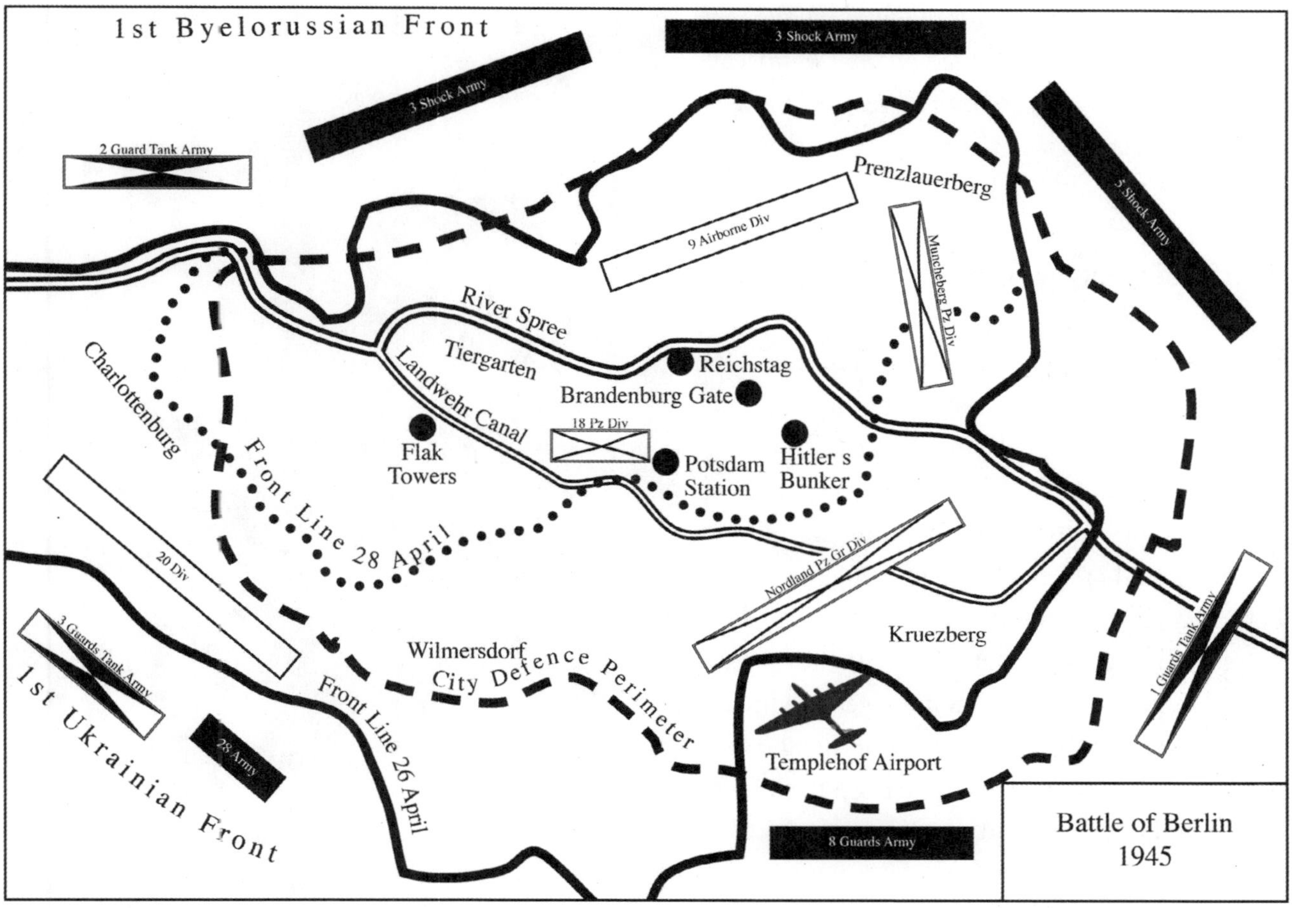

IN EARLY 1945, the race to Berlin was on. Although the Soviets had three army groups poised on the Oder-Neisse Line (now the Polish border) Montgomery's 21st Army Group was moving at such a pace it was thought they might get to the German capital first. Montgomery proposed using his overwhelming strength in a single thrust from the Ruhr that would take Berlin and finish the war. However, Eisenhower vetoed his plan.

Throughout the invasion, Eisenhower had favoured Montgomery over his own generals. Now he switched his resources to General Omar Bradley's 12th Army Group in southern Germany. He thought Bradley's forces could make a quick dash for the area around Dresden, where they could join up with the Red Army. This would then cut Germany in two. Eisenhower's fear, however, was that Hitler might abandon Berlin and retreat to the mountainous region of southern Germany, to continue the fight.

On 28 March, Eisenhower sent an outline of his plans to Stalin and asked about the Soviet plans. Churchill protested vigorously when he found out. He wrote to the ailing Roosevelt, pointing out the political necessity of taking Berlin as 'the supreme symbol of defeat'. But Churchill had another agenda. He was a fervent anti-Communist and he had been one of the architects of the 1919 Allied intervention into Russia, which attempted to strangle the Bolshevik state at birth. He now feared that the Russians might roll on across western Europe and he had even made plans to fight Stalin by re-arming the German army after Hitler's death. He wrote at the time:

If the Russians take Berlin, will not the impression that they have been the

overwhelming contributor to the common victory be unduly imprinted on their minds, and may this not lead them into a mood which will raise grave and formidable difficulties in the future?

It was of the utmost necessity that Berlin be taken by an Anglo-American force.

However, leaving the politics aside, Eisenhower was correct in military terms and his staff backed him. Stalin sent a reply on 2 April, in which he agreed that the plan for their two armies to meet up near Dresden was strategically sound. As a result, he said, he would only send a second-rate force against Berlin which had 'lost its former strategic importance'. Nothing could have been further from the truth. Stalin was a politician not a general. He knew the political importance of taking Berlin and he suspected that Eisenhower was playing a trick on him. Before he replied, he had spoken to his two senior field marshals, Ivan Konev and Georgii Zhukov. They were great rivals and both had begged for the chance to take Berlin. He gave them each forty-eight hours to come up with a plan.

Although Stalin told Eisenhower that he intended to attack Berlin in May, Konev and Zhukov were clear that he wanted to do it before that, even though their armies were exhausted after weeks of heavy fighting. Konev's 1st Ukranian Front – or Army Group – was on the eastern bank of the River Neisse, some seventy-five miles southeast of Berlin. He proposed starting his offensive by employing 7,500 guns in a two-and-a-half-hour artillery bombardment. At dawn, he would lay smoke and then force a river crossing with two tank armies and five field armies – over 500,000 men in all. He would keep his tanks on his right. They would smash through the German defences and then swing northwest and dash for Berlin. Unfortunately, two of the armies within his planned force were only the subject of a promise – they could not be relied upon.

Zhukov's 1st Belorussian Front was on the Oder river, fifty miles east of Berlin, with a bridgehead on the western side of the river at Küstrin.

His plan was to begin by using 10,000 guns in a pre-dawn bombardment. He would then turn 140 anti-aircraft searchlights towards the German defenders, thereby blinding them while he attacked. Two tank armies and four field armies would stream out of the Küstrin bridgehead, with two more armies on each flank.

With complete air superiority, and 750,000 men at his disposal, Zhukov was confident of a quick victory.

After Hitler had committed suicide, it seemed there was nothing left to fight for, but there were still bands of fanatical Nazis who maintained pockets of resistance.

Stalin gave Zhukov the green light because he was closer to Berlin and also better prepared. However, he encouraged the rivalry between the two field marshals by informing Konev that he was free to make a dash for Berlin if he thought he could get there before Zhukov. The starting date for the offensive was set at 16 April. The two field marshals had just thirteen days to prepare.

The Americans entered the race on 15 April when Lieutenant-General William Simpson's Ninth Army crossed the Elbe. The only obstacle between the Ninth Army and Berlin was the remainder of the German Twelfth Army, commanded by General Walther Wenck. This force would be able to do little to prevent Simpson from making a dash for the capital. However, Eisenhower ordered Simpson to halt on the Elbe until the link-up with the Red Army had been made at Dresden.

Three red flares lit up the skies over the Küstrin bridgehead at 04.00 on the following morning. They were followed by the biggest artillery barrage that had ever been mounted on the eastern front.

The Reichstag, Germany's parliament building, was a key objective for the Red Army. A fire there in 1933 had been used as an excuse for the beginning of Hitler's repression.

Mortars, tanks, self-propelled guns, light and heavy artillery – along with 400 Katyusha multiple rock launchers – pounded the German positions. Entire villages were blasted into rubble. Trees, steel girders and blocks of concrete were hurled into the air. Whole forests caught fire. Men were deafened by the guns and blinded by the Russian searchlights, a new and not altogether successful tactic. After thirty-five minutes of bombardment, the Soviets attacked.

In his fortified bunker under the Reichschancellery, Hitler still believed that he could win. He predicted that the Russians would suffer their greatest defeat at the gates of Berlin because his maps told him so. They were still covered by the little flags that represented SS and Army units. Unfortunately, most of these little flags were just that – little flags. The units they represented had long since ceased to exist or were so chronically under strength

that they were next to useless. Anyone who pointed this out was dismissed. Even Guderian was relieved of his position as Chief of the General Staff on 28 March for suggesting that it was time to negotiate.

Hitler also sacked *Reichsführer* Heinrich Himmler, the chicken farmer who had become Hitler's secret policeman and the architect of the Holocaust, from his position as Commander of the Army Group Vistula – which had not seen the Vistula, the river that runs through Warsaw, for some time. He was replaced by a veteran military man, Colonel-General Gotthard Heinrici. At his disposal was the Third Panzer Army, under General Hasso von Manteuffel, which occupied the northern part of the front. The centre was held by General Theodor Busse's Ninth Army while the south was held by the depleted army group of Field Marshal Ferdinand Schörner. And he could call on thirty other divisions in the vicinity of Berlin.

Heinrici was an expert in defensive warfare. He had pulled his front line troops back on the eve of the Soviet attack so that Zhukov's massive bombardment fell on empty positions. The Ninth Army had dug in on the Seelow heights, blocking the main Küstrin–Berlin road and Zhukov's men, who were attacking further down the road, suffered terrible casualties. The Russians eventually overwhelmed the Seelow line by the sheer weight of numbers, but then they came up against more German defences, reinforced by General Karl Weidling's 56th Panzer, and were halted. Stalin was furious. He ordered Konev, who was making good progress to the south, to turn his forces on Berlin. And on 20 April Marshal Konstantin Rokossovsky's 2nd Belorussian Front made a separate attack on von Manteuffel.

Busse's Ninth Army began to disintegrate at this point and Zhukov got close enough to Berlin to start bombarding the city with long-range artillery. Konev's forces were also approaching from the south and the German capital was caught in a pincer movement. To ensure the Americans did not snatch their prize at the last moment, both Zhukov and Konev sent forces to meet up with Simpson on the Elbe. They made contact at Torgau on 25 April, only to find that he was sitting there facing no-one. Two days earlier, Wenck had been ordered back for the defence of Berlin. On 28 April he had reached the suburbs of Potsdam where he had met with fierce Soviet resistance. He managed to extricate his force and then tried to link up with the remains of the Ninth Army. At that point he moved westwards in the hope of surrendering to the Americans. Hitler cursed his treachery, and ordered his arrest. Busse and Wenck would struggle through the forests south of Berlin and surrender to the Americans.

What propaganda minister Joseph Goebbels now called 'Fortress Berlin' was defended by 90,000 ill-equipped boys from the Hitler Youth and elderly men from the *Volkssturm* or Home Guard. The two million Berliners still trying to go about their business in the ruined city joked: 'It will take the Russians exactly two hours and fifteen minutes to capture Berlin – two hours laughing their heads off and fifteen minutes to break down the barricades.'

Himmler and other top Nazis then left the city but Hitler refused to go. For a while he pretended that the situation could be reversed and he issued a barrage of orders to his non-existent armies. Then, as the Soviets drew the noose tighter and 15,000 Russian guns began to pound the city, Hitler abandoned his pretence of being in control and announced that he would commit suicide before the Russians arrived.

As Soviet troops entered the city, Hitler sacked his designated successor, Göring, for trying to take over while he was still alive, and Himmler, for trying to put out peace feelers to the British and the Americans. Grand Admiral Karl Dönitz was named as his new successor. Then the news came that Mussolini was dead. Captured while trying to escape into Austria in a German uniform, he was executed along with his mistress, Claretta Petacci, on 28 April, and their bodies were hung upside down in the Piazza Loreto in Milan. On 29 April, Hitler married his faithful mistress Eva Braun. He dictated his will and his final political testament on the following day. That afternoon, Hitler and his wife of one day committed suicide in their private quarters. Their bodies were burnt in a shallow trench in the Chancellery Gardens.

The troops of both Zhukov and Konev were now in the city. However, Konev was ordered to halt to give Zhukov's men the honour of raising the Red Flag on the Reichstag. Zhukov's resultant popularity was quickly seen as a threat by Stalin, who banished him to obscurity in 1946.

There were still pockets of resistance in the city, and those who remained in Hitler's bunker tried to negotiate surrender terms. The Soviets would accept nothing but unconditional surrender – which General Weidling conceded on 2 May. The surrender of the German forces in northwestern Europe was signed at Montgomery's headquarters on Lüneburg Heath on 4 May. Another surrender document, covering all remaining German forces, was signed with more ceremony at Eisenhower's headquarters at Reims. And at midnight on 8 May 1945, the war in Europe was officially over.

It is not known how many people perished in the Battle of Berlin. Estimates put the number of German dead as high as 200,000 and the Russian losses at 150,000. The Soviet troops then went on an orgy of drinking, looting and raping. It is thought that as many as 100,000 women were raped – often publicly – during that period in Berlin, and an estimated two million in the whole of eastern Germany. The Russians often shot their victims afterwards. Other women committed suicide. In one district of Berlin alone, 215 female suicides were recorded in three weeks.

At the Yalta conference in the Crimea in February 1945 it had been agreed that Berlin would be divided between the four powers – Britain, France, the US and the USSR. By the time the Four Power Control Commission arrived to take control, the orgy was over. Almost immediately, the Cold War started. The part of the city in the hands of the western powers became West Berlin – an enclave of democracy and free-market capitalism, deep inside the region dominated by the Soviet Union, which extended for a hundred miles to the west of the capital. This situation was to remain as a bone of contention for the next fifty-five years, until the reunification of Germany in 1990.

Dien Bien Phu

A French Defeat

1954

At Dien Bien Phu, a French colonial army with American backing were decisively defeated by a local Vietnamese army. For centuries, Vietnamese fighters had fought off the Chinese and they went on to defeat the Americans too.

THE FRENCH COLONY of Indochina comprised the countries of Vietnam, Cambodia and Laos. During World War II, it was occupied by the Japanese and the British took the Japanese surrender there in 1945. The British rearmed the Japanese to keep order until the French could send a force because they were anxious to re-establish the legitimacy of their own colonies in the Far East.

However, there was a rival for power in Vietnam, which was the Viet Minh, a Communist and nationalist group who had fought the Japanese with American backing. On 2 September 1945 its leader, Ho Chi Minh, announced the Democratic Republic of Vietnam. Talks were held with the French colonists but when these broke down the Viet Minh began a guerrilla war with the intention of freeing Vietnam from French rule.

The war continued inconclusively for the next eight years. During that time, the French managed to maintain control of most of south Vietnam, while the Viet Minh held on to the rural areas of the north. In 1953, the Korean War came to an end. This allowed the Chinese to divert large quantities of arms to their Communist comrades in Vietnam. Now well equipped, the Viet Minh's Red Army, under General Vo Nguyen Giap, quickly doubled in size. The French dismissed them as a bunch of backward peasants but Giap was about to demonstrate the fact that he had created a well-armed, well-disciplined army.

That same year, General Henri Navarre was appointed as the new French commander-in-chief in Vietnam. Determined to break the stalemate, Navarre adopted a new strategy. He would lure the guerrillas out of their jungle strongholds and then force Giap into a conventional pitched battle, when he would defeat him.

The place he picked for this battle was a small valley in northwest Vietnam that contained a tiny village called Dien Bien Phu. It was 150 miles west of Hanoi, just twenty-five miles from the border with Laos and seventy-five miles from the Chinese border to the north. The battle location was right in the middle of Viet Minh territory. A successful action would effectively split the enemy's territory into two, thereby cutting them off from their supply routes through Laos and China. The village was surrounded by open ground so the guerrillas would have to commit themselves to conventional warfare.

Dien Bien Phu was also a good place from the logistical point of view. It had links to Sam Neua, the French base in Laos, and the French garrison at Lai Chau on the Song Da River to the north. And it had its own air strip.

If the guerrillas would not come to Dien Bien Phu then the French were in a good position to send patrols out into the surrounding area. Either way, the Viet Minh would be finished if Navarre succeeded in taking northwest Vietnam from the guerrillas.

On the morning of 20 November 1953, sixty-seven C-47 Dakotas dropped three battalions of French and colonial Vietnamese paratroopers over Dien Bien Phu. They were battle-hardened soldiers who had seen action in Indochina and World War II. However, they immediately found themselves in trouble. Viet Minh soldiers from the 149th Regiment were on an exercise in the valley at the time. They rushed for defensive positions and engaged the Sixth Colonial Parachute Battalion while they were still in the air. By the time they landed they discovered that they were fighting a full-scale battle for the drop zone. Their struggle was intensified when they could not find the machine-guns, mortars and other heavy weapons that had been dropped with them. Also, very few of their radios had survived the drop, so communications had to be conducted by runner.

The Second Battalion of the Parachute Chasseurs Regiment were of no assistance when they landed to the south. They were scattered and it took several hours to form them up into fighting units. Nevertheless the Sixth Colonials managed to force the guerrillas back into the village and then flush them out. The First Colonial Battalion helped mop up areas of strong resistance after they jumped at 15.00 hours. Meanwhile the Viet Minh main force retreated in good order, taking the villagers with them. After the action, thirteen of the French were dead and forty wounded.

The Eighth Vietnamese Parachute Battalion and the First Foreign Legion Parachute Battalion were dropped on the following day. With them came the commanding officer of the parachute battalions, Colonel Pierre Charles Langlais, who broke his leg on landing, and Brigadier-General Jean Gilles, who would take command of the entire operation.

By 22 November there were 4,500 French troops on the ground at Dien Bien Phu. A lot of them were without equipment, which had been scattered down the valley in the air-drops. The engineers then set about building fortifications but the Viet Minh quickly cut all the roads to Dien Bien Phu. It was estimated that the engineers would need 36,000 tons of material and equipment to fortify the base. This would now have to be supplied by air.

It would take 12,000 flights to carry that amount of material in C-47 transport aircraft. Although the US sent larger C-119 transports the task was still found to be impossible. In all, the engineers received just 4,000 tons – including 3,000 tons of barbed wire – just eleven per cent of their requirements.

The French sent out reconnaissance missions in force in an attempt to make contact with their forces in Laos. When this failed, they confined themselves to patrolling the surrounding area. They seldom made contact, although there was evidence of Viet Minh activity. Giap wanted to avoid any engagement until he was good and ready.

He knew that he would have to besiege the fort at Dien Bien Phu with superior numbers if he were to defeat the French. He calculated that it would take just 5,500 troops to seal the valley. These men would have to be supplied. Heavy vehicles were available, but the roads could be washed out by monsoon rains or knocked out by French bombing. Accordingly, he set up supply lines that depended on mules, bicycles and human bearers.

The French positions bristled with twenty-four 150mm howitzers, four 155mm howitzers, thirty-two heavy mortars and the firepower of ten M-24 tanks – the tanks had arrived by air in parts. This was all the firepower they would need because they were confident that it would be impossible for the Viet Minh to bring artillery pieces into the rugged terrain. Colonel Piroth, the commander of the artillery batteries at Dien Bien Phu, staked his reputation on the boast that in the unlikely event that any enemy artillery appeared, he would silence it before three rounds had been fired.

However, the French had not counted on the organizational ability of Giap and the determination of the Viet Minh. Through jungles and over mountains they managed to manhandle 140 field howitzers, between seventy and eighty recoilless rifles, fifty heavy mortars, thirty-six light anti-aircraft guns and twelve Katyusha rocket launchers, of the type used in the battle for Berlin.

Instead of concentrating on their own logistical problems, the French used their transport aircraft for flying high-ranking British and American delegations into the area, in the hope of winning the support of their governments. Although the French ducked the awkward questions of the military men, US Vice-President Richard Nixon, who visited the base, was impressed. The Cold War was at its height and America wanted to see the French crush the Communist threat in Southeast Asia.

In an effort to isolate Dien Bien Phu, the Viet Minh sent its 316th Division against Lai Chau. The French were forced to airlift the garrison out. Lacking the required air transport, 2,000 soldiers were left to make the six-mile hike to Dien Bien Phu. Only 175 men arrived, not one of them an officer.

At Dien Bien Phu, the Viet Minh had already won the battle of logistics. If French planes could not land due to bad weather or anti-aircraft fire, the garrison would have to do without. The French had also lost the battle of intelligence. Confined to the valley, they had no idea of what they were up against. The Viet Minh positions were well camouflaged. Concentrations of soldiers in the surrounding hills were hidden beneath the jungle foliage and the Viet Minh had built dummy positions to further confuse the picture.

On the other hand, Viet Minh spotters could look down from the hills and watch the French prepare

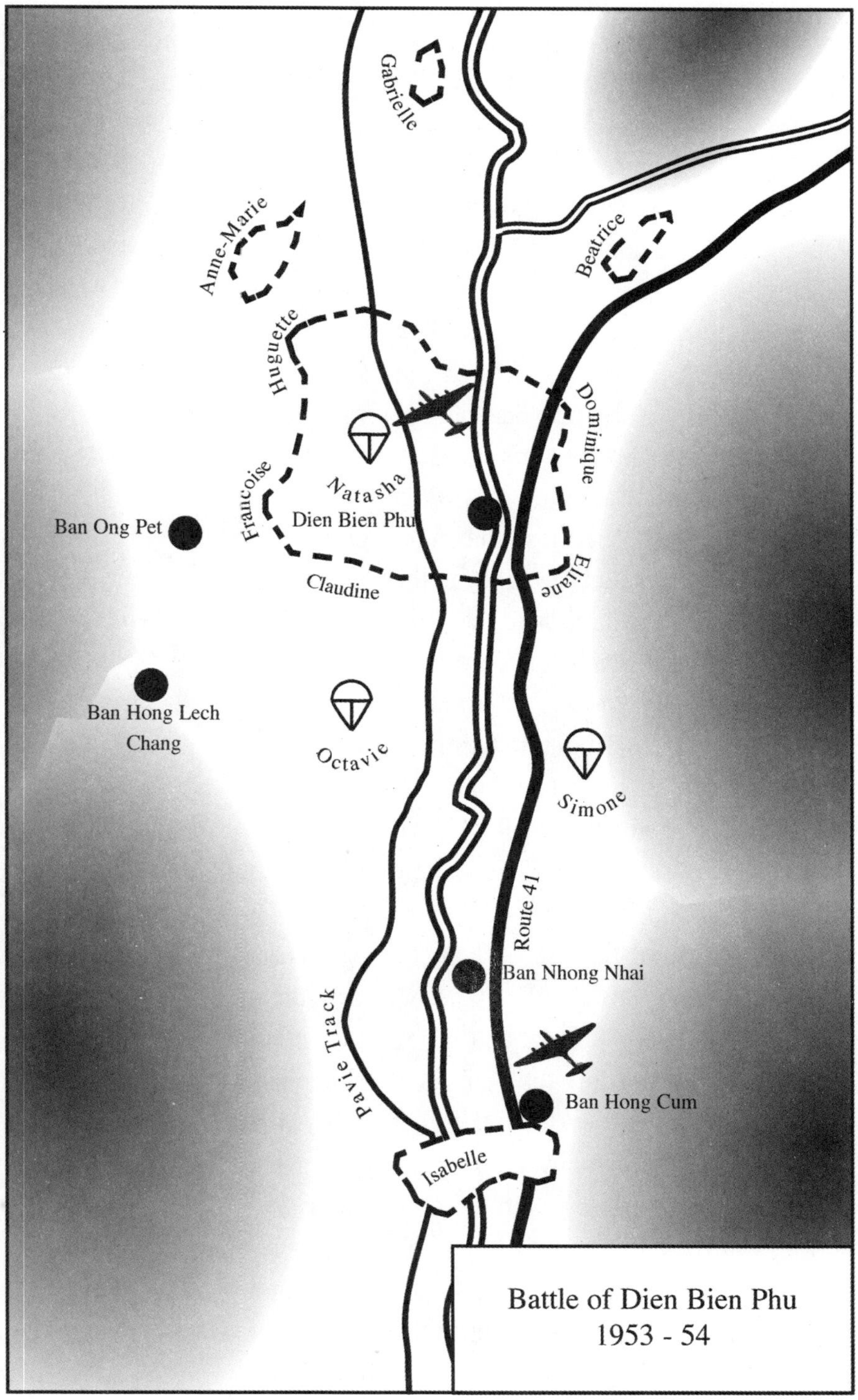

Battle of Dien Bien Phu
1953 - 54

their defences. When the battle started, Giap's men had accurate maps showing every detail of the French Fortress and the troop deployments. Also the Viet Minh had the advantage of fighting on their own territory.

As well as having more guns, the Viet Minh outnumbered the defenders eight to one. A further advantage was that half the French garrison were colonial troops from south Vietnam. They were easy to demoralize and they deserted when the going got tough.

The French defences consisted of a series of interlocking fortified strongpoints, which had been given – predictably – women's names. Claudine, Elaine, Dominique, Huguette and Françoise surrounded the airstrip and the village. Anne-Marie protected the northwest; Gabrielle defended the road to the north, some two miles out; Beatrice sat on Route 41 to the northeast; and four miles to the south was Isabelle. This was a safety area to which the French could withdraw if they lost the main complex. It guarded the pass out of the valley to the south and it had its own makeshift airstrip.

Eventually, the French concentrated 6,500 men at Dien Bien Phu. They were supported by a number of fighter-bombers that operated from the main airfield. Against them, Giap had assembled five divisions, one of which was composed entirely of artillerymen and engineers. The siege of Dien Bien Phu was now under way.

The Viet Minh began by launching guerrilla actions to harass the defenders. These were costly to the French: between November 1953 and the end of February 1954, they lost the equivalent of one battalion. Although the thirteen battalions that defended Dien Bien Phu were assured that they were up to strength, the losses told. These harassing actions were costly in ammunition too. Given the logistical situation, the French Headquarters in Hanoi gave instructions to ration ammunition. Only a set number of rounds could be used each day in engagements with the enemy. The Viet Minh suffered no such restrictions,

As the harassment increased, the French veterans readied themselves for an all-out attack. Intelligence reports indicated that it would come in mid-March. On the night of 12 March, Colonel Christian de Castries, General Gilles' successor, was briefing his officers about the forthcoming attack. At the same time General Giap was issuing orders for a full-scale attack at 17.00 hours the next day.

The French spotted troop movements around Gabrielle to the north and Beatrice to the northeast around 13 March, but it was still not clear where the Viet Minh attack would come. Everything fell silent

at around 17.00. The tension was palpable. However, the French began to think that they had been mistaken about the attack as the minutes ticked by.

Then, at 17.14, shells began falling on Beatrice. The men of the Third Battalion, the Thirteenth Demi-brigade of the French Foreign Legion holding the outpost, were under attack. The Viet Minh artillery quickly destroyed Beatrice's 105mm guns and knocked out the command post, killing Colonel Gaucher. Then two regiments of the 312th Viet Minh Division appeared, less than a hundred yards away, and charged the perimeter.

By 21.00 they were inside the wire and the other French batteries had to stop firing in support because they risked hitting their own men. The fighting continued until shortly after midnight, when Beatrice fell quiet. The only noise that broke the silence was that of French soldiers crying out to identify themselves as they pulled back to the main complex. Less than 200 men made it. Three-quarters of the battalion had been wiped out in less than seven hours.

The French were stunned by the speed and strength of the attack. Colonel de Castries called

Three battalions of French paratroopers sent to take the strategic town of Dien Bien Phu landed where a regiment of Vietnamese soldiers were on an exercise, with disastrous consequences.

The Vietnamese attacked in waves. These were cut down. But the French had not expected them to be able to manhandle their artillery over the mountains to such a remote location.

Hanoi for more men and ammunition. But he had a problem. Due to the accuracy of the Viet Minh artillery, the airstrip had to be closed when the undamaged strike aircraft had flown out on the following morning.

Later that day the Fifth Vietnamese Parachute Battalion dropped in. De Castries considered making an attempt to retake Beatrice from the Viet Minh, but the clouds over the valley were too low for air support.

At 18.00 hours that evening the Viet Minh began shelling Gabrielle. This time two regiments attacked – the 88th and the 165th Regiments of the elite 308th Viet Minh Division. It was a carbon copy of the attack on Beatrice. The outpost was defended by an Algerian battalion, some Legionnaires and eight heavy mortars. Heavy hand-to-hand fighting continued all night, but in the morning the French still held Gabrielle. De Castries quickly counterattacked with six of his ten tanks, two companies of Legionnaires and a battalion of Vietnamese. Withering fire arrested their progress 1,000 yards from Gabrielle, but they managed to evacuate the remaining 150 Algerians before withdrawing.

When the situation was reported back to Hanoi, the French commanders found it hard to believe that two heavily-fortified outposts and two and a half battalions had been lost in just forty-eight hours. To add to the garrison's problems, General Navarre, the commander in Saigon, and General Cogny, who had just taken over in Hanoi, vied with each other for command.

Morale collapsed at Dien Bien Phu. After seeing most of his artillery destroyed, Colonel Piroth, who had boasted that the Viet Minh would never loose off more than three rounds, retired to his bunker where he committed suicide with a hand grenade.

On 16 March more French troops were airlifted in as a moral-boosting exercise. At the same time, the Third Thai Battalion deserted Ann Marie en masse, leaving the outpost unmanned. Some of them set off for home and others dug themselves in along the Nam Noua River, beyond Beatrice, in order to watch the outcome of the battle.

Colonel de Castries realised that he was out of his depth. On 24 March he handed over effective command to Colonel Langlais and Major Bigeard, commander of the Sixth Parachute Battalion, while remaining nominally in charge himself. They realised that the situation was hopeless, but they felt that they may yet save the garrison if they made the Viet Minh pay dearly enough.

So far the Viet Minh's assaults on Beatrice and Gabrielle had been costly. Giap slowed the pace, because he hoped that he could slowly strangle the garrison. His engineers also began digging tunnels under the French positions, which were then packed with high explosives.

The Viet Minh attack had come to a halt, so on 30 March Giap reverted to the tactics that had given him Beatrice and Gabrielle. After an artillery bombardment, the 312th and 316th Divisions attacked Dominique and Elaine. Four days of hand-to-hand fighting followed, with positions changing hands more than once. The French fired more than 13,000 rounds of 105mm shells in one day, but they still failed to dislodge the Viet Minh.

After a hiatus of two days, Giap sent the 308th Division against Huguette. This was where Bigeard had concentrated his men. They held on to Huguette and at the end of the action more than 800 Viet Minh were found hanging from the perimeter wire. Bigeard's paratroopers also managed to take back one of the posts in Elaine, further boosting morale.

Giap's forces were now exhausted. He took the rest of April to regroup. After all, the beleaguered French garrison was not going anywhere. By 1 May, they only had enough rations for three days and ammunition enough for one last action. At 22.00 hours, Giap began a general offensive.

Over the next five days, the Viet Minh took position after position, shrinking the French perimeter each day. Somehow Langlais and Bigeard managed to keep the Algerian and Vietnamese colonial troops fighting alongside their paratroopers. On 6 May a French aircraft attempted to give ground support, but only succeeded in causing the French more casualties. Later that day, Giap used his Katyuska rocket launchers to blow up what remained of the French ammunition dump. With that, the colonial troops deserted.

There was now nowhere for the French to make a last stand as Giap began detonating the explosives in the tunnels the Viet Minh engineers had dug weeks before. On 7 May the Viet Minh swept in. Major Bigeard attempted a counterattack with two companies of paratroopers and the remaining tank. However, Dien Bien Phu was overrun later in the afternoon. Isabelle surrendered on the following day.

The siege had lasted for fifty-six days. The French forces had lost 2,000 troops, a further 5,000 were wounded and 7,000 had been taken prisoner – only half of them would survive captivity. The Vietnamese counted 8,000 dead and 15,000 wounded.

Dien Bien Phu ended French colonial power in Indochina. While the battle was raging, a peace conference was taking place in Geneva. It was decided that the French administration in the south and the Viet Minh in the north should remain in place until there was an election to unite the country. The US was a guarantor of that accord. However, when it became clear that the Communists would win any election, the US declared that there could be no free and fair elections. They established a puppet regime in the South, and announced that North and South Vietnam should remain permanently divided. These events set the stage for the Vietnam war, which began eleven years later.

A–Z of Battles

Picture Credits

AFP / Getty Images
p. 153
Ann Ronan Picture Library / HIP / TopFoto
p. 99
Art Archive / Victoria and Albert Museum London / Eileen Tweedy
cover painting '*The Battle of Waterloo*' by Félix Philippoteaux, 1874
Corbis
pp. 9, 27, 34, 44, 56, 60, 77, 84, 105, 113, 116, 119, 126, 132, 144, 198, 205, 206
Hulton Archive
pp. 39, 41, 49, 80, 82, 87, 94, 99, 102, 108, 125, 130, 135, 139, 143, 158
Mary Evans Picture Library
pp. 53, 63, 67, 156, 163, 167, 178
Picture Desk
p. 30
TimeLife / Getty Images
pp. 6, 15, 18, 88, 149, 191
Topham Picturepoint
22, 71, 91, 123, 168, 175